Sport and leisure in social thought

Above all else, this book is written for undergraduate and graduate students who over the years have asked for a single text that will introduce them not only to sociological theory, but also the sociology of sport and leisure. The book attempts to capture the breadth of sociological thinking about sport and leisure. Too often a doctrinal quality is given to particular sociological traditions of social thought. It is as if a particular theory is fully developed and all that remains is to test it against 'the facts'. Specialist texts have tended to champion particular traditions of thought so that the breadth and diversity of sociological traditions which are relevant in understanding sport and leisure has been under-estimated. This book attempts to transcend this situation. It consists not only of a discussion of the major sociological traditions but also shows how sport and leisure has contributed to our understanding of contemporary sociological themes such as the body, globalisation, social space, the environment, consumption, nationalism and social inequality.

Grant Jarvie is Professor of Sport and Leisure Research at Heriot-Watt University; **Joseph Maguire** is Senior Lecturer in the Sociology of Sport at Loughborough University.

Sport and leisure in social thought

Grant Jarvie and Joseph Maguire

London and New York

First published 1994
by Routledge
11 New Fetter Lane, London EC4P 4EE

Simultaneously published in the USA and Canada
by Routledge
29 West 35th Street, New York, NY 10001

© 1994 Grant Jarvie and Joseph Maguire

Typeset in Baskerville by LaserScript, Mitcham, Surrey
Printed and bound in Great Britain by
Biddles Ltd, Guildford and King's Lynn

British Library Cataloguing in Publication Data
A catalogue record for this book is available from the British Library

Library of Congress Cataloging in Publication Data
A catalog record for this book has been requested

ISBN 0–415–07703–6 (hbk)
ISBN 0–415–07704–4 (pbk)

Contents

Acknowledgements

The research for this text was made possible through small research monies from the University of Warwick and Loughborough University of Technology. Polity Press are to be thanked for their permission to reproduce Table 1 in Chapter 9. Eric Dunning, David Frisby and Alan Tomlinson have all commented on various sections of this book. The meticulous preparation of the manuscript is entirely due to Carolyn Ison. We thank her yet again for all her work over the years.

Introduction
Sport and leisure in social thought

This book is not a comprehensive history of sociological thought about sport and leisure but rather a selective history of some of the major traditions of social thought which have informed an ever increasing body of research into the sociology of sport and leisure. As opposed to the terms perspective or framework, the word tradition has been deliberately used throughout this book because it conveys more of a sense of both change and continuity within and between different ways of thinking about sport and leisure. We have suggested that it is probably more fruitful to see various social and political positions as encompassing broad traditions of social thought rather than logically sealed paradigms and problematics. Above all else this book is written for all those undergraduate and graduate students who over the years have asked us and others for that single text which will introduce them not only to sociological theory but also to the sociology of sport and leisure. Some may think we have failed, but it is our belief that while a number of specialist texts have tended to reflect particular traditions of social thought, no one general text has attempted to capture the contemporary breadth of sociological thinking about sport and leisure.

Analytically speaking there has been a sociological debate about sport and leisure for a quarter of a century, maybe longer. Indeed long before nineteenth-century sociological thought (Comte, Spencer, Marx) sought to define the social, both in terms of society as a complex structural whole and its relation with specific institutions, Adam Ferguson talked about sport as a necessary component of civic life.[1] Writing in the eighteenth century Ferguson saw sport as a type of collective ceremony through which community solidarity could be demonstrated. For Marx, communist society offered the opportunity to hunt in the morning, fish in the afternoon and breed cattle in the evening. Durkheim saw certain religious ceremonies as having 'an outward appearance of recreation'.[2]

It has often been suggested that sport and leisure have been peripheral or even meaningless objects of sociological enquiry. Research for this book necessitated engaging with many of the classical sociological texts and while one cannot say whether Weber played football, or Rosa Luxembourg enjoyed painting, or Adam Ferguson watched shinty, it is clear that Marx, Weber, Durkheim, Simmel and others all viewed sport or leisure as anything but peripheral. On a more contemporary note we know not only that Anthony Giddens supports Tottenham Hotspur Football Club and that the current director of the Economic and Social Science Research Council supports Derby County, but more importantly that sport and leisure have also figured in contemporary traditions of social and political thought such as feminism, postmodernism, figurational sociology and cultural studies, to name but a few. We have also attempted to show how sport and leisure research has contributed to an understanding of contemporary sociological themes such as the body, globalisation, social space, religion, the environment, consumption, the emotions, nationalism and cultural identity.

Numerous developments have undoubtedly contributed to a burgeoning interest in the sociology of sport and leisure but at least three sets of considerations appear to have been of decisive importance: (i) while sport and leisure may mean different things to different people – fun, pain, alienation, pleasure, freedom – to escape from the world of leisure – and, to a lesser extent, sport – is virtually impossible. One need only consider the place of sport or leisure within people's lives, or the emotional psyche of various social formations during World Cup tournaments, or the way in which certain sport and leisure practices act as symbols of inclusion and exclusion, status and marginality, or the way in which sport and leisure have contributed to the economy or social welfare policies, to realise that sport and leisure are popular facets of a lived way of life for many people; (ii) a transcendence of a general belief that sport and leisure were somewhat autonomous or separate from society or politics or problems of social development gave rise to a growing recognition that sport and leisure were far too complex to be viewed as simple products of voluntary behaviour or totally autonomous entities. Like sociology itself early critical thinking about sport and leisure tended to begin with the breakdown of the classical, voluntarist model. Much of the early 1960s work in this area not only challenged the myth of autonomy but also illustrated that changing world conditions and social relations affect everything and everyone, including the structure, meaning and organisation of sport and leisure; and (iii) a proliferation of organisations, university modules and courses, specialist journals and academic societies has helped not only to support a distinct sociology of sport and leisure but also to illustrate that such areas of concern do in fact connect and contribute to many classical sociological concerns and disputes, such as the future of organised or disorganised capitalism, the transition from rural to industrial society, the importance of an individual's life and the relationship between personal troubles and public issues.

The development of sociological thinking about sport and leisure has been the result of collaborative, communicative and, to a lesser extent, a gladiatorial interaction of individuals, social groups and communities. It is perhaps one of the strengths and weaknesses of this area that so many traditions of social thought have been presented as being doctrinal. Even the slightest glimpse of the respective fields would probably suggest that there is a high correlation between the type of cultural capital which different writers have at their disposal and the form of sociology that they defend as the only legitimate one. At times a great deal of intellectual curiosity and energy has been spent ensuring that one favoured tradition of thought counts for more than others rather than examining whether the basis for both the diversity and fragmentation of knowledge and rivalry is itself premised upon a false basis. It is as if a particular theory or position is all in place and all that remains is to run more substantive areas through it. Nor have we attempted to provide a consistently critical stance within each chapter. This is not to say that we have not been critical but that we have not approached each tradition of social thought from a set position. It is our belief that the critique and counter-critique which has plagued the sociology of sport and leisure over the last decade has failed to recognise the cultural diversity and common ground which does in fact exist between different traditions of social thought. One of the consequences of this malaise is that while various specialist texts have tended to reflect and champion particular traditions of social thought, no one general text has attempted to reflect generally pon the contemporary breadth of sociological thinking about sport and leisure. This then is what *Sport and Leisure in Social Thought* attempts to do.

This book, as we have said, is a selective account of sociological thought about sport and leisure. A text of this nature could easily become a shopping list of great names. We have tried to avoid this by concentrating upon major themes of sociological relevance as well as significant thinkers. Inevitably critics will look to see if person A or theme B is adequately covered or even omitted. We could have, for example, included a chapter on structuration theory and the immense contribution that Giddens has made to contemporary sociology. Yet although Giddens himself commented upon sport in the 1960s and more recently upon the cultural significance of Paul Gascoigne's tears during the 1990 World Cup in Italy, at a general level structuration theory has not yet pushed itself to the forefront of the sociology of sport and leisure. Ways of seeing things are seldom conducted from a neutral standpoint and the selection of thinkers and themes for this text has been based largely upon those which have been at the forefront of sociological thinking about sport and leisure either in the past or at the time of writing.

Grant Jarvie
Joseph Maguire

NOTES AND REFERENCES

1 A. Ferguson, *Essay on the History of Civil Society*, Edinburgh, Edinburgh University Press, 1767/1967.
2 For an excellent introduction to leisure in the work of early classical sociological thinkers, see N. Parry and F. Coalter 'The Sociology of Leisure: A Question of Root or Branch?' in *Sociology*, no. 2, 1973, pp. 220–31. A more recent overview of the Sociology of Sport and Leisure can be found in C. Rojek and E. Dunning (eds) *Sport and Leisure in the Civilising Process, Critique and Counter-Critique*, London, Macmillan, 1992, pp. 1–35.

Chapter 1

Functionalism, solidarity and social stratification

The literature on functionalist thought stretching from Durkheim to Parsons is vast. As a tradition of social thought, functionalist concerns and methodological assumptions have influenced a substantial body of research into sport and leisure. During the late 1960s and early 1970s it played a key part in the early development of the sociology of sport in North America and on both sides of what was then the European 'iron curtain'. The work of both Durkheim and Parsons has been subject to recent critical re-evaluation.[1] Yet in many ways it has been a traditional reading of their works that has been the hallmark of functionalist thinking about sport and leisure.

A consistent theme of functionalist thought, and one derived from Durkheim, is that sociology is concerned with the impact that large scale structures of society have on the thoughts and actions of individuals. The key to tracing this impact lies in grasping the existence of what Durkheim termed social facts. Social facts are both cultural norms and social structures that are external to and constrain and regulate social actors. Examples of social structures and cultural norms would include the bureaucracy of an organisation such as the Arts Council, and the emphasis in sport on achievement-striving, effort and competition. As social facts are things they can be studied empirically – sociology entails an attempt to establish the pattern that lies behind all observable phenomena. This is what Durkheim argued in this connection:

> ... Social facts are to be treated as things. ... Things include all objects of knowledge that cannot be conceived by purely mental activity, those that require their conception of data from outside the mind, from observations and experiments, those which

are built up from the more external and immediately accessible characteristics to the less visible and more profound.[2]

For Durkheim, social facts were external to the individual and were invested with coercive power. This power enables them to 'impose' their influence on individuals. In language development, such social facts are internalised. They rule individuals from within, becoming an integral part of the self. Society 'enters' the individual as a moral force. The task thus facing sociologists is to study the ways in which social facts are impregnated with moral elements. Some dominant themes of functionalist thought have concerned social cohesion, social order and the ways in which individuals are integrated into society.

Several crucial questions arise with regard to Durkheim's account of social facts. How do social facts control human actions? What role does an individual's subjective state play in social life? If social cohesion rests on the autonomy of moral action, how can 'society' be external to the individual? On these questions Durkheim was ambivalent. Though he argued that individuals act in conformity to constraining influences, he also suggested that the individual interprets external facts in specific ways. Durkheim concluded:

> . . . nothing collective can be produced if individual consciousnesses are not assumed; but this necessary condition is by itself insufficient. These consciousnesses must be combined in a certain way; social life results from this combination and is, consequently, explained by it.[3]

Generally, however, functionalist work is portrayed as stressing that society is less the product of collective human action and more a constraining abstraction. The social milieu is the determining factor, while an individual's subjective state plays a more passive role. Durkheim, and other writers working within functionalist traditions, have been accused of adopting a 'mechanistic' and 'deterministic' approach. It is possible, however, to see Durkheim's early writings as an over-reaction to the then pervasive methodological individualism and atomism. That is, Durkheim was critial of voluntaristic, subjective and psychological approaches and, to counter their influence, sought to emphasise that the primary unit of sociological analysis must be the social milieu. The social was irreducible. Hence, sociology must be concerned with social facts: objective datums that exist independent of individuals, of their psychology and their interaction with others. Despite this forthright emphasis, Durkheim's later work is seen to revolve around the unresolved problem of human action and a constraining social milieu. As Durkheim argued more than once, the unity of society develops only through moral action.

Social facts then are viewed as objective entities but they also contain a significant subjective element. These social facts, combining within the individual's consciousness, form what Durkheim termed 'collective representations' of the social world. That is, collective symbols through which society becomes conscious of itself. They are not reducible to individual consciousness. Durkheim argued that the states which constitute collective consciousness 'differ specifically from those which constitute the individual consciousness' and that this 'specificity comes from the fact that they are not formed from the same elements'. While individual consciousness resulted from the 'nature of the organico-psychological being taken in isolation' collective consciousness emerged out of 'the combination of a plurality of beings of this kind'.[4] Collective life is thus reflected in collective representations. In turn these representations become autonomous realities independent of individuals.

The functionalist perspective that emerged out of Durkheim's shadow was further developed in Parsons' later work.[5] Drawing on Parsons' general theoretical model, it is possible to establish the basic assumptions on which functionalism rests. Societies are viewed as wholes, that is as a system of interrelated parts. These parts perform a specific function within the system and contribute to the integration and adaptation of the system as a whole. Reference to 'system' is not surprising given that it is a concept central to all forms of functionalism. Examining the functional relation of parts to whole, society is understood as a structure of elements possessing a patterned form. The task for functionalists is to discern those parts that are essential for the survival, evolution and adequate functioning of the system.

Such parts perform special functions and are called 'functional prerequisites'. They cater for the generalised conditions necessary for the maintenance of the system. Several have been identified. These include the provision for an adequate relationship of the individual to the environment, role differentiation and role assignment, communication, shared cognitive orientations, goals and suitable means of achieving these. The regulation of affective expression, socialisation and social control of deviant behaviour are also crucial to the maintenance of social order.[6]

It is important to grasp that the integration of parts of the system, termed the sub-system, is never perfect. Durkheim's work highlighted the fragile and unstable nature of social solidarity within advanced societies. Though the basic tendency of social systems veers towards equilibrium, elements of mal-integration will always be present. In functionalist thinking therefore, particular consideration is paid to the role of social control mechanisms.

Functionalists thus argue that deviance, tension and strains are dysfunctional elements that tend to become institutionalised or resolved in the direction of social integration. This is reached through value consensus. The principles underlying this consensus legitimise the existing social, economic and political structure. Change is possible, and, as noted earlier, Durkheim was not primarily concerned with 'the problem or order', but with the problem of 'the changing nature of order'. Social change is viewed as adaptive and gradual, and where more rapid change does occur, it tends to do so in cultural institutions. The basic institutional framework remains intact.

Parsons identified four 'functional imperatives' which are characteristic of systems. For Parsons, a system, if it is to survive, must be able to cope with external change (adaptation). Further, a system must be able to define and secure its primary goals (goal attainment). In addition, a system must regulate the inter-relationship both between its component parts and among the other three functional imperatives (integration). Finally, a system must nurture, sustain and regenerate both the motivation of individuals and the cultural patterns that create and enhance the motivation (pattern maintenance).[7]

Building on these assumptions, Parsons argued that these four functional imperatives are linked to four action systems. For Parsons, these action systems were conceptual tools with which to understand the 'ordered structure of systems'. They do not exist in the real world. The biological organism is the action system that handles the adaptation function. It does so by adjusting to and transforming the external world. The goal attainment function is performed by the personality system. This is achieved by defining system goals and mobilising resources to attain them. The integration function is undertaken by the social system that ensures that its component parts are suitably controlled. The cultural system performs the pattern maintenance function by providing actors with the appropriate norms and values that motivate them for action.

The problem of order dominates both the functional imperatives and the action systems identified. For Parsons systems have the property of and tend toward self-maintaining order or equilibrium. His theoretical analysis was thus focused on outlining the ordered structure of systems. Consequently, his work has been viewed as too static, mechanical and structured. Gone is the insight that Durkheim concerned himself with, namely, the changing nature of order.[8] Functionalist thinking about sport and leisure has tended to follow several familiar themes.

The social functions of sport and leisure practices

Several key features of functionalist accounts of sport and leisure can be identified. The role that sport and leisure play in socialisation and the learning of culturally 'appropriate' values is examined. In addition, the 'functional' relationship between sport, leisure and work is explored. Further, the contribution that sport and leisure make to the 'functional' requirements of social systems is considered.[9] For functionalists, sport is a social institution that transmits values to participants. It functions to maintain the larger society. Sport is not unique in this respect. As with other leisure activities, sports contribution is inter-related with other aspects of society. These include the family, education and religion. In each of these areas sport and leisure activities find regular expression.

Closer inspection of functionalist research reveals that several questions about sport and leisure repeatedly surface. How is sport and leisure inter-related with other social institutions? How does sport and leisure promote social values, norms, statutes and roles? How does sport and leisure function as an integrative mechanism within society? Underpinning each of these questions is a functionalist objective that seeks to establish how social phenomenon contribute to the 'functional prerequisites' or 'imperatives' of society.

Sport and leisure is seen as a cultural subsystem of society. They serve specific functions. The rules of sports are, for example, widely agreed and this is perceived to both reinforce and reflect the notion of consensus in society. Sport reflects existing cultural values. Fair play and achievement striving are valued.[10] Sport also aids in pattern maintenance and tension management. That is, sport is seen to teach people the basic values and norms of the society in which they live and performs a useful socioemotional function. Besides tension management, feelings of camaraderie and community and the reassuring seasonal rituals of the sporting calendar, all contribute to social cohesion.[11] Early work maintained that participation in sport helps to create suitably motivated workers necessary to maintain productivity in industrialised societies. More recently functionalist writers have argued that the social drama of sport encourages spectators and players, both young and old, to accept dominant cultural values. Focusing on youth team sport, some functionalist writers have concluded that sport participation teaches young people valuable lessons about life in their societies.[12]

Sport and leisure practices integrate members into the society. These practices do this through 'collective representations'. Community teams and voluntary organisations are good examples of this. A similar identification with international teams results in sport functioning as a cohesive political force. Such sentiments find expression in the wider society. At the height of the Vietnam war, Spiro Agnew, then vice-president of the United States of America, commented that athletics was 'one of the few bits of glue that holds society together'. Functionalists are thus concerned to ask questions about how sport creates and strengthens the social relations necessary for people to work together in constructive ways. Lever's portrayal of Brazilian soccer provides a classic example of this. She maintains that 'sports help complex modern societies cohere' and concludes that 'spectator sport is one mechanism that builds people's consciousness of togetherness'.[13]

Through its dominant ethos, sport, as some observers argue, also reinforces the learning of achievement orientations and aids in the learning of social roles. Functionalists have been keen to examine the part that sport plays in justifying and reaffirming the important goals in social systems.[14] Sport is also seen to play an important role in adaptation. In increasingly technologically advanced societies, sport is one of a few areas where it is still possible for human beings to develop the physical skills and well-being that are essential to their survival as a species.[15] It is no surprise then that functionalist thought also finds expression in an account of the making of 'modern' sports and societies.

The division of labour: From mechanical to organic solidarity and the making of modern sports and societies

Durkheim was interested in the question of what held society together. Hence, in his idea of sociology as a science of morals, his concern was with regulation and community. In examining the historical evolution of societies, Durkheim focused on the movement from 'mechanical' to 'organic' solidarity. Attention was therefore given to the social problems engendered by this transition and the problematic nature of the social bonds that united individuals with each other and with society as a whole.[16] Though functionalist work has thus been associated primarily with the issue of order, this is not necessarily an accurate portrayal of Durkheim's position. That is, as Giddens notes, Durkheim was not primarily concerned with 'the problem of order', but with the problem of 'the changing nature of order' in the context of a definite conception of 'social development'.[17] What was this conception of social development?

Durkheim's analysis was based on a conception of two ideal types of society. In one, marked by mechanical solidarity, there was a relatively undifferentiated social structure and little or no division of labour. Unity was maintained because all people are generalists: the individual was so directly and harmoniously linked with society that their individual action was always spontaneous, unreflective and collective. In moving from a society marked by mechanical solidarity to one characterised by organic solidarity, unity was born out of necessity. Because of the very differences between people stemming from an increased specialisation of tasks and responsibilities, people needed others to survive. The increase in the sheer number of people and of the interaction between them involved the development of a division of labour and social differentiation. The social structure was characterised by a high level of interdependence, yet the individual was no longer enveloped by the collective conscience. People developed greater individuality and personality.

This transition, Durkheim argued, would not result in harmonious social differentiation if the process remained unregulated by a consensus or moral beliefs.[18] Durkheim was thus concerned to examine issues of law, anomie, the collective conscience and collective representations. These issues reflected his preoccupation with the moral elements of social life and, especially, the decline of the common morality that he believed characterised societies marked by mechanical solidarity. The application of functionalist thought to the study of the emergence of modern sport has surfaced in what is conventionally termed the general theory of industrial society or modernisation theory. Several social historians, anthropologists and sociologists have been associated with this approach. Just as Durkheim explored the shift from mechanical to organic societies, writers working within this modernisation theory have contrasted what they term 'traditional' with 'modern' societies.[19]

Traditional societies are those deemed to have existed prior to industrialisation. These societies had organisation structures and values markedly different from our own. Based primarily around agricultural production, a less specialised division of labour was also evident. Social order was based on tradition, superstition and religious ritual. The family, community, labour, leisure and religion were all highly inter-related and each were features of localised cultural expression. The dominant values emphasised collective duties and obligations. Individualism was suppressed.[20]

Gradually, industrialisation emerged out of this setting. A combination of new ways of thinking, innovations in technology and changes in the demographic composition were key factors in this process. A more complex and specialised division of labour developed. Historians, whose work is underpinned by such thinking, conclude that this transformation produced unprecedented material affluence and created a separate and expanding sphere of leisure time. The emergence of sport and 'new' leisure practices was a manifestation of this broader transformation from traditional agrarian to modern industrial society.[21] During the eighteenth and nineteenth centuries, traditional folk pastimes were replaced by the new world of modern sport. Folk pastimes had been in tune with the wider society. Unorganised, localised, with no written rules or controlling institutional bodies, folk sports were closely connected to the religious and agricultural calendars. Bound up in established rituals and the conventions of the prevailing social hierarchy, folk sports were swept away with other aspects of 'merrie' England.

This modernisation perspective views modern sports as fundamentally different. This transformation is seen as a measure of the broader social changes that occurred. Modern sports are more organised, structured and regulated. An elaborate system of regional, national and international organisations emerged to control and regulate sports. Sport gradually became more specialised, bureaucratised and its values oriented around individual achievement. Codification, organisation and legitimation processes aided the broader institutionalisation of sport in society.

This breakdown of tradition in folk pastimes, as well as in other aspects of popular culture, was marked by a relative absence of conflict between social groups. People actively chose to give up old customs and adopt new ways of living. This process was both progressive and democratic. Modern leisure opened up many new opportunities for a greater number of people. Their efforts were evaluated less on ascribed values and more on achieved criteria. Modern sports and leisure forms were thus in tune with more rational ways of living.

This perspective can be encapsulated by the comments of Walvin when he concluded that 'leisure is itself a product of industrial society'. He also argued that 'as England became a highly populated, urban and industrially dominated society the way people chose (and were encouraged) to spend their free time changed dramatically'.[22] Aspects of functionalist thinking can be found in the work of many writers. Both Roberts and Dumazedier see leisure as having three major functions: recreation, the free development of the individual, and recuperation.[23] Leisure activities allow individuals to adapt to their particular social situation. Leisure time activities compensate for the unrewarding and unsatisfying aspects of life. Functionalist thinking has also been applied to other aspects of the contemporary leisure sphere.

Suicide, the elementary forms of the religious life and the sports phenomenon

To illustrate some of Durkheim's concerns regarding the moral elements of social life, discussion of his work on suicide is of assistance. While Durkheim recognised that suicide was a personal act, he also argued that it was profoundly social. Indeed, the incidence of suicide was closely related to the problem of social cohesion and social bonds. Durkheim was not concerned with studying why any specific individual committed suicide. Instead, he was interested in explaining suicide rates. That is, he focused his attention on why one group had a higher rate of suicide relative to another. Avoiding psychological explanations, Durkheim

tended to assume that any relevant biological, genetic, psychological or socio-psychological factors would remain constant from
one group to another or from one time period to another. If it
could be established that there was variation in suicide rates from
one group to another or from one time period to another, then
such variations would be due to sociological factors. Durkheim
termed these 'social currents'. These social currents were 'social
facts' just as much as legal and moral regulations, and had the
same objectivity and ascendency over the individual. What Durkheim wrote regarding this issue has the potential to cast light on
sport and leisure behaviour more generally and is worth citing at
some length:

> The great movements of enthusiasm, indignation, and pity in a
> crowd do not originate in any one of the particular individual
> consciousnesses. They come to each one of us from without and
> can carry us away in spite of ourselves. Of course, it may happen
> that, in abandoning myself to them unreservedly, I do not feel
> the pressure they exert upon me. But it is revealed as soon as I
> try to resist them. Let the individual attempt to oppose one of
> these collective manifestations, and the emotions that he denies
> will turn against him (sic). Now, if this power of external
> coercion asserts itself so clearly in cases of resistance, it must
> exist also in the first-mentioned cases, although we are un-
> conscious of it.[24]

Different collectivities were seen to have different collective con-
sciences and collective representations and, in turn, to produce
different social currents that had differential effects on suicide
rates. Durkheim thus focused on historical studies of changes in
the suicide rates within a given collectivity. He identified four main
types of suicide and concluded that the degree of cohesion presented in a society would generate a tendency to certain forms of
suicide. Too little or too much integration generated egoistic or
altruistic suicides. Too little or too much regulation produced
anomic or fatalistic suicides.

It is not appropriate to go into the details of the types of suicides
identified nor the social structures that cause suicides. It is important, however, to grasp two essential features of his argument. First,
the state of society produces either strong or weak suicidal
currents. Second, the extent to which a particular individual is
affected depends on the nature of the social bonds and the degree

of his/her integration within the social group. Again, Durkheim's concern with the nature and consequences of the forms of social cohesion characteristic of modern societies is evident. Societies marked by organic solidarity are characterised by an absence of strong regulative norms and a lack of integration. It is no surprise then that it was this type of society that generated a greater incidence of egoistic and anomic suicides. Durkheim was at his most forceful when he argued:

> The conclusion from all these facts is that the social suicide-rate can be explained only sociologically. At any given moment the moral constitution of society establishes the contingent of voluntary deaths. There is, therefore, for each people a collective force of a definite amount of energy, impelling men to self-destruction. The victim's acts which at first seem to express only his personal temperament are really the supplement and prolongation of a social condition which they express externally.[25]

At first sight it might appear that Durkheim's interest in religion, especially 'primitive' religion is somewhat tangential to his other work. He studied 'primitive' religion, not because of any interest in that religious form *per se*, but because such a study could reveal some of the essential and permanent aspects of humanity. It is also possible to justify the study of sport and leisure on the same grounds. Durkheim's concern with the issue of social cohesion surfaced in this discussion of religion.

Religion was viewed as the ultimate 'nonmaterial social fact'. Religion had both constraining and enabling features. That is, it not only had the capacity to constrain individuals within a specific set of 'beliefs' and 'rules', but also to elevate them above their ordinary abilities. Focusing on the religion of the aborigine tribes of Australia, Durkheim sought to highlight the exact differences between modern and traditional social systems. Aboriginal tribal societies were seen as representing the simplest type of organisation known to ethnography. Durkheim argued that through a study of these societies it was possible to reveal all that is 'essential' to social organisation in general and religion in particular. He began his classic study of religion by observing:

> We are not going to study a very archaic religion simply for the pleasure of telling its peculiarities and its singularities. If we have taken it as the subject of our research, it is because it has

seemed to us better adapted than any other to lead to an understanding of the religious nature of man, that is to say, to show us an essential and permanent aspect of humanity.[26]

Given the uniform and pervasive nature of religion in primitive societies, Durkheim felt able to equate religion with the collective conscience. It was an all-embracing collective morality. In contrast, in modern societies religion occupies an increasingly narrow domain and instead of being the collective conscience, it become is one of several collective representations. Functionalists tend to view sport and some leisure forms in similar terms. Despite this shift, the various collective representations of modern societies do have their origins in the all-embracing religion of primitive societies.

What religions in both primitive and modern societies have in common is a fundamental division of the known and knowable into two classes that embrace all that exists but exclude each other. These two classes are known as the sacred and the profane. The sacred class refers to certain phenomena that are set apart from everyday life and are deemed forbidden. In forming the essence of religion, such phenomena induce an attitude of reverence, respect, mystery, awe and honour. In contrast, the profane reflects the everyday, the mundane and the utilitarian.

The main features of religious systems can thus be discerned. The differentiation between the sacred and the profane, and the elevation of some aspects of social life to the sacred level, are necessary though not sufficient conditions for the development of religion. In addition, a set of religious beliefs that expresses the nature of the sacred must be developed. Further, a set of religious rites must be formulated and the construction of a 'church' or the emergence of a single overarching moral community must occur. These elements, sacred objects, a set of beliefs and rites and the development of a church or moral community are all interwoven. There are some striking parallels with sport and leisure practices.

The sets of beliefs and rites exist in their purest form in the aborigine totem. For Durkheim, totemism was a religious system in which certain things, particularly animals and plants, become regarded as sacred objects of the 'clan'. By examining this most elementary of religions, Durkheim hoped to discover the causes leading to the rise of the religious sentiment in humanity. He argued that totemism is the symbolic representation of the collective conscience and that the latter is an anonymous and impersonal force. On this basis he concluded that the sacred stems from the collective conscience whose source is society itself. How is this religion generated? Here, Durkheim refers to the role of 'collective effervescence'. This appears to arise at times of great moment in history when a collectivity reaches new and heightened levels of collective exaltation. In turn, this can lead to significant changes in the general structure of society.

What is the source of the feelings expressed in sports contexts? What functions do such feelings serve? Lever is in no doubt. Sport is a social institution that 'holds together the people of the metropolis and heightens their attachment to the locale'. She concludes that the 'pomp and pageantry of sport spectacles create excitement and arouse fervour, and do for the people of the metropolis what religious ceremonies did for people in communal societies'.[27] In what way can sport, and indeed leisure events more generally, be said to act as a form of 'surrogate religion'?

In his work on religion, Durkheim acknowledged that secular events could be equally successful in reaffirming the common sentiments of a collectivity. They would do so by creating sacred things out of ordinary ones. Durkheim noted the overlap when he observed:

> Representatives rites and collective recreations are even so close to one another that men pass from one sort to the other without any break of continuity. The characteristic feature of the properly religious ceremonies is that they must be celebrated on a consecrated ground . . . but there are others in which this religious character is somewhat effaced, though it has not disappeared completely. They take place outside the consecrated ground which proves that they are already laicized to a certain degree.[28]

Within a Durkheimian tradition, sport and leisure practices are seen as one of several available 'collective representations'. Through these people represent to themselves, in symbolic form, the power of the social groups in which they live. These collective representations symbolise the structures and moral codes of society. By so doing, sport and leisure activities help to create and sustain, yet also be influenced by, existing social relations to which these symbolic structures relate.

Durkheim, as noted, separated out the sacred from the profane. How can sport be seen to belong to the realm of the sacred? Durkheim himself offers some clues when he noted that:

> It is a well-known fact that games and the principal forms of art seem to have been born of religion and that for a long time they retained a religious character. We now see what the reasons for this are: it is because the cult, though aimed primarily at other ends, has also been a sort of recreation for men (*sic*).[29]

Several dimensions of this can be highlighted.[30] Coles, for example, draws a direct parallel between the experience of the soccer spectator and the rites of aborigines described by Durkheim. In both, a social process is at work that 'regenerates and amplifies the feelings expressed in a group context'.[31] From this review we can see that Durkheim discusses the 'recreative and aesthetic element' of religion, compares the rites to 'dramatic representations' and relates them to 'games and the principal forms of art'. These observations are best illustrated in the following passage drawn from Durkheim's study of the elementary forms of religious life:

> The world of religious things is a partially imaginary world, though only in its outward form, and one which therefore lends itself more readily to the free creations of the mind. Also, since the intellectual forces which serve to make it are intense and tumultuous, the unique task of expressing the real with the aid of appropriate symbols is not enough to occupy them. A surplus generally remains available which seeks to employ itself in supplementary and superfluous works of luxury, that is to say, in works of art. There are practices as well as beliefs of this sort. The state of effervescence in which the assembled worshippers find themselves must be translated outwardly by exuberant movements which are not easily subjected to too carefully defined ends. In part, they escape aimlessly, they spread themselves for the mere pleasure of so doing, and they take delight in all sorts of games.[32]

Following Durkheim, functionalists regard sport as being best understood as a symbolic representation of community and personal identity. A feeling of the sacred can and is evoked in that context. A heightened sense of the social significance of the occasion is also evident. Two things need to be borne in mind. Durkheim argued that religion is the means by which human beings come to explain and understand their societies, and that the main symbol of religious force in society is the totem.[33] It is not difficult to see sports teams as performing a similar function. Sports teams are created or adopted as totems. For some members of society, teams can become the concrete symbol of their 'insider' identity and power.

It is not solely the team itself that can act in this way. Modern sport activities enable people to represent to themselves both the society of which they are members and the ordinarily hidden, but intimate relations they have with it. Stone, for example, shows how modern wrestling is a 'passion play'.[34] A bout involves the contestants symbolically wrestling with decisions underpinned by the moral codes of good and evil. This process can also operate at an inter-societal level. That is, athletes come symbolically to represent their society's identity, power and effectiveness. Sometimes, as in the case of the Argentinian soccer star Diego Maradona, the 'hand of God' is seen to be at work!

Displays of this nature can evoke powerful episodes of collective behaviour. These displays seemingly not only propel the individual into the sacred realm, but also influence people's emotional mood more generally. Durkheim's account of Aboriginal rites casts light on this issue:

> When they are once come together, a sort of electricity is formed by their collecting which quickly transports them to an extraordinary degree of exaltation. Every sentiment expressed finds a place without resistance in all the minds, which are very open to outside impressions. . . . This effervescence often reaches such a point that it causes unheard-of actions. The passions released are of such an impetuosity that they can be restrained by nothing.[35]

Drawing on the Durkheimian notion that public ceremonial occasions simultaneously increase social integration and lessen the incidence of suicide, Curtis, Loy and Karnilowicz examined the possible connection between this phenomenon and sport events.[36] Other functionalist research had attested to the integrative role which major sport events play in modern societies. Examining the period around the World Baseball Series final and American football's 'SuperBowl Sunday' they compared these events with two American civil holidays, the Fourth of July and Thanksgiving Day. They concluded that there is support for the notion that the incidence of suicide does 'dip' before and during major sporting ceremonies.

Several features can be identified that appear to support the idea that sport belongs to the realm of the sacred. Viewing sport as a form of symbolic dialogue, Ashworth argues that sport is cut off in time and space from the 'profane' aspects of social life.[37] As such, in modern Western societies, it 'symbolises the strict requirements of how a dialogue should be conducted'. There are also many rituals and taboos that surround sport. The opening and closing ceremonies, the medal and award ceremonies, the ritual shaking of hands or bowing towards your opponent, the uniforms, symbols of excellence and trophy rooms celebrating past victories and heroes/heroines all point to the sacredness of sport. In cricket, this phenomenon is vividly shown by the status of the Long Room at Lord's, the spiritual home of English cricket.

Rituals and taboos draw a clear line between the sacred and the profane. Such rituals and taboos help to resolve the fundamental contradiction between individual wants and collective needs by providing a basic lesson about religion and moral authority. The individual learns that freedom and happiness can only exist in their association with, and submission to, sacred order. Sport and certain leisure forms both generate and express people's capacity to grasp and understand this order. The rituals and taboos that structure the sport experience reveal society and social relations to the individual. They serve to organise people's knowledge of the past and the present and their ability to imagine the future. Although these rituals and taboos tend to aid in the development of social consensus, they can also dramatise social cleavages and conflicts in life outside the sports and leisure arena.

Stratification, sport and leisure practices and social mobility

Echoing Parsons' general theoretical model, functionalists view social stratification as a permanent, necessary and inevitable feature of human societies. Such reasoning is closely related to two other functionalist assumptions: that social phenomena perform some positive function in society, and that certain 'functional prerequisites' have to be met. Stratification performs exactly this function. The stratification system is viewed as a structure that is made up of a system of positions that carry different degrees of prestige. It is the device by which societies ensure that the most important positions are conscientiously filled by the most qualified and suitable people. Two crucial questions arise. How does society instil in individuals the desire to fill certain positions, and once occupying such positions, how does it ensure that such individuals fulfil the requirements of these positions? This is accomplished by a distribution of rewards.

This problem of social placement emerges due to several reasons. First, some positions in society are seen as more functionally important than others. Second, some positions are more pleasant to occupy than others. Third, some positions require different abilities and talents. Building on this basis, functionalists tend to argue that not everyone has the talent to fill the more functionally important positions. An exclusive few make the necessary sacrifices in order to fill these positions. The talented few are only induced if differential rewards are attached to such positions. A system of unequal rewards is thus built into a hierarchy of positions in society. These rewards include social prestige, high salary and sufficient leisure time.

At least two additional points need to be made. Such a system does not come about due to a conscious plan, rather it is the result of an 'unconsciously evolved device'.[38] Nevertheless, it is a device that every society does and must develop if it is to survive. The distribution of unequal rewards inherent in stratification systems becomes, over time, part of the social system and causes structured inequalities to persist across generations. Hence, society also needs a device to ensure that individuals can move up or down social stratification hierarchies. This is accomplished, in part, through social mobility and educational provision.

In keeping with functionalist thought on stratification systems more generally, sociologists of sport and leisure in both North America and the former 'Eastern bloc' have tended to use the categories that make up these systems in a very limited way. When the concept of social class has been referred to, it is seen as one variable among several, that can affect sport and leisure. More often than not, however, class is discarded in favour of occupation. Consider Parker's analysis of types of work and resulting patterns of leisure.[39]

Focusing on the perceived fusion or polarity between work and leisure Parker argues that the former occurs when people refuse to divide up their lives between work and leisure. When polarisation does occur the corresponding functions of leisure are identified as 'spillover' or compensatory. Work may be said to spill over into leisure to the extent that leisure is the continuation of work experiences and attitudes. In some instances leisure activities 'compensate' for the dissatisfactions felt in work. Parker identifies three basic work-leisure patterns: extension, opposition and neutrality. Each of these patterns is associated with several work and non-work variables. The type of work-leisure pattern experienced is closely related to the degree of autonomy allowed and level of education required in the occupation setting.

Whatever the merits of this approach, the wider explanatory significance of stratification systems is overlooked. Narrow and more immediate concerns have attracted functionalist researchers. A network of stratification systems operates cross-culturally and this eases or inhibits access to specific sports and the realisation of performers' full potential. In studies conducted in a range of modern industrial societies, functionalists have established a pattern of involvement in sport along class lines. Both the type and form of sport and leisure activities and the frequency and length of involvement is influenced by social class. This observation holds true for both participants and spectators. Functionalist work has also shown that there is a pattern to the recruitment and occupation of leadership positions in sport organisations.[40]

The precise form that the stratification system takes varies from one country to the next. This, of course, also influences the pattern with regard to sport and leisure forms. The issue of gender or of 'race' is given greater attention in some countries. In the United States of America considerable research efforts have been given to establishing the pattern and level of involvement of 'black' Americans. Attention has focused on recruitment and retention strategies employed by 'white' coaches and managers regarding, for example, their 'black' and Hispanic players. Particular interest has centred on the pattern of distribution by playing position of ethnic minorities in sports such as American football, basketball and baseball. This phenomenon is commonly called 'stacking'. Functionalist work has usually shown the existence of informal quotas, unequal distribution of 'primary' playing positions and the precarious career span of ethnic minorities.[41] Concern for the rights of women and ethnic minorities has also led functionalist researchers to examine the role that sport plays in social mobility. To what degree can or does sport serve as an avenue of social mobility? Despite such research, critics usually regard functionalist work as reinforcing rather than challenging the status quo.[42]

Concluding thoughts

There are several well-established criticisms that can be made of functionalist work. Functionalism is viewed as inherently ahistorical. That is, it concentrates on, at best, contemporary or more usually, abstract societies. This charge is however, open to debate. Certainly, its practitioners, both in mainstream sociology and within the subdisciplines of the sociology of sport and leisure, have tended to avoid historical analyses, but this need not be the case. Durkheim, as noted, was interested in the problem of the changing nature of order. While Parsons is more usually associated with this charge, Robertson and Turner seek to defend him in this regard.[43] As was mentioned earlier, some work of note has been produced with regard to the emergence of modern sport.

Although Parsons retained a strong interest in comparative religious systems a neglect of comparative studies in sport and leisure has been evident.[44] Recently, however, attention has been paid to the cross-cultural modernisation of sport and leisure. This has occurred within the broader debate regarding globalisation generated by nonfunctionalist writers within the sociology of sport.[45] Nevertheless, functionalists more usually argue that institutions can only be understood in the context of the society in which they operate. If that is so, then cross-cultural studies appear to be ruled out. Closely related to this perceived inability to grasp the significance of time-space relations, is the charge that functionalists are unable to deal effectively with the process of social change. Attention focuses on static structures contributing in some reified way to the functional needs of society.

Just as damning is the inability to deal effectively with conflict. More often than not conflict is overlooked or downplayed. When it is examined, for example in the area of collective violence, the broader social context tends to be neglected.[46] One further substantive criticism may be levelled at functionalism, namely, that the approach has an oversocialised view of the social actor. Social actors are viewed as passive and are constrained by cultural and social forces that lie outside their control.[47] For some, functionalism lacks a dynamic, creative sense of the social actor. Again, this criticism is disputed in the more recent debates concerning the functionalist tradition, and within the sociology of leisure, functionalism still has its supporters.[48]

These general criticisms have led some to conclude that there is a conservative bias in functionalism. This is attributable not only to what it ignores, but also to what it chooses to focus on. Whatever the merits of the debate, it would appear that functionalism has a rather narrow approach to the study of sport, leisure and society. Certainly this viewpoint has been put forward repeatedly in the sociology of sport and leisure.[49] Gruneau cleverly turns the functionalist tradition on itself when he argues that the maintenance of inequality is the primary social function of sport.[50] This inequality it is argued is based on three key functional assumptions. First, that achievement and recognition through competitive processes serve to integrate people in their society. Second, that sport fosters and makes explicit social stratification. Third, sport provides an avenue for achievement and upward social mobility. As Gruneau points out however, the maintenance of this inequality does not serve the purposes of the system. It serves those who occupy positions of power.[51]

By implication this is also a critique of the functionalist analysis of stratification. Several more reservations can be stated. How adequate is the measurement of the functional importance of specific sport and leisure occupations? Why is elite-level tennis worth more than badminton? How adequate is the measurement of the functional importance of positions in sport and leisure? Who makes these decisions and what criteria do they use? Functional analyses arguably overlook the influence of power and cultural relations upon the distribution of rewards. Even if this was not the case, how adequate are the mechanisms of matching ability to position? Issues of class, gender and racial bias are acknowledged as important. Although functionalist work does note that some roles are based on ascribed as opposed to achieved criteria, the analysis tends to be viewed in terms of individual bias. The institutionalised nature of inequality is overlooked.

The absence of an adequate theory of power is seen to pervade functionalist writing. The concept of social needs that is employed confuses the needs and interest of specific groups of people with the needs and interests of all. By viewing the development and functioning of modern sport and leisure as an adaptive response to change, and to the nature of society as it is today, the cultural struggle and resistance that was and is part of this is neglected.[52] Given these criticisms, the question arises whether functionalism has any continuing relevance for scholars and students of sport and leisure?[53]

What value has functionalist thought in the late twentieth century? The more enduring aspects of this tradition appear to hinge around the development of neo-functionalism or a re-evaluation of Durkheim and Parsons.[54] Exponents of neo-functionalism suggest that they have overcome several of the criticisms outlined.[55] Robertson and Turner argue that Parsons has been misunderstood and that his theory of the structure of social action, and his work on religion, and economic and medical sociology, continues to have relevance.[56] They argue that there are four answers to the question, why read Parson? These are: his work is a sustained and systematic attempt to develop social theory; his writings represent one of the few attempts to locate what would be the minimal requirements for a general theory of the social sciences; his substantive research relates explicitly to 'actually existing' capitalism, and his critique of utilitarian rationalist economism remains one of the most cogent attacks on the core logic of the positivistic variant of social science. Neither this revisionism nor this reassessment of Parsons has, as yet, surfaced in the study of sport and leisure.

NOTES AND REFERENCES

1 For an extensive discussion on this re-evaluation, see J. C. Alexander (ed.) *Durkhemian Sociology: Cultural Studies*, Cambridge, Cambridge University Press, 1991; and R. Robertson and B. Turner, 'Talcott Parsons and Modern Social Theory – an appreciation', *Theory, Culture and Society*, no. 6, 1989, pp. 539–58.

2 E. Durkheim, *The Rules of Sociological Method*, New York, Free Press, 1895/1964, p. xiii.

3 ibid, p. 103.

4 ibid, p. 104.

5 In some respects, there are crucial differences between this approach inspired by Parsons' later work and his earlier work on action theory; whether there is a direct linkage between this and his later, structural-functional, theorising is a matter of some debate. We are more centrally concerned here with this later work which sought to discern those parts of society that are essential for the survival, evolution and adequate functioning of the system. See R. Robertson and B. Turner, op. cit., 1989.

6 For a more extensive discussion of functionalism and its place within the development of social theory, see Alan Swingewood, *A Short History of Sociological Thought*, London, Macmillan, 1984; and G. Ritzer, *Sociological Theory*, New York, Knopf, 1988.

7 T. Parsons, *The Social System*, Glencoe, Free Press, 1951; T. Parsons, *Societies*, Englewood Cliffs, Prentice Hall, 1961; and T. Parsons and G. Platt, *The American University*, Cambridge, Harvard University Press, 1973.

8 Again, however, this charge is subject to debate, see R. Robertson and B. Turner, op. cit., 1989.
9 These themes are evident in the work of G. Luschen, 'Social Stratification and Social Mobility among Young Sportsmen' in J. Loy and G. Kenyon (eds) *Sport, Culture and Society: A Reader on the Sociology of Sport*, Toronto, Macmillan, 1969, pp. 258–76; and S. Parker, *Leisure and Work*, London, Allen & Unwin, 1983.
10 A degree of consensus exists cross-culturally on this issue.
11 For evidence to support this thesis see R. Frankenburg, *Village on the Border*, London, Cohen & West, 1957; and C. Stevenson and J. Nixon, 'A conceptual scheme of the social functions of sport', *Sportswissenschaft*, no. 2, 1972, pp. 119–32.
12 These issues have preoccupied a number of functionalist writers such as G. Luschen, op. cit, 1969; R. Lipsky, 'Towards a Political Theory of American Sports Symbolism', *American Behavioural Scientist*, no. 21, 1978, pp. 345–60; and H. Nixon, *Sport and the American Dream*, New York, Leisure Press, 1984.
13 J. Lever, *Soccer Madness*, Chicago, Chicago University Press, 1983, p. 3. The specific reference to Spiro Agnew can be found in C. Lasch, *The Culture of Narcissim: American Life in an Age of Diminishing Expectations*, New York, Warner Books, 1979, pp. 202–03.
14 The reinforcement of wider goal attainment activities is viewed as an important function of sport, see J. Loy, G. Mcpherson and G. Kenyon, *Sport and Social Systems*, Reading, Addison Wesley, 1978. The precise role performed by sport varies from one society to the next. Different aspects of sport experience are highlighted and serve to reinforce the appropriate goals and means to secure those goals in the overall social system, see H. W. Morton, *Soviet Sport*, New York, Collier, 1963. Further, physical competition is inherent in sport and allows for aggressive norms to find safe expression, see P. Goodhart and C. Chataway, *War Without Weapons, the Rise of Mass Sport in the Twentieth Century and its Effect on Men and Nations*, London, Allen & Unwin, 1968. Sport is thus viewed as a valuable agency of social control. Any conflicts that flow from this or other aspects of sport are viewed as dysfunctional and in need of eradicating if system stability is to be maintained.
15 Functionalists have also emphasized the important role that sport played in less developed societies.
16 E. Durkheim, *The Division of Labour in Society*, New York, Free Press, 1893/1964, pp. 153–4.
17 A. Giddens, *Capitalism and Modern Social Theory*, Cambridge, Cambridge University Press, 1971.
18 E. Durkheim, op. cit., 1893/1964, pp. 172–3.
19 For a more extensive discussion of this point see R. Gruneau, 'Modernisation or Hegemony: two views on sport and social development' in J. Harvey and H. Cantelon (eds) *Not Just a Game: Essays in Canadian Sport Sociology*, Ottawa, Ottawa University Press, 1988, pp. 9–32.
20 ibid, p. 26.

21 Such sentiments are evident in J. Betts 'The Technological Revolution and the Rise of Sport 1850–1900', *Mississippi Valley Historical Review*, no. xl, 1953, pp. 231–56; B. Dobbs, *Edwardians at Play, Sport 1890-1914*, London, Pelham Books, 1973; R. Mandell, *Sport, a Cultural History*, New York, Columbia University Press, 1984 and J. Walvin, *Leisure and Society 1830–1950*, London, Longman, 1978.

22 J. Walvin, op. cit., 1978, p. viii.

23 See J. Dumazedier, *Towards a Society of Leisure*, New York, Free Press, 1967 and K. Roberts, *Leisure*, London, Longman, 1981.

24 E. Durkheim, op. cit,. 1895/1964, pp. 4–5.

25 E. Durkheim, *Suicide: a Study in Sociology*, London, Longman, 1897/1964, p. 299.

26 E. Durkheim, *The Elementary Forms of Religious Life*, London, Allen & Unwin, 1912/1971, pp. 1–2.

27 J. Lever, op. cit., p. 14.

28 E. Durkheim, op. cit., 1912/1971, p. 380.

29 ibid, p. 381.

30 A number of writers have pointed to the symbolic role which play and sport perform. J. Huizinga, *Homo Ludens: A Study of the Play Element in Culture*, Boston, Beacon Press, 1955.

31 R. Coles, 'Football as a Surrogate Religion?' in M. Hill (ed.) *A Sociological Yearbook of Religion in Britain*, London, SCM Press, 1975, pp. 61-77.

32 E. Durkheim, op. cit., 1912/1971, p. 381.

33 ibid, p. 382.

34 G. Stone, 'Wrestling – the Great American Passion Play' in Eric Dunning (ed.) *The Sociology of Sport*, London, Cass, 1971, pp. 301–35.

35 E. Durkheim, op. cit., 1912/1971, pp. 215–16.

36 J. Curtis, J. Loy and W. Karnilowicw, 'A Comparison of Suicide – dip effects of major sports events and civil holidays', *Sociology of Sport Journal*, no. 3, 1986, pp. 1–14.

37 C. Ashworth, 'Sport as Symbolic Dialogue' in Eric Dunning, op. cit., 1971, pp. 40–6.

38 K. Davis and W. Moore, 'Some Principles of Stratification' *American Sociological Review*, no. 10, 1945, pp. 242–9.

39 S. Parker, op. cit., 1983.

40 The existence of a network of stratification systems operating cross-culturally has been subject to systematic review by J. Loy, G. Mcpherson and G. Kenyon, op. cit., 1978. Although this type of research is more developed in North America, similar work has been conducted in most European countries since the 1960s. For instance see J. Eggleston 'Secondary Schools and Oxbridge Blues', *British Journal of Sociology*, no. 16, 1965, pp. 232–42; W. Nowak, 'Social aspects of Polish boxers and their environment in the light of questionnaires and surveys', *International Review of Sport Sociology*, no. 4, 1969, pp. 137–50; and R. Renson, 'Social status symbolism of sport stratification, *Hermes*, no. 10, 1976, pp. 433–43.

41 Again this research is more developed in North America and has been usefully surveyed by J. Coakley, *Sport in Society: Issues and Controversies*, St Louis, Mosby, 1990.

42 J. Loy, G. McPherson and G. Kenyon, op. cit., 1978, conclude that there is little evidence to support the notion that sport can or does provide an avenue of social mobility.

43 R. Robertson and B. Turner, op. cit., 1989.

44 ibid, p. 548.

45 For a greater discussion of this debate, see the collection of papers published in *Sociology of Sport Journal*, no. 3, 1990; no. 4, 1990; no. 1, 1991; and no. 2, 1991.

46 This seems to apply whether sport violence or wider societal violence is under consideration.

47 A survey of functionalist literature on socialisation and sport appears to confirm this. See for example J. Loy and A. Ingham, 'Play Games and Sport in the Psychological Development of Children and Youth' in G. Garrick (ed.) *Physical Activity: Human Growth and Development*, New York, Academic Press, 1973, pp. 257–302; and J. Coakley 'Socialisation and Youth Sports' in C. Rees and A. Miracle (eds) *Sport and Social Theory*, Champaign, Human Kinetics, 1986, pp. 50–84.

48 Critical accounts of this would include P. Cohen, *Modern Social Theory*, London, Heinemann Books, 1968; A. Gouldner, *The Coming Crisis of Western Sociology*, New York, Basic Books, 1970; C. Wright-Mills, *The Sociological Imagination*, New York, Oxford University Press, 1959 and D. Wrong, 'The Oversocialised Conception of Man', *American Sociological Review*, no. 26, 1961, pp. 183–93. More recently G. Robertson and B. Turner, op. cit., 1989, have sought to rehabilitate aspects of functionalist thought.

49 For a sound overview of this scenario see R. Gruneau, 'Sport, Social Differentiation and Social Inequality', in D. Ball and J. Loy (eds) *Sport and Social Order: Contributions to the Sociology of Sport*, Reading, Addison-Wesley, 1975, pp. 117–84.

50 ibid, 1975.

51 ibid, 1975.

52 Such points are elaborated upon by P. Donnelly and K. Young, 'Reproduction and Transformation of Cultural Forms in Sport. A Contextual Analysis of Rugby', *International Review for the Sociology of Sport*, no. 20, 1986, pp. 19–37, and John Hargreaves (ed.) *Sport, Culture and Ideology*, London, Routledge & Kegan Paul, 1982, pp. 30–61.

53 G. Luschen and A. Rutten, 'The Specificity of Status Crystallisation and the Meaning of Sport'. Paper presented at the *World Congress of Sociology*, Madrid, 1990, July 9–13.

54 J. C. Alexander, op. cit., 1991, and G. Robertson and B. Turner, op. cit., 1989.

55 J. C. Alexander and P. Colomy, 'Towards Neo-Functionalism', *Sociological Theory*, no. 3, 1985, pp. 11–23.

56 G. Robertson and B. Turner, op. cit., pp. 551–2.

Chapter 2

Interpretative sociology: Rationalisation, cultural pessimism and the search for meaning

A diverse range of writers and theoretical strands are associated with interpretative sociology.[1] Exploring the conceptual, methodological and empirical projects of and possible links between our chosen writers, Simmel and Weber, is no easy task. Indeed, there exists considerable debate regarding both the nature of their specific work and the degree of similarity (and difference) between them.[2] Here, we suggest that there is sufficient overlap to warrant joining them and viewing them as examples of best practice in interpretative sociology.[3] Several reasons for adopting this strategy can be offered.

The linkage between Simmel and Weber on methodological grounds has been thoroughly explored. In certain respects – particularly with regard to concepts such as *verstehen*, the ideal types, interaction, social action, forms of sociation, value judgements and critiques of positivism – there is arguably considerable overlap.[4] Reference to these features of their work assists in evaluating interpretative sociology and how students studying leisure and sport can benefit from a knowledge of these methodological positions.[5] But this is not the primary reason why we have chosen to link Simmel and Weber. Given that we wish to explore the cultural problems associated with late modernity – and the position of leisure and sporting practices in this regard – it is these two writers who shared important substantive concerns on this general area.

In discussing the linkage between Simmel and Weber, Lawrence Scaff persuasively argued that both need to be understood as being 'caught up in a maelstrom of essentially cultural problems associated with modernity'.[6] For Scaff, these problems include urbanisation, metropolitan life, the experience of work, the fate of religious, ethical and aesthetic life-orientations, individual freedom and constraint, the impact of the objective and subjective cultures and the process of rationalisation.[7] It can be argued that social life in Western societies of the late twentieth century continues to be characterised by such problems.

We are fortunate not only with regard to the powerful light that Simmel and Weber cast on these problems, but also that both considered an array of issues and topics that relate to the fields of the sociology of leisure and sport, and did so in discussing these broader cultural problems. These common Simmelian and Weberian interests include, but are no means exhausted by, art, music, fashion, play, games and the role of clubs.[8] Simmel and Weber not only shared these common substantive interests, but they also reached not too dissimilar a view on how people would cope with the cultural problems identified.[9] Both shared a cultural pessimism that stemmed from what Weber termed the 'iron cage' of social life and which Simmel believed derived from the impact of objective culture on subjective experience. Their writings on these cultural problems are marked by a search for meaning, but neither seemingly can escape the melancholy and disenchantment of modernity. Significantly, both writers probed, sometimes in a tangential way, sometimes in a more direct manner, what role these phenomena played for people in making sense of, or coming to terms with, the modern predicament.

Simmel, sociation and the societal labyrinth

In contrast to the 'positivistic' tradition that was emerging in Europe in the late nineteenth century, Simmel's sociological gaze centres on forms of interaction between active human beings. For Simmel, such interaction is a complex, dynamic process. It involves the expression of meanings in a dense multi-layered reciprocal exchange between knowledgeable social actors. His 'formal' sociology is grounded in this concept of interaction or 'reciprocal effect'. Simmel paints an image of a 'web' to convey how the countless number of actions of people creates these reciprocal effects and what people thus call 'society'. The 'threads' of this web 'are spun, dropped, taken up again, displaced by others, and interwoven with others'.[10] Everything interacts in some way with everything else. This is what Simmel had to say:

> Without the interspersed effects of countless minor syntheses, society would break up into a multitude of discontinuous

systems. Sociation continuously emerges and ceases and emerges again . . . the whole gamut of relations that play from one person to another and that may be momentary or permanent, conscious or unconscious, ephemeral or of grave consequence . . . all these incessantly tie men together. Here are the interactions among the atoms of society. They account for all the toughness and elasticity, all the colour and consistency of social life.[11]

For Simmel, then, society is not a 'thing', a reified totality lying outside human consciousness. 'Society', according to Simmel, 'is only the synthesis or the general term for the totality of these specific interactions. . . . Society is identical with the sum of these relations'.[12] At first sight, there appears little room here for the study of large scale or more permanent features of society. Though this has been a dominant image of Simmel, it may be a misrepresentation in several respects.

Clearly Simmel was keen to unveil the 'immeasurable number of less conspicuous forms of relationship and kinds of interaction' that characterise human socieities.[13] He was also aware that these interactions interweave to form interactions of a more enduring kind. As he noted, the 'interactions we have in mind when we talk about "society" are crystallised as definable, consistent structures such as the state and the family'.[14] The institutions and social structures of 'society' then constitute the forms taken by the social content of the interaction he describes. Seeing such interconnections involves a question of distance. As Simmel remarks:

> When we look at human life from a certain distance, we see each individual in his precise differentiation from all others. But if we increase our distance, the single individual disappears, and there emerges, instead, the picture of a 'society' with its own forms and colours – a picture which has its own possibilities of being recognised or missed. . . . The difference between the two merely consists in the difference between purposes of cognition; and this difference, in turn, corresponds to a difference in distance.[15]

The reader is thus left with the question whether the sole object of sociological study is interaction or something more than the everyday cut and thrust of social life? In Simmel it is possible to find different conceptions of the purpose and subject matter of sociology. Clearly sociation is a key building block of Simmel's framework. By deploying the notion of distance, Simmel was attempting to avoid concentrating exclusively on individuals. Writing in 1896, Simmel observed:

> If society is to be an autonomous object of an independent discipline, then it can only be so by virtue of the fact that, out of the sum total of individual elements which constitute it, a new entity emerges; otherwise, all problems of social science would only be those of individual psychology.[16]

Here, again, arise the knotty problems of the individual and society, agency and structure. What did Simmel mean by 'a new entity'? As Frisby notes, Simmel uses the terms society and sociation interchangeably. Simmel indeed sees 'society everywhere, where a number of human beings enter into interaction and form a temporary or permanent unity'.[17] This double usage is evident throughout his work. We can illustrate this with reference to his examination of the connections between sociability, 'social games' and play:

> In the game, they [people] lead their own lives; they are propelled exclusively by their own attraction. For even where the game involves a monetary stake, it is not the money . . . that is the specific characteristic of the game. To the person who really enjoys it, its attraction rather lies in the dynamics and hazards of the sociologically significant forms of activity themselves. The more profound, double sense of 'social game' is that not only is the game played in a society (as its external medium) but that, with its help, people actually 'play' 'society'.[18]

Simmel is thus highlighting that the game is not only located in society but, as a social form, the game is society and society is the game. Though Simmel was referring to gambling, the relevance to sport and games more generally is clear. Indeed, this passage provides, in embryonic form, a more general theory of sport. Despite this use of society and sociation in the double sense outlined, the reader will, however, search in vain in Simmel's formal sociology for a general theorisation of society. Yet, if one examines Simmel's study of the rationalisation of social life and, in particular, his work *The Philosophy of Money*, a different facet of his framework comes to the fore.[19] That is, a probing of the broader genesis of the 'labyrinth' that human interaction creates. It is sufficient to note, at this stage, that social structures are composed of the actions and interactions of innumerable human beings that characterise 'sociation'. This process of sociation, or interaction, is the form in which individuals grow together into units that satisfy their needs. Simmel understood the role of leisure practices in this light.[29]

How is the task of investigating these reciprocal forms of sociation to be undertaken? For Simmel, sociologists have to immerse themselves substantively in day-to-day sociation. To capture the interplay between people, sociologists also have to deploy 'relational' concepts that are sensitive to the interweaving of human actions. Only when sociologists have substantively investigated the complex and multi-layered forms and dynamics of sociation, can they grasp how the 'new entity', 'society', comes about. Given that Simmel argued that 'society is everywhere', sociologists could legitimately study the so-called 'serious' or 'mundane' forms of sociation. It is fortunate that Simmel chose to examine an array of leisure activities to illustrate insights. He also recommended and conducted work that was concrete, comparative and historical in nature. This type of study explored the inevitable contradictions associated with the interweaving of human actions. He was also concerned to show how this interweaving in turn constructed a labyrinth, a dense matrix of interaction. This was, of course, concomitantly structuring the ongoing sociation that formed the focus of his detailed empirical enquiries.

Several advantages can be derived from studying 'the delicate, invisible threads that are woven between one person and another'.[21] The focus sociation allows scope for the exploration of human agency. As such, society is seen as the product of socially mediated human action. Thus a reified view of society is avoided. This individual endeavour is not, however, seen as a separate entity from society. The trap of individualism is side-stepped. By focusing on the day-to-day, the lived experience of social life can be placed centre frame. The puzzling, contradictory features of human existence are shown in a more colourful and less opaque light. By turning to the substantive base of his work several more advantages can be identified.

Social geometry, conflict, space and the metropolis

The discussion of 'social geometry' is linked to Simmel's work on conflict and competition. This allows scope for consideration to be given to his references to play and games, (and, very occasionally, sport). In the present context, a more extensive analysis of Simmel's study of an Alpine journey will be undertaken. Given that Simmel argues that the main motivation for such journeys lies in an escape from the social space of the city, this section concludes with an account of some aspects of his work on modernity and life in the metropolis. In a series of essays, Simmel pointed to the various elements that characterise social relations. These include numbers of people, degrees of distance, positions, and the degrees of self-involvement and symmetry. These elements interweave in different combinations in different types of interaction (sport and leisure practices being no exception). It is sufficient to highlight the shift in interaction involved in what Simmel refers to as a dyad and a triad:

> The difference between the dyad and larger groups consists in the fact that the dyad has a different relation to each of its two elements than have larger groups to their members. Although, for the outsider, the group consisting of two may function as an autonomous, super-individual unit, it usually does not do so for its participants. Rather, each of the two feels himself confronted only by the other, not by a collectivity above himself.[22]

The inclusion of a third person, the transformation of the dyad into a triad, causes a radical and fundamental change. For Simmel, this triad has the possibility of obtaining a meaning beyond the individuals involved. In the cut and thrust of triadic interaction, occurring over time and space, an entangled web of larger and larger groups forms. One consequence of this is that the individual becomes increasingly separate from this emerging structure – even though the individual is part of its composition. The individual grows more alone, isolated and segmented from others within the groups with which he/she interacts.

Here we see one of the contradictions that Simmel suggests characterise everyday life. That is, while this emerging structure (society) allows for the emergence of individuality and greater freedom, it also impedes, constrains and ultimately threatens, such choices. Game contests clearly show the processes involved. Consider games such as chess or tennis and compare this with more fluid, multi-person games such as basketball, soccer and rugby. Games in general, and sport games in particular, are of course, patterned by the very same elements that characterise social relations.[23] In the following passage we try to spell out how Simmel's ideas can apply to sport.

Sports are a particular form of sociation and are also part of the wider matrix of interaction. Sport contests provide almost paradigmatic examples of interaction with different degrees of symmetry of reciprocity and degrees of distance and closeness (vertical and horizontal). Examples include not only different types of games, (invasion, striking and fielding) with different numbers of participants and objectives therein, but also different degrees of symmetry of reciprocity and closeness that distinguish sports cultures more broadly. These different degrees of symmetry and close- ness would involve the varying quality of and strategies deployed by the interacting teams. They would also include referee–player, coach–athlete and elite performer and fans, agents and media personnel entanglements.

Though individuals, in sport contests, enter reciprocal interaction with each other, this should not be taken to suggest that this reciprocity is synonymous with notions of order and harmony. This was not Simmel's position. Simmel sees conflict as central to understanding the web of group affiliations. In spelling this out, we will also discuss its implications for the study of sport and games. Simmel sees conflcit as part of the dynamic by which people are attracted to or repelled by, each other. This occurs within a series of uneasy, shifting combinations, interactions and groups. Allies and foes are mutually entangled and this entanglement is in a constant process of flux that undergoes different rates of change – sometimes slower, sometimes more rapid.

Conflict is understood in Simmelian terms as involving a 'synthesis of elements that work both against and for one another'.[24] Simmel concludes that 'conflict itself resolves the tension between contrasts'.[25] This process is also evident in the unifying features of sport. Different degrees of reciprocity and closeness exist within and between teams. Without mutual acceptance of the rules governing the contest, no resolution of the anticipated conflict between the teams can be attempted. As rivals, opponents are bound to each other. In this connection, Simmel discussed at some length the role of antagonistic games. He observed:

> In its sociological motivation, the antagonistic game contains absolutely nothing except fight itself. . . . But there is something else more remarkable: the realisation of precisely this complete dualism presupposes sociological forms in the stricter sense of the word, namely unification. One unites in order to fight, and

one fights under the mutually recognised control of norms and rules . . . these unifications . . . are the technique without which such a conflict that excludes all heterogeneous or objective justifications could not materialise. What is more, the norms of the antagonistic game often are rigorous and impersonal and are observed on both sides with the severity of a code of honour – to an extent hardly shown by groups which are formed for co-operative purposes.[26]

Again, though he does not explicitly do so, Simmel could easily have referred to antagonistic sport games such as Association football or rugby to make these very points. Players in these sports are involved in a fierce physically contested struggle. Yet this antagonistic contest would not be possible if the players did not agree to abide by a set of rules voluntarily entered into. In these sport forms, as in others such as boxing, elements of exchange, conflict and sociability characterise encounters between rival opponents. Even with bitter rivals, a reciprocal set of rights and responsibilities govern the contest. According to Simmel the study of conflict is the study of competition. Again, this analysis is heavily laden with implications for the sociological study of leisure and sport. For Simmel, competition is a particular form of conflict in which opposing elements are synthesised. Discussing various types of competition, Simmel observes:

In many other kinds of conflict, victory over the adversary not only automatically secures, but itself is, the prize of victory. In competition, instead, there are two other combinations. Where victory over the competitor is the chronological first necessity, it itself means nothing. The goal of the whole action is attained only with the availability of a value which does not depend on that competitive fight at all. . . . The second type of competition perhaps differs even more greatly from other kinds of conflict. Here the struggle consists only in the fact that each competitor by himself aims at the goal, without using his strength on the adversary.[27]

A variety of examples is given by Simmel to illustrate these types of competition. Referring to the second type of competition where the competitor aims at the goal, without using force to prevent his/her opponent(s) from producing their optimal performance, Simmel notes that 'this strange kind of fight is exemplified by the runner who only by his fastness . . . aims to reach his goal . . . the subject of the final goal and the object of the final result inter-weave in the most fascinating matter'.[28] Simmel could have added the Alpine climber or skier to his example of the runner.

If sport contests highlight webs or networks of interaction/sociation, so too do clubs. Here too, there is an interweaving of conflict and co-operation. Professions and various occupational groups, such as doctors and lawyers, show a synthesis of elements that work both against and for one another. Significantly, for present purposes, Simmel discusses the role that 'social clubs' play in counter-balancing the presence – or absence – of serious com-petition in the lives of specific groups. Simmel notes:

> Thus, the members of a group in which keen competition prevails will gladly seek out such other groups as are lacking in competition as much as possible. As a result businessmen have a decided preference for social clubs. The estate-consciousness of the aristocrat, on the other hand, rather excludes competi-tion within his own circle; hence, it makes supplementations of that sort (i.e. social clubs) largely superfluous. This suggests forms of socialisation to the aristocrat which contain stronger competitive elements – for example, those clubs which are held together by a common interest in sports.[29]

Whatever the precise applicability of these insights to other coun-tries, and to a later period, the general tenet of Simmel's line of reasoning does appear relevant. In this way, within the context of a theory of culture, he is providing a framework in which to examine leisure. Intriguing though this reference to 'sports' and sports clubs might be, it is not developed. Instead, the reader has to look to Simmel's treatment of an Alpine journey to pick up the threads of this analysis. Just as the bourgeois trader or landed aristocrat uses clubs for different purposes, so too, according to Simmel, do different groups interact with 'nature'.

In his essay entitled, 'The Alpine Journey', Simmel questions the wholesale opening up of nature. In an earlier period the individual could escape the mediocrity of urban life and experi-ence the solitude provided by the Alps. Now, the transport revolu-tion, and the presence of increasing numbers of excursionists, had standardised this experience, and thus undermined this escapism. His pessimism about the possibilities of human existence is also evident in this context. In addition, however, Simmel challenges the justification for climbing and walking provided by the upper strata. He disputes whether such activities have any educational value and suggests that the upper strata 'seeks shamelessly to cloak its own pleasures with objective justification'.[30] Instead, Simmel probes the 'excitement and euphoria', the 'momentary rapture' provided by the physical act of climbing. In discussing these competing claims, he concludes:

> The clearest expression of this error is the confusion of the egoistic enjoyment of alpine sports with educational and moral values. . . . One forgets that the forces deployed are a means to goals which have no moral claim and indeed are often unethical; as a means for momentary enjoyment, which comes from the exertion of all one's energies, from playing with danger and the emotion of the panoramic view. Indeed, I would place this enjoyment as the highest that life can offer. The less settled, less certain and less free from contradiction modern existence is the more passionately we desire the heights that stand beyond the good and evil whose presence we are unable to look over and beyond.[31]

Here we have both an analysis of Alpine climbing and a more general explanation for the motivation that lies behind the types and forms of leisure that characterised Simmel's period. If people in the late twentieth century are increasingly less settled, less certain and less free, due to the contradictions of modern existence, then this may explain the growing centrality of sport/ leisure/adventures. Though Simmel regards the joy gained from 'playing with danger' as 'the highest that life can offer', no explanation for the source of this human need for enjoyment is provided.

One motivation for undertaking such journeys, and seeking out new adventures, was to escape from the 'contradictions of modern existence'. That is, from the contradictions between 'objective culture' and 'subjective culture' that were so evident in the metropolis. In turning our attention to this, it is also relevant to consider Simmel's work on social space.[32] Not surprisingly, in painting an image of the metropolis, Simmel points to the web or network of intersecting spheres. These entangled social circles include the division of labour, distribution, communications, money economy, commodity exchange and intellectual/cultural circles. Simmel's work on the metropolis shows how relevant his work is to those questions of culture generated by the problems associated with late modernity.

In his appraisal of Simmel, Frisby stresses this relevance by noting how, in the former's study of the metropolis, emphasis is placed 'upon the sphere of circulation and exchange, not merely of money and commodities but also social groups and individuals, a dynamic interaction of social circles'.[33] But the impact of this sphere of circulation and exchange on the social groups, and individuals involved, can be quite profound. The circulation and exchange of goods, commodities, images and practices creates a need in metropolitan people to create a distance between their inner selves and the kaleidoscope of impressions they are confronted with. According to Simmel, this social distance can be created by various forms of differentiation, social, physical and psychological. Clearly, leisure practices reflect these forms of spatial distance. The exclusion of specific groups from clubs and leisure forms, the segregation of sport practices on lines of gender, and the quest for novelty, adventure and excitement promised by tourism, mountaineering and seafaring, are all examples of the establishment of types of social distance. The key to understanding leisure then appears to lie in the metropolis and the problems engendered there by modernity.

Some of these issues of social distance are connected to Simmel's work on social space. Such work has, we believe, considerable significance for both the socio-geographic study of leisure and sport forms and for an analysis of crowd behaviour at sports stadia, pop concerts and the like. For Simmel, sociation involves the use and experience of space. Sociation involves sharing space. In this way social relations can be said to assume a spatial form. This space/place functions as a context for action. Several basic qualities of sociation involving a spatial dimension are identified by Simmel. These include: the exclusivity or uniqueness of space; the partitioning of space; the degree of fixity that space offers to social forms; spatial proximity and distance and finally movement through space. Before spelling out, in bare bones form, the implication of this for the study of leisure and sport forms of sociation, one additional but crucial insight that he offers needs to be highlighted. Simmel's work on the sociology of space involved neither spatial determinism (as is the tendency with some geographical studies of leisure and sport), nor social constructionism. In this way he could conclude that the city is 'not a spatial entity with sociological consequences, but a sociological entity that is formed spatially'.[34] Likewise, to paraphrase Simmel, the sports stadium, concert hall or theatre are not spatial entities with sociological consequences, but are sociological entities that are formed spatially.[35]

If the basic qualities of sociation involving a spatial dimension are borne in mind, then sport and leisure 'places' can be understood in a different way from more positivist geographical studies. Consider the different exclusivity or uniqueness associated with places such as Wimbledon and the Woodstock pop festival. Think about the partitioning of space in the form of national parks, nature reserves and sites of special scientific or scenic interest. Reflect on the gradual development of spatial boundaries in sport and the growing separation of performer from spectator. Ponder the intimacy and degree of intermingling involved in the 'local pub' and contrast this with the segregation of rival groups of football supporters. Observe the global movement of musicians, artists and sports stars performing in the redesigned spatial amphitheatres of late modernity, such as the Sydney opera house, Toronto's Skydome and the new section of the Louvre in Paris. Recognise how the media–sport production complex – as a part of the 'objective culture' to which Simmel drew attention – shrinks space. No longer do we have to be physically present – (at the Olympics, for example) – people can 'be together' without sharing space. Taken together, these basic qualities of sociation involving spatial dimension provide a powerful lens by which to refocus attention on the time–space dimensions of leisure and sport practices.

The philosophy of money, leisure and modernity

Judging by the range, depth and subject matter of *The Philosophy of Money*, Frisby is correct to claim that Simmel developed an important theory of modern society.[36] Simmel was, of course, not alone among late nineteenth- and early twentieth-century writers in probing the problems associated with modernity. It is appropriate too, at this point, to note that both Simmel and Weber sought to examine those problems with reference to the general process of rationalisation. Here we see a common thread appearing between these two writers. Whereas Weber was concerned to trace the disjunctures between the social system and the life world, Simmel was keen to probe the separation of objective culture from subjective culture. Unlike Weber, however, who, as we will show, sought to trace these disjunctures through examining the historical genesis of large-scale social formations, Simmel focused on small-scale social processes. He did so to illuminate the separation he detected in cultural life.

In this way, Simmel was concerned to show how individuals actually experience modernity in everyday life. Such a strategy is, of course, in keeping with his general view on sociology. If, as Frisby maintains, Simmel viewed modernity as being associated with 'the dissolution of our contact with the external world through concrete practice', then the study of the experience of modernity becomes vital. The study of how people actually cope with the growing separation of themselves from society becomes vital.[37] Examining the themes concerning the separation of objective and subjective culture, it becomes clear, in *The Philosophy of Money*, that people do produce the culture of modernity, but because of their ability to reify social reality, this cultural world comes to have a life of its own. The world of objective culture comes to dominate social actors who, in everyday interaction, continually help to re-create it. With modernity, objective culture grows and expands. Different components of this cultural realm become not only more extensive but also increasingly intertwined. The growth and expansion of the money economy (in the modern metropolis) transforms cultural forms into external objects. For Simmel 'every day and for all sides, the wealth of objective culture increases, but the individual mind can enrich the forms and contents of its own development only by distancing itself still further from that culture'.[38]

Though subjective culture is used as a refuge by the individual, the overall impact is the domination of objective culture over subjective culture. With the division of labour and the growing complexity associated with entangled social circles of urban interaction, culture itself becomes more rationalised and less fulfilling. Individuals too, are affected. They become more indifferent, calculating and alienated. The estrangement of individuals from others and a growing inner restlessness are related themes that Simmel explores in *The Philosophy of Money*. As he observes:

> The lack of something definite at the centre of the soul impels us to search for momentary satisfaction in ever-new stimulations, sensations and external activities. Thus it is that we become entangled in the instability and helplessness that manifests itself as the tumult of the metropolis, as the mania for travelling, as the wild pursuit of competition and as the typically

modern disloyalty with regard to taste, style, opinions and personal relationships.[39]

Simmel thus paints a pessimistic view of life in the modern metropolis. Subjective culture becomes rationalised, personally less enriching and dominated by objective culture. Objective culture is seen as the 'great leveller' of standards and talent. It creates – in the money economy – mass consumption. 'Cheap trash' is produced for this mass of consumers. Individual culture atrophies. Yet, out of this passivity comes the emergence of what Simmel terms 'excitement' and 'stimulation', and a desire for novel, constantly updated, attractions. Here is what he says:

> There emerges the craving today for excitement, for extreme impressions, for the greatest speed in its change . . . the modern preference for 'stimulation' as such in impressions, relationships and information – without thinking it important for us to find out why these stimulate us – also reveals the characteristic entanglement which means: one is satisfied with this preliminary stage of the genuine production of values.[40]

In the emerging 'boundless pursuit of pleasure', non-fulfilling activities are avidly consumed. Could he have had sport in mind? For Simmel, 'there is perhaps no psychological phenomenon that is so unreservedly associated with the metropolis as the blasé attitude. . . . A life in boundless pursuit of pleasure makes one blasé because it agitates the nerves to their strongest reactivity for such a long time that they finally cease to react at all'.[41] The individual becomes atomised, isolated, more dependent, less knowledgeable and is enslaved by an overwhelming objective culture. This then, for Simmel, is the 'tragedy of culture'.

Yet, another aspect of *The Philosophy of Money* emphasizes the contradictory nature of the processes involved. Just as it is subjective culture that creates and re-creates the objective culture that then comes to dominate it, the development of human potential comes to depend, in part, on this very expansion of objective culture. The irony is, therefore, that there are some 'liberating effects' to this process. Several can be identified. These include the extent to which this process allows individuals to engage with many more people; the obligations of the people involved become specific and not so all-embracing; a greater range of gratifications are available and people enjoy more 'freedom' to develop their individuality. People also have a greater potential to protect their 'inner selves'. Could not some leisure activities act as an enclave in which these liberating effects can be maximised? Despite the contradictory nature of these interconnected processes, the general theme of *The Philosophy of Money* is, as noted, the 'tragedy of culture', the triumph of the objective culture over the subjective experience. Frisby concludes his evaluation by noting that the themes found in *The Philosophy of Money* provide a foundation for the development of a 'sociology of . . . leisure, the emotions and the aesthetics of modern life'.[42]

A central theme of *The Philosophy of Money* concerns the issue of consumption. Simmel believed, as noted, that the satisfaction derived from this consumption was not that fulfilling or authentic. The consumption of cultural goods and spectacles reflected less the meeting of real needs and desires, but more the creation of mass markets of the money economy. In this way, leisure became associated with the possession of things and the escape from the mundane existence of everyday life. Here, as Frisby notes, we can see another example of the contradictory features of social life that Simmel examines. Though leisure provided a form of escape, it too was increasingly reflecting the everyday consumption that individuals find fulfilling.

The possession of cultural artefacts reflected more the dominance of objective culture over subjective culture then the skilled choice of the individual. Though the metropolis was the 'genuine showpiece of this culture', where new sights, sounds, smells, tastes and feelings could be found, to what extent these exciting cultural practices reflected real needs remained in doubt. Given that these centres were sites for the production, consumption, circulation and exchange of goods and services, they could provide a bewildering choice. But it was a choice determined by the market. Further, these glitzy places of entertainment were 'non-serious', apolitical and provided a diet of shallow amusement and a superficial intoxication of feelings.

Yet, in some leisure activities, metropolitan dwellers could find an escape from the demands of external life. In leisure forms such as sociability, art, music and travel, 'real' opportunities for 'genuine individuality' could be created and experienced. The Alpine journey, as noted, provided an opportunity for personal enrichment. Adventure, travel and tourism were the frontiers of human imagination, feeling and fulfilment. Even these, Simmel maintained, were under threat. The standardisation and commercialisation of these leisure forms deeply compromised their potential.

Based on such an analysis, Frisby concludes that several inferences and insights can be drawn from Simmel. First, the concept of leisure itself needs critical examination. The term itself is ideologically laden, reflecting dominant commercial and ideological interests. Second, leisure is not an autonomous sphere: it is closely interwoven with the 'serious side of life'. After all, leisure for some, is labour for others. Third, leisure can never be adequately associated, a priori, with creativity. Commodified and objectified leisure forms appear shallow and superficial and not fulfilling. Fourth, the very success of the exploitation of the countryside and wilderness as a compensation for metropolitan life results in a diminution of this as an escape route. We bring 'our' objective culture with us!

Whatever the merits of this line of thought, clearly Simmel was a perceptive observer of people, at leisure. His general theoretical position emphasised that in the study of any forms of sociation it was possible both to trace its interconnection with other interactions and to view it as a locus of meaning for the totality of interactions. There are grounds to suggest that this observation provides an important justification for and insight into the sociological study of leisure and sport.

Weber, *verstehen*, ideal types and historical sociology

Just as Simmel sought to avoid reifying social life by emphasizing the study of 'sociation', Weber's fundamental unit of investigation is the individual. Only the individual, for Weber, is capable of 'meaningful social action'. People have motives for action. Their behaviour is guided by subjective meanings. People also have their ideas and explanations as to why they behave as they do. These ideas and actions form part of any comprehensive account of their conduct. This led Weber to conclude that 'such action exists only as the behaviour of one or more individuals'.[43] On this basis, he observed that 'society' is never more than the plurality of interactions of individuals within specific social contexts. Units such as the 'state' or the Church (or the International Olympic Committee), are examples of 'collectives' that are 'solely the resultants and modes of organisation of the particular acts of individual persons, since these alone can be treated as agents in a course of subjectively understandable action'.[44] 'Collectives' cannot think, feel or interpret social life – only people can.

The task of sociology then, involves 'rendering intelligible' the subjective basis of social life. To get at the motives for social action, it is necessary to penetrate the subjective understanding of individuals. To do this, the sociologist must account for the meanings and concepts that govern her/his behaviour. For Weber, however, the task of sociology was not only to show empathetic understanding, but also to provide a causal explanation for such conduct. Sociology's claim to being a science involved an 'interpretative understanding of social action in order . . . to arrive at a causal explanation of its course and effects'.[45]

Clearly, *verstehen* analysis is useful in exploring the subjective meanings of social actors. These actors are always faced with choices. One specific course of action is always chosen in preference to the many others available. Such choices are powerfully influenced by social actors' perceptions of the limits and opportunities available with regard to specific courses of action. Because of this, there develops a 'patterning' to social life. Though social action is choice ridden, it is not random. A pattern emerges that allows sociologists to attempt to construct an 'understandable sequence of motivation' and thereby enabling them to undertake causal analysis. Such causal analysis does not, Weber maintains, produce 'laws', but generates statements of tendency regarding the nature, course and consequences of human interaction.

The meaning of social action may be analysed in two senses. First, concerning the concrete meanings expressed by individual actors. Second, regarding the 'ideal type' meaning associated with a specific course of conduct held by a hypothetical actor. We will deal with the concept of ideal type in due course. For now, note that Weber believed that no rigid separation existed between these modes of analysis. Not all social action, however, is equally understandable. Behaviour involves a weaving together of understandable and non-understandable features. For Weber, some behaviour was only partially understandable – he included religious fervour in this category. Indeed, the more 'foreign' the behaviour, the more difficult for the social scientist to view the course of conduct through the actors' eyes. Weber pointed out, however, that a full recapitulation of an experience is not necessary for the task of providing a version of the experience that would be analytically intelligible. Weber observed, 'one need not have been Caesar in order to understand Caesar'.[46] While he believe that, 'recapturing an experience is important for accurate understanding', it was not 'an absolute precondition for its interpretation'.[47]

Weber identified two types of *verstehen*. The first related to a direct observational understanding where observing the act was sufficient to reveal what was going on. However, to understand why the act was taking place, the sociologist needed to have recourse to explanatory understanding. Taken in isolation, the act would defy interpretation. By placing it in an intelligible 'sequence of motivation', that is, in a wider context of meaning, the sociologist would be able to grasp the motives and subjective meanings of the social action. This probing of the intervening motivational link between the observed act and its meaning to the actor, entailed relating the particular behaviour to a broader normative code of conduct with reference to which the individual acts.

To help in this task of tracing 'sequences of motivation', Weber developed the concept of ideal type. Its function for Weber was 'the comparison with empirical reality in order to establish its divergencies or similarities . . . and to understand and explain them causally.[48] Ideal types were viewed as providing the technical means of analysing the probability that actors will follow one course of action rather than another. Ideal types then, are conceptual abstractions that highlight the core features of specific social formations. This is what Weber had to say in this connection:

> An ideal type is formed by the one-sided accentuation of one or more points of view and by the synthesis of a great many diffuse, discrete, more or less present and occasionally absent concrete individual phenomena, which are arranged according to those one-sidely emphasised viewpoints into a unified analytical construct. . . . In its conceptual purity, this mental construct . . . cannot be found empirically anywhere in reality.[49]

By examining a range of different empirical cases, the core features of a specific form could be identified. While no one example conforms to the ideal type, each case would be the distillation of these principal features. In generating a series of hypotheses about voluntary sport organisations, Wendy Frisby clearly had this in mind when she noted that:

Weber's theory of bureaucracy provides a framework for investigating the structure and meaning of modern amateur sport by focusing on the historical and cultural context in which organisational structures emerge and examining the effects of structure on the attainment of instrumental objectives and resource acquistion, while considering the consequences of a shift in power as control is taken out of the hands of the worker, or in this case, the participant.[50]

Weber was keen to emphasise, however, that it was illusory to imagine that the researcher could ever capture the 'true essence' of reality. Reality was too complex, too interconnected and always subject to different readings. Weber's advice was to avoid looking for some mythical essence and instead focus on the ways specific cases differed in their consequences for social action. This is what Frisby attempts to do. As a tool of analysis, the ideal type was to be used as a yardstick to compare and contrast empirical cases. The discrepancies would thus become the object of study. Used along with substantive research, it would enable the researcher to determine the causes that led to differences between the ideal type and empirical reality. The research would thus be able to rank various factors involved in a given historical case and assign a relative significance to each.

Weber's use of ideal types relates both to his view of the status of sociology as a science and its relation to history. Ideal types, coupled with the *verstehen* method, enabled the sociologist to conduct their interrogation of the meaning of social action based upon techniques that were capable of being replicated. These techniques would thus be verifiable and in accord with the conventional canons of scientific method. In this regard, Weber did not rule out the use of statistics to complement, support and confirm the findings gleaned through *verstehen* analysis. This analysis, coupled with the deployment of ideal types, was a necessary prelude to causal explanation. Regarding sociology's relation to history, Weber saw that ideal types would be generated by sociologists so that causal analysis of history could be undertaken. Sociology's 'preliminary task' was oriented towards the development of these clear concepts. Given that Weber viewed historical processes as the combination of many different factors and antecedents (which varied in their relative importance), ideal types would enable the researcher to establish an ordering of

importance and causal significance. For Weber, historical sociology was concerned with both particularity and generality. The
probing of this interconnection would be accompanied by the
utilisation of general concepts such as ideal types and different
types of causation.[51] But the assessment of the precise sequence of
events was not seen as connected to a specific logic of history. Any
assessment therefore would need to be substantively grounded
and based on a notion of a balance of probabilities. That is, causal
explanation for Weber involved the question of probability that an
event would be followed or accompanied by another event.

The value of this approach to the sociological study of leisure
and sport has been examined by a range of authors.[52] In assessing
its worth, Alan Ingham, for example, believed that Weber provided a 'cure' for the positivist 'malaise' he identified as plaguing
the sociology of sport during the 1960s and 1970s. Ingham concluded that Weber was valuable to the sub-discipline of the sociology of sport for several reasons. Drawing on Weber enabled the
researcher to grasp that sport (and leisure) are part of a historical,
meaningful human creation, a part of sociocultural reality.
Indeed, sport cannot, he argued, be isolated analytically from
public issues and insistent human troubles that characterise socio-
cultural reality. Using Weber's substantive work as a benchmark,
Ingham observed that sport needed to be studied in an inder-
disciplinary manner.[53] Continuing this Weberian theme, he noted
that the sociologist of sport, through part of a broader socio-
cultural reality also has the power to confront and investigate it.
The knowledge generated from such enquiries cannot be objective
(in the natural scientific sense), it can only be a partial and one-
sided explanation of certain aspects of reality. Those aspects
selected for investigation reflect the value significance assigned to
them by the sociologist of sport/leisure. Considered in the light of
the arguments actually presented by Weber, the fact-value debate
that characterises some North American sociology of sport is seen
by Ingham as specious. There is, however, more to this debate than
Ingham conveys.

In his essay 'Science as a Vocation', Weber discusses the ethical
stance of the scientist.[54] Although acknowledging that science contributes to the growth of knowledge, Weber argues that this does
not in itself add to our understanding of how people should live,
or assist in deciding whether certain values are better than others.
Hence scientists, or so Weber believed, should jettison any hope

that they will, in generating some all-encompassing 'truth', be able to transform the social world. In addition, the scientist should avoid using the lecture theatre as an opportunity to express political beliefs masquerading as scientific fact. The curtailment of personal values, the maintenance of 'intellectual integrity' and the single-minded pursuit of knowledge are dominant themes in Weber's vision of a scientist's vocation. For Weber, the scientist cannot tell people what to do. Given his exposure to American university life, and hence the burgeoning college sports programmes, at the turn of the century, it is perhaps less surprising that he contrasted the ethical stance of the scientist with that of the football coach. This is what he had to say:

> Those of our youth are in error who react to all this by saying, 'Yes, but we happen to come to lectures in order to experience something more than mere analyses and statements of fact'. The error is that they seek in the professor something different from what stands before them. They crave a leader and not a teacher. . . . To be sure, if the teacher happens to be a football coach, then, in this field, he is a leader. But if he is not this (or something similar in a different field of sports), he is simply a teacher and nothing more. . . . Fellow students! You come to our lectures and demand from us the qualities of leadership, and you fail to realise in advance that of a hundred professors at least ninety-nine do not and must not claim to be football masters in the vital problems of life, or even to be 'leaders' in matters of conduct.[55]

The task facing sociologists of sport and leisure – perhaps especially for those working in contexts where an emphasis is placed on high performance sport, a traditional notion of physical education, or some form of social intervention – is no easy matter. Following a Weberian approach entails, if we take Weber at his word, the adoption of an 'heroic' vocational stance and doing substantive research. This also involves, as Ingham correctly observed, doing so in a way that recognises that there is no single theory of sport and that sociological research cannot generate 'laws', only statements of tendency regarding sport and leisure developments.[56] Given these key points, and having outlined some of the main methodological concepts of Weberian sociology, let us see to what extent this appraisal of its usefulness for the sociology of sport and leisure is accurate.

Rationalisation and body cultures

The rationalisation process is the unifying theme of Weber's empirical studies. The tendency towards rationalisation is made up of several interlocking themes. Each, in varying degrees, affected the course and development of Western societies. This rationalisation process involved not only the emergence of a particular form of consciousness, but also new forms of discipline that regulated, controlled and organised the development and expression of human bodies.[57] In mapping out the main features of this rationalisation process reference will be made to several institutions and areas of life where new forms of consciousness emerged and developed. In addition, however, we will examine how this process manifested itself in both the emergence of quite distinctive body cultures and the broader making of modern sport.

For Weber, rationalisation was seen as a broad collective process that permeated Western societies from the Reformation period onwards. The actions of individuals were increasingly reduced to prosaic calculation – action oriented to routine administration of a world dominated by large-scale organisations and a specialised division of labour. This process led to the destruction of human vitality and freedom. In addition, a sense of disenchantment with the world was engendered and a gradual elimination of magical thought and practice occurred. Why should tracing the development of 'formal' rationality be central to an understanding of the dilemmas facing contemporary people?

Several interlocking elements can be identified. Rationalisation processes undermined the then existing coherent and unified, mainly religious, world views. In turn, these processes generated a growth in multiple secular belief systems. As part of this process, a modern pluralist culture began to develop. As this general process gathered momentum individuals became trapped in a world that they helped create but increasingly undermined their creativity and autonomy of action. Out of this rational social action is produced a world that is essentially meaningless, lacking in moral direction and dominated by bureaucratic structures. In one telling passage, Weber powerfully conveys the nature of the processes involved as he saw then:

> The Puritan wanted to work in a calling; we are forced to do so. For when asceticism was carried out of monastic cells into everyday life, and began to dominate worldly morality, it did its

part in building the tremendous cosmos of the modern economic order. This order is now bound to the technical and economic conditions of machine production which today determine the lives of all the individuals who are born into this mechanism, not only those directly concerned with economic acquisition, with irresistible force. Perhaps it will so determine them until the last ton of fossilised coal is burnt. In Baxter's view the care for external goods should only lie on the shoulders of the 'saint like a light cloak, which can be thrown aside at any moment'. But fate decreed that the cloak should become an iron cage.[58]

Let us look at how this 'iron cage' emerged in a little more detail. Weber's historical sociology was concerned to explore the regularities and patterns of action within cultural formations. In this connection, he was keen to explain the specific features and conditions of modern Western societies. The key for Weber lies in understanding the origins, nature and effects of rationalisation. From his comparative studies of religions and other institutions, Weber observed that rationalisation processes were inhibited in the East but facilitated in the West. Why should this have been so?

Though Weber identified several different types of rationality, here discussion will centre on two main forms. In one type, formal rationality, conduct is organised according to rationally calculable principles. A form of means–end calculation is undertaken by the individual. This calculation occurs with reference to universally applied rules, laws and regulations. Over time, such formal rationality was to become the dominant feature of the rationalisation process as it unfolded in the West. It found expression in a range of institutions, economic, religious, legal and scientific. Accompanying its spread was the emergence, according to Weber, of a bureaucratic form of domination and a rational-legal authority. Let us illustrate this in bare bones form with reference to the sphere of work. As rationalisation processes penetrate the work sphere several changes occur. There is a general extension of the productivity of labour. There also develops a tendency for workers to be separated from the means of production. Work practices also become subject to more efficient means of administration. Concomitantly, technological advances, designed to enhance productivity, gather momentum. The social practices that govern such productivity become increasingly impersonal and specialised. For Weber, the individual becomes a mere 'cog' in the machine.

In contrast to this, Weber highlighted what he termed 'substantive rationality'. In this type of rationality, individuals make choices to achieve specific ends based on a system of values. With the growing ascendancy of formal rationality, this form of rationality, and the value systems underpinning it, became increasingly marginalised. What were the dynamics involved in this process? In his work, Weber highlighted how the Calvinistic quest for salvational security gave rise – by a process of unintended consequences – to a culture that emphasised reason, stability, coherence, discipline and mastery of the natural world. This Calvinistic quest generated a new form of possessive individualism. This, in turn, legitimated the pursuit and possession of money and created a culture dedicated to both work and the transformation of the human environment. As a part of the demagification of the world, Calvinism denied the magical efficacy of the Christian sacraments. The role of charismatic leaders was also downplayed. And, in creating a culture that was sympathetic to the study of the natural sciences and intellectual inquiry, Calvinism paradoxically helped the emergence of the modern scientific world-view.

The iron cage to which Weber pessimistically refers was formed out of the objectification of material culture and the projection of asceticism into the external world of production, labour and all styles of life. In this regard, Weber comments that 'one of the fundamental elements of the spirit of modern capitalism, and not only of that but of all modern culture: rational conduct on the basis of the idea of the calling, was born . . . from the spirit of Christian asceticism'.[59] This asceticism undertook to reshape the social world and permeate all aspects of life. For Weber, it had gained 'an inexorable power over the lives of men'.[60] Discussing this Puritan idea of the calling and asceticism, Weber also highlighted its impact on the pastimes of people. Weber noted that:

> This asceticism turned with all its force against one thing: the spontaneous enjoyment of life and all it had to offer. This is perhaps most characteristically brought out in the struggle over the Book of Sports which James I and Charles I made into law expressly as a means of counteracting Puritanism, and which the latter ordered to be read from all the pulpits. The fanatical opposition of the Puritans to the ordinances of the King,

permitting certain popular amusements on Sunday outside of Church hours by law, was not only explained by the disturbance of the Sabbath rest, but also by resentment against the intentional diversion from the ordered life of the saint, which it caused. And, on his side, the King's threats of severe punishment for every attack on the legality of those sports were motivated by his purpose of breaking the anti-authoritarian ascetic tendency of Puritanism, which was so dangerous to the state.[61]

Clearly then, this process was, at least in its early stages of development, a contested affair. While the feudal and monarchical forces protected the pleasure seekers against the forces unleashed by these processes, Puritans continued to emphasise the principles of ascetic conduct.[62] Weber developed this reference to the 'sports' and pastimes of people by highlighting the ambivalent status they enjoyed:

> The Puritan aversion to sport, even for the Quakers, was by no means simply one of principle. Sport was accepted if it served a rational purpose, that of recreation necessary for physical efficiency. But as a means for the spontaneous expression of undisciplined impulses, it was under suspicion; and in so far as it became purely a means of enjoyment, or awakened pride, raw instincts or the irrational gambling instinct, it was of course strictly condemned.[63]

Sport was not the only target. As we have already pointed out, the demagification of society was one feature that characterised the rationalisation process. It is not surprising, therefore, that other aspects of people's pastimes that had such 'magical' connections would be frowned upon. Weber records that 'the Puritan's ferocious hatred of everything which smacked of superstition, of all survivals of magical or sacramental salvation, applied to the Christmas festivities and the May Pole and all spontaneous art'.[64]

We have already suggested that rationalisation processes found expression in a range of cultural activities and institutions. Sport and the pastimes of the people were clearly no exception. The impact of these processes is one, as suggested, where the individual is increasingly disenchanted. Whereas the ethos of vocation adopted by Calvinists once led to a sense of inner-worldly accomplishment, for Weber, contemporary people are faced with a situation that lacks meaning. Examining responses to the domination of formal rationality, Weber noted that people attempt to justify their life activity by either surrendering completely or by embracing the compulsions of 'mundane passion'. Before completing the final part of *The Protestant Ethic and the Spirit of Capitalism* (where this argument is located), Weber had, as we noted earlier, visited America. This country was seen to best illustrate the trends involved. For Weber, the American social order was being 'stripped of its religious and ethical meaning'. What is most revealing, given our present concern to probe what role sport and leisure practices played for people in making sense of, or coming to terms with, the modern predicament, is that Weber believed that this social order was assuming the character of sport. This is what Weber wrote:

> Where the fulfilment of the calling cannot be related to the highest spiritual and cultural values, or when, on the other hand, it need not be felt simply as economic compulsion, the individual generally abandons the attempt to justify it all. In the field of its highest development, in the United States, the pursuit of wealth, stripped of its religious and ethical meaning, tends to become associated with purely mundane passions, which often actually give it the character of sport.[65]

Sport (college or professional) was, for Weber, part of the negative portrayal of the contemporary world. Modern people could find no comfort there – though as we will highlight in the next section, Weber did see some hope in the role that art and music could play. For now, however, let us turn attention to how rationalisation processes have affected body cultures and the making of modern sport.

The emergence of a particular form of consciousness is a well-established feature of the rationalisation process to which Weber refers. An equally important but neglected theme is the development of new forms of discipline that supervised the body.[66] Brian Turner, for example, develops this strand in Weber's writings by noting that it casts light on the subordination and regulation of instinctual gratification. In traditional societies, human needs were restricted to immediate gratification and production – a natural relation existed between need and economy. With the unfolding rationalisation processes however, came both a disciplining of energies and an amplification of needs. This process involved a transition from internal religious restraints on people's passions (emotions), to an external secular amplification and display of desires. This secularisation and rationalisation of the body is evident in several areas, taken together these areas provide a framework by which to understand the transformation of the human body in Western societies. First, the body ceases to be a feature of religious culture – people's bodies are no longer enveloped in a religious system of meaning and ritual. Second, bodies became increasingly incorporated into a bio-medical scientific discourse. Third, internal restraints seen to be controlling the body appear to shift to outside the body. Fourth, bodies become symbols of worth and prestige signifying status to the bearer of a specific body. Fifth, modern societies emphasize both overt displays of personal status and a narcissistic drive towards self-fulfilment.[67]

If we examine the development of body cultures, the processes outlined stand in stark relief. The transformation of dance and the scientisation of exercise, the emergence of formal gymnastics (German and Swedish varieties) and the increasing work-like regimes, scientific testing and dietary manipulation of elite performers, are all areas that highlight rationalisation processes.[68] We also noted earlier that Weber observed that Puritans did accept the value of exercise as a suitable component of education. Turner correctly observes that this provided the rationale for the nineteenth-century acceptance of sport and training as a form of character building and as part of 'rational recreation'.[69] Besides these areas, Turner also points to the artistic representation of the body and the transformation of dietary practices – with a blend of medical and moral discourses – as showing rationalisation processes being at work.[70]

If attention is given to the broad process involved in the making of modern sport, then Weber's work has also provided a framework for writers to consider this issue. Here we will consider the work of Allen Guttmann.[71] For Guttmann, the emergence of this scientific world-view is the key to explaining the making of modern sports, or what he terms the transition from ritual to record. He highlights seven interrelated themes that he contends provide the framework for understanding this transition. The details of this analysis need not delay us here. In each of these areas Guttmann draws on a Weberian framework to support his case. On this basis he concludes:

One great advantage of the Weberian model is that it enables one to see in the microcosm (modern sports) the characteristics of the macrocosm (modern society) – secularism, equality, specialisation, rationalism, bureaucratic organisation, and quantification. These six characteristics, plus the quest for records which appear even more strikingly in sports than in the rest of the social order, are interdependent, systematically related elements of the ideal type of a modern society. They derive from the fundamental Weberian notion of the difference between the ascribed status of traditional society and the achieved status of a modern one.[72]

Whatever the merits of this approach, and Gruneau for one believes (correctly in our judgement) that he provides an overly optimistic interpretation of Weber and the sporting condition, Guttmann has demonstrated of some elements of a Weberian analysis of the making of modern sports.[73] Guttmann concludes in the following manner:

> Sports themselves, originating in the spontaneous expression of physical energy, have their source in the irrational. . . . Sports are an alternative to and, simultaneously, a reflection of the modern age. They have their roots in the dark soil of our instinctive lives, but the form they take is that dictated by modern society.[74]

While rightly pointing to the paradoxical nature of modern sports, we must note that Weber himself was rather dismissive about the potential of the 'compulsions of mundane passions' to act as an alternative to our modern age. In fact, Weber suggested that if an alternative was possible, then it would be found in a retreat into aestheticism.

Art, music and styles of life: Seeking solace in aestheticism

In developing the theme regarding people's responses to the problems and dilemmas posed by modernity, an account of Weber's portrayal of the origins and function of Western art, music and styles of leisure practices is required. In doing so, it is also necessary to examine some specific aspects of Weber's work on religion. In this way it is possible to see how artistic creativity came to perform the function that Weber assigns to it. Weber's work on religion is vast. Here, we wish to focus on that strand of Weber's work that examined the role religion played in forging a broader state of mind of which the capitalist element is a central part. Weber's overriding concern was to probe the relationship among a variety of world religions and the unique development in the West of the emergence of a rational type of capitalist economic system. He examined several world religions and showed how either their structure and/or system of ideas acted as impediments to the rise of rationality. The realm of the sacred in these religions proved a powerful sphere of resistance to the possible flowing of rationalisation processes. Outside the West, the balance of factors favoured the retention of traditional modes of thinking, feeling and acting.

In the West, however, it was a different matter. In *The Protestant Ethic and the Spirit of Capitalism*, Weber probes the origins of the peculiar spirit that eventually made captialism possible. We have already noted that Weber argued that 'rational conduct based on the idea of the calling' was one of the 'fundamental elements of the spirit of capitalism' and that this was 'born' from the spirit of Christian asceticism. It needs to be stated however, that Weber was not suggesting that capitalism was the result of Protestantism in general or Calvinism more specifically. Weber abhorred recourse to mono-causal explanations. Religious forces were only part of the equation. A range of other historical factors was also involved. Throughout *The Protestant Ethic and the Spirit of Capitalism*, Weber highlights how in the pursuit of wealth, the development of frugality and the consecration of material activity, individuals felt that they were serving God and fulfilling a calling. No aspects of life were left untouched by the rationalisation processes that were set in train by these actions. Whatever the merits of this approach, Weber himself did not see this work as the final word. He himself concluded that 'the next task would rather be to show the significance of ascetic rationalism . . . for the content of practical social ethics. . . . Only then could the quantitative cultural significance of ascetic Protestantism in its relation to other plastic elements of modern culture be estimated'.[75] It is possible to examine the development of art and music in this spirit. Weber recognised the interrelated relationship between religion, art, music and rationalisation processes. At an earlier stage in human societies there also existed a close relationship between artistic creation and religion. This was especially so when such creative activities gave expression to religious values:

Since its beginnings, religion has been an inexhaustible fountain of opportunities for artistic creation, on the one hand, and of stylising through traditionalisation, on the other. This is shown in a variety of objects and processes: in idols, icons, and other religious artefacts; in the stereotyping of magically proved forms, which is a first step in the overcoming of naturalism by a fixation of 'style'; in music as a means of ecstasy, exorcism, or apotropaic magic; in sorcerers as holy singers and dancers; in magically proved and therefore magically stereotyped tone relations – the earliest preparatory stages in the development of tonal systems.[76]

Observe Weber's reference to the development of tonal systems. In music, and in painting, the effects of rationalisation processes would not only contour the shape of creativity, but would also lead to growing antagonism between these forms of human endeavour and religion. Indeed, the more art developed into an autonomous sphere, which Weber saw as stemming from the onset of 'lay education', the more art tended to acquire its own set of constitutive values. This antagonism increased with the growth of secular intellectualism. With these processes, those elements in art that were compatible with religious fervour were diminished. Art took over the function of 'this-worldly salvation'. It provided a refuge or 'salvation from the routines of everyday life'. Before teasing out how this relates to the retreat by contemporary people into aesthticism, some of the key features of art and music, as they developed in the Western rationalisation process, need highlighting.

In his study of music, Weber points to how, in its Western form, it became based on tonality, polyphony and the study of counterpoint. Modern Western musical notation facilitated structural composition, but left little room for improvisation. That is, it became highly rationalised. This is evident in the emergence of 'classical' music – symphonies and operas – and in the development of musical instruments – piano and violin. More concise notation, the establishment of a well-tempered scale, the harmonious tonal range and the standardisation of various instruments into specific groups are all seen as part of the rationalisation of Western music.[77] Paradoxically, 'spontaneous' musical creativity was being reduced to routine procedures based on rational principles, yet this process also enabled Western composers and musicians to express themselves in what became known as 'classical' music. Rationalisation processes led to a 'transformation of the process of musical production into a calculable affair operating with known means, effective instruments and understandable rules'.[78] Similarly, in painting, sculpture and architecture there developed the rational utilisation of lines and the emergence of a spatial perspective from the Renaissance period on. Turner also observes that there was an intimate connection between the representation of the nude in Western art and the growth of individualisation and secularisation.[79]

Echoing Simmel's analysis of the function of art, Weber believed that art developed as a distinctive and autonomous sphere of value. It had become a source and setting for inner experiences that provided the possibility of transcending the routines of everyday life. For Weber, the significance of art lies in its opposition to rationalisation. The mundane and the routine are left behind.[80] The artistic realm, therefore, not only appropriates the aesthetic as salvation from theoretical and practical rationality, but also involves an attempt to 're-create the aesthetic as a genuine sphere of redemption bearing cosmic significance for an entire way of life'.[81] The paradoxical feature of this process was, as Scaff notes, that the growth of specific forms of art that cultivated inward cultural redemption was not possible without the new technologies of publication, communication and metropolitan life. Here, again, we see the clash between the individuals' subjective culture and the objective culture of the city to which Simmel referred. Would the solace provided by aestheticism prove an illusion?

These leisure practices also perform other functions. Chief among these is the role they play in the pursuit and maintenance of status. In his discussion of ethos and style of life, Weber refers to the process by which status is closely related to the adoption and pursuance of specific styles of life associated with particular social positions. Weber shares with Simmel a concern over the conspicuous consumption of goods, services and leisure practices. In this connection, Weber discusses several areas that are of interest. These include the games of the ancient and medieval world, duelling and the role of clubs in both America and Germany. These areas are tied together by Weber's concern to explore the role that status plays in society.

Clearly, in both the ancient and medieval world, physical activity games played an important role in the culture of European warrior groups. Such games reinforced dominant values

emphasising aggression and discipline and sharpened the necessary skills required for combat. This was not the only function of
such activities. Weber intriguingly refers, for example, to the role
of agon in the 'glorification of knightly heroism' and the 'important bond' that such activities forged in the Hellenic world against
barbarians.[82] Weber goes on to note that:

> Inevitably the game also occupies a most serious and important
> position in the life of these knightly strata; it constitutes a
> counterpole to all economically rational action. However, this
> kinship with an artistic style of life, which resulted from this
> aspect of the game, was maintained also directly by the aristo-
> cratic ethos of the dominant feudal stratum. The need for
> 'ostentation', glamour and imposing splendor . . . is primarily a
> feudal status need and an important power instrument.[83]

Considered in this light, leisure practices are closely connected to
issues of power, control and the 'serious' side of social life. Not
only do they perform practical functions relating to tasks conducted in different contexts (military skills), but also confer
and/or deny prestige and status to different social groups. This
line of thinking is also evident in Weber's discussion of athletic and
social clubs in American and Germany. In probing the function of
clubs in America, Weber provides some relevant insights into
contemporary leisure practices. To gain admission to exclusive
clubs or associations was, he maintained, a 'ticket to ascent'. Exclusion from the 'boys club at school', the 'athletic club or Greek
letter society' at university, or the 'notable clubs of businessmen
and the bourgeoisie' and that of the 'metropolitan plutocracy', was
usually to end up as 'a sort of pariah'.[84] Continuing in this vein,
Weber concludes:

> In America . . . affiliation with a distinguished club is essential
> above all else. In addition, the kind of home is important . . .
> and the kind of dress and sport. . . . This is not the place for a
> more detailed treatment. There are masses of translating
> bureaus and agencies of all sorts concerned with reconstructing
> the pedigrees of the plutocracy. All these phenomena, often
> highly grotesque, belong in the broad field of the European-
> isation of American 'society'.[85]

It is clear from this that while these clubs and societies were
performing the role of status enhancement, not all provided

solace and comfort for the troubles of metropolitan life. This was the crucial difference identified by Weber in comparing these clubs with the aesthetic functions performed by art and music groups and salons. Comparing the national character of America and Germany, Weber again assessed the role that sport could play in this regard. He did so in quite disparaging terms. Contrasting Prussian duelling clubs with Anglo-Saxon clubs, Weber observed:

> The most stupid Anglo-Saxon club offers more of a cosmopolitan education, however empty one may find the organised sports in which the club often finds its fulfilment. The Anglo-Saxon club with its often very strict selection of members always rests upon the principle of the strict equality of gentlemen and not upon the principle of 'pennalism', which bureaucracy cherishes so highly as a preparation for discipline in office.[86]

For Weber, it was the aesthetic components of art and music – and not sport – that provided a potential salvation from the routines of life. Sport was 'empty', 'mundane' and a 'compulsive passion' that provided no alternative to but rather was a complementary feature of the rationalised iron cage of contemporary people's existence. With the ongoing commodification of art, can this enclave any longer be seen to provide the salvation to which Weber referred?

Concluding thoughts

As representatives of interpretative sociology, Simmel and Weber arguably cast considerable light on the cultural problems associated with modernity. Both emphasise the need to probe how people actually experience these problems. They also provide coherent frameworks through which to understand the place of leisure and sport practices in these broader cultural problems. Nevertheless, we want to offer some criticisms of the inherent nostalgia that can be detected in their work. Conversely, we will also suggest that both writers have considerable potential for those seeking to examine leisure and sport practices in a modernist and/or postmodernist manner. (See chapter 9.)

Drawing on Turner's criticisms of theories of modernity, we suggest that Simmel and Weber share four main weaknesses in their position on modernity.[87] In their accounts of the modernisation (rationalisation) process, the dominant emphasis is on incorporation – the iron cage or the tragedy of culture. The more positive and liberating dimensions of these processes are either overlooked, downplayed or ambiguously developed. In addition, in their observations on modern leisure – especially in its popular forms – reference is made to 'mundane passions', 'momentary rapture' and the shallow 'excitements' provided by metropolitan life. Both tend to adopt a somewhat disapproving Puritan tone to such hedonistic practices. This issue relates to a third criticism. Both adopt a dismissive, elitist manner by which popular culture is denigrated, and high culture (art and music and excluding sport), is praised for its potentially liberating effects. Some of their observations on crowd psychology would not be out of place in mass society theory. Finally, their views on the incorporation of the working classes into modern consumerism seem too orderly and overlooks the contested nature of this process.

To some, this evaluation may seem harsh. Other writers see Simmel and Weber as contributing not solely to questions of modernity, but to questions of modernism and postmodernity. The Weinsteins, for example, see Simmel as less a cultural pessimist and more 'an internal critic of modernism'.[88] Similarly, Scott Lash emphasises the 'thoroughly modernist nature' of Weber.[89] Whatever the merits of these positions, clearly both Simmel and Weber have a considerable amount to offer the sociology of sport and leisure.

NOTES AND REFERENCES

1 This appraisal of interpretative sociology centres around the cultural problems associated with modernity. We are only too aware that, as a consequence of this decision, no examination of the symbolic interactionist and phenomenological strands of the interpretative tradition is undertaken. We regret this. Here we are thinking of the work of Mead, G. H., *Mind, Self and Society: From the Standpoint of a Social Behaviourist*, Chicago, University of Chicago Press, 1934/1962; Goffman, E., *Encounters: Two Studies in the Sociology of Interaction*, Indianapolis, Bobbs-Merrill, 1961 and Schutz, A., *The Phenomenology of the Social World*, Evanston, Ill, NorthWestern University Press, 1932/1967. Both Mead and Goffman wrote about sport, socialisation and the role of games in interaction. These strands have proved extremely useful in North American sociology of sport and to a lesser extent, in the sociology of leisure. See Fine, G. A., 'Small groups and culture creation: the idioculture of little league baseball teams', *American Sociological Review*, no. 44, 1979, pp. 733–45; Stone, G. P., 'American Sports: Play and Display' in Dunning, E., *Sociology of Sport*, London, Cass, 1970, pp. 47–65; Zurcher, L., 'The Staging of emotion: a dramaturgical analysis', *Symbolic Interaction*, no. 5, 1982, pp. 1–22.

2 The secondary literature on these two writers is enormous. For discussion of Georg Simmel, see Frisby, D., *Simmel and Since: Essays on Georg Simmel's Social Theory*, London, Routledge, 1992; Frisby, D., *Sociological Impressionism: A Reassessment of Georg Simmel's Social Theory*, London: Routledge, 1992, 2nd Edition; Levine, D., (ed.) *Georg Simmel: Individuality and Social Forms*, Chicago, University of Chicago Press. For an appraisal of Max Weber, see Turner, B. S., *Max Weber: From History to Modernity*, London, Routledge, 1992; Scaff, L., *Fleeing the Iron Cage. Culture, politics and modernity in the thought of Max Weber*, Berkeley, University of California Press, 1989; Parkin, F., *Max Weber*, London, Tavistock, 1982; Schroeder, R., *Max Weber and the Sociology of Culture*, London, Sage, 1992; Whimster, S. and Lash, S., (eds), *Max Weber, Rationality and Modernity*, London, Allen & Unwin, 1987.

3 The following section is informed by the work of Lawrence Scaff who makes a powerful case for the overlap between Simmel and Weber (see Scaff, L., op. cit., 1989). See also the discussion in Turner, B. S., op. cit., 1992, especially Chapter 9.

4 For an appraisal of this see Lichtblau, K., 'Causality or Interaction? Simmel, Weber and Interpretative Sociology', *Theory, Culture and Society*, no. 8, 1991, pp. 62.

5 For example see Ingham, A. G., 'Methodology in the sociology of sport: from symptons of malaise to Weber for a cure', *Quest*, no. 31, 1979, pp. 187-215; and Stuck, M. F., 'An application of Georg Simmel's sociology to team sport', *Physical Educator*, December, 1982, pp. 190–3.

6 Scaff, L., op. cit., 1989, p. 122.

7 ibid., 1989, p. 123.

8 In this section Weber discusses at some length the role of art, music and religion. Weber, M., 'The social psychology of the world religions' in *For Max Weber* (translated and edited by Gerth, H. H. and Wright Mills, C., New York, Oxford University Press, 1946, pp. 341–2.

9 In this section Simmel discusses the relationship between sociability, art, play and games. Simmel, G., 'Sociability' in Wolff, K. H., *The Sociology of Georg Simmel*, New York, The Free Press, 1950, Chapter 3, p. 43.

10 Simmel, G., 'The Problem of Sociology' in Wolff, K. H., (ed.) *Essays in Sociology, Philosophy and Aesthetics*, New York, Harper Torchbooks, 1959, p. 328. See also the special edition on Simmel in *Theory, Culture and Society*, 1991, p. 8.

11 Simmel, G., 'Sociability' in Wolff, K. H., op. cit., 1950, Chapter 1, pp. 9–10.

12 Simmel, G., *The Philosophy of Money*, Bottomore, T. and Frisby, D. (eds. and trans.) London, Routledge & Kegan Paul, 1978, p. 175.

13 Simmel, G., 'Sociability' in Wolff, K. H., op. cit., 1950, Chapter 1, p. 9.

14 ibid., 1950, p. 9.

15 ibid., 1950, p. 8.

16 Simmel, G., 'Zur Methodik der Sozialwissenschaft', *Jahrbuch fur Gesetzgebung, Verwaltung und Volkswirtschaft*, no. 20, 1896, pp. 575–85, cited in Frisby, D., op. cit., 1992, pp. 12–13.

17 ibid., 1992, p. 12.

18 Simmel, G., *Conflict and the web of group-affiliations*, Wolff, K. H. and Bendix, R. (trans.) New York, The Free Press, 1955, p. 50. Loy, McPherson and Kenyon, in their discussion of paradoxical features of sport and of social life, find it perfectly reasonable to substitute the word sport for Simmel's discussion of sociability. See Loy. J. W., McPherson, B. and Kenyon, G., *Sport and Social Systems*, Reading, Ma: Addison-Wesley, 1978, p. 420.
19 Simmel, G., *The Philosophy of Money*, op. cit., 1978.
20 See Frisby, D., op. cit., 1992, pp. 118–34 for an account of Simmel on leisure.
21 Simmel, G., 'The Problem of Sociology' in Wolff, K. H., (ed.), op. cit., 1959, p. 327.
22 Simmel, G., 'The Isolated Individual and the Dyad' in Wolff, K. H., op. cit., 1950, Chapter 3, p. 123.
23 Stuck, M. F., op. cit., 1982, pp. 190–3.
24 Simmel, G., op. cit., 1955, p. 14.
25 ibid., 1955.
26 ibid., p. 35. For further discussion see Loy, J. W., McPherson, B. and Kenyon, G., *Sport and Social Systems*, Reading, Ma: Addison-Wesley, 1978, pp. 110–12.
27 ibid., 1978, pp. 57–8.
28 ibid., 1978, pp. 58–9.
29 ibid., 1978, pp. 156.
30 Simmel, G., 'The Alpine Journey', *Theory, Culture and Society*, no. 8, 1991, p. 95.
31 ibid., 1991, p. 97.
32 Simmel's work has numerous insights that could be profitably taken up by the emerging and related sub-discipline of the geography of sport.
33 Frisby, D., op. cit., 1992, p. 101.
34 Simmel, G., cited in Frisby, D., op. cit., 1992, pp. 112–13. For further discussion of Simmel and space see Lechner, F. J., 'Simmel on Social Space', *Theory, Culture and Society*, no. 8, 1991, pp. 195–203. An example of the type of geography we have in mind is J. Rooney, *The Recruiting Games*, Lincoln, University of Nebraska, 1987.
35 Such insights could be profitably used in conceptualising sport and leisure stadium disasters such as at Hillsborough, the stadium of Sheffield Wednesday. It was at this ground in 1989 that ninety-five football supporters lost their lives as a result of crowd crushing.
36 Frisby, D., op. cit., 1992. See Chapter 4.
37 ibid., 1992, p. 66.
38 Simmel, G., *The Philosophy of Money*, op. cit., 1978, pp. 44–8.
39 ibid., 1978, p. 484.
40 ibid., 1978, p. 275.
41 Simmel, G., Die Grossstadte und das Geistesleben, *Jahrbuch der Gehe-Stiftung zu Dresden*, no. 9, cited in Frisby, D., op. cit., 1992, p. 55.
42 Frisby, D., op. cit., 1992, p. 79.
43 Weber, M., *Economy and Society: an outline of Interpretative Sociology*, edited by Roth, G. and Wittich, C., New York, Bedminster Press, 1968, p. 13.
44 ibid., 1968, p. 13.

45 Weber, M., *The Theory of Social and Economic Organisation*, New York, Free Press, 1964, p. 118.
46 Weber, M., op. cit., 1968, p. 5.
47 ibid., 1968, p. 5.
48 Weber, M., *The Methodology of the Social Sciences*, edited by Shils, E. and Finch, H., New York, Free Press, 1949, p. 43.
49 ibid., 1949, p. 90.
50 Frisby, W., 'Weber's Theory of Bureaucracy and the Study of Voluntary Sport Organisations' in Dunleavy, A., Miracle, A. and Rees, C. R., *Studies in the Sociology of Sport*, Fort Worth, Tx: Texas Christian University, 1982, pp. 53–71.
51 Weber, M., op. cit., 1949, p. 69, 'Adequate causation' entailed the cumulative build up of socio-cultural tensions in which any number of different critical events could provide the spark that would set events following the specific pattern determined by this cumulative build up. 'Chance causation', in contrast, was a social event caused by one unique and unrepeatable 'spark'.
52 See Ingham, A. G., op. cit., 1979, pp. 187–215.
53 ibid., 1979, pp. 211–12.
54 Weber, M., 'Science as a Vocation', op. cit., 1946.
55 ibid., 1946, pp. 149–50. It is also possible that Weber was implicitly raising issues of authority and charisma.
56 As an example of this approach see Ingham, A. G., 'American Sport in Transition: the Maturation of Industrial Capitalism and its Impact upon Sport'. Unpublished doctoral dissertation, University of Massachusetts, 1978.
57 For further discussion of this see Turner, B. S., op. cit., 1992, Chapter 7.
58 Weber, M., op. cit., 1992, p. 181.
59 ibid., 1992, p. 180.
60 ibid., 1992, p. 181.
61 ibid., 1992, pp. 166–7.
62 Weber was using the term 'sport' which embraced a wider range of pastimes than would be accepted in the contemporary period as sport. See Brailsford, D., *Sport and Society: Elizabeth to Anne*, London, Routledge & Kegan Paul, 1969, for further details.
63 Weber, M., op. cit., 1992, p. 167.
64 ibid., 1992, p. 168.
65 ibid., 1992, p. 182.
66 This section draws on arguments presented by Turner, B.S., op. cit., 1992.
67 ibid., 1992. See also Lasch, C., *The Culture of Narcissism*, New York, Warner Books, 1979, for a powerful analysis of sport following this line of argument.
68 See Hoberman, J., *Mortal Engines: The Science of Performance and the Dehumanisation of Sport*, New York, Free Press, 1992.
69 See Bailey, P., *Leisure and Class in Victorian England: Rational Recreation and the Contest for Control 1830–1885*, London, Routledge, 1978.
70 Turner, B. S., op. cit., 1992, Chapter 7.

71 Guttmann, A., *From Ritual to Record: the Nature of Modern Sports*, New York, Columbia University Press, 1978.
72 ibid., 1978, pp. 80–1.
73 Grunneau, R., *Class, Sports and Social Development*, Amherst, Ma: Unviersity of Massachusetts Press, 1983, pp. 44–6.
74 Guttmann, A., op. cit., 1978, p. 89.
75 Weber, M., op. cit., 1992, pp. 182–3.
76 Weber, M., *Religious Rejections of the World and their Directions*, op. cit., 1946, p. 341.
77 Weber, M., op. cit., 1972, pp. 14–15.
78 Weber, *The Rational and Social Foundations of Music*, Carbondale, Southern Illinois University Press, 1958, p. 11.
79 See Weber's discussion of this in Weber, M., *Religious Rejections of the World and their Directions*, op. cit., 1946, pp. 342–3.
80 For further discussion of this see Scaff, L., op. cit., 1989, pp. 73–120.
81 ibid., 1989, p. 104.
82 Weber, M., op. cit., 1968, p. 1367.
83 ibid., 1968, p. 1166.
84 Weber, M., *The Protestant Ethic and the Spirit of Capitalism*, op. cit., 1946, p. 309.
85 ibid., 1946, p. 310.
86 Weber, M., 'National Character and the Junkers', op. cit., 1946, p. 388.
87 Turner, B. S., op. cit., 1992, see pp. 132–8.
88 Weinstein, D. and Weinstein, M. A., 'Simmel and the Theory of Postmodern Society' in Turner, B.S., (ed.) *Theories of Modernity and Postmodernity*, London, Sage, 1990, pp. 75–87, p. 76.
89 Lash, S., 'Modernity of Modernism? Weber and Contemporary Social Theory' in Whimster, S. and Lash, S., (eds) *Max Weber, Rationality and Modernity*, London, Allen & Unwin, 1987, pp. 355–77, p. 356.

Chapter 3

Beyond conventional pluralism

The critical epoch of debate between Marxism and pluralism is to be found in the past. It was a debate which had at its core different views about the relationship between economic and political power. In its normative dimension it was a debate that revolved around the compatibility or otherwise of socialism and a form of representative democracy.[1] It is difficult to find a consistent meaning or interpretation of the term pluralism, especially given that the term has been applied to quite different types of social organisation. Conventional pluralism tends to assert that individual citizens have little or no direct influence upon the political decision making process. Pluralist societies tend to be characterised by the presence of large, well integrated groups representing significant divisions of interests and tastes. Various groups are limited in their power by the fact that the interests of other groups have to be taken into account. Thus competing interest groups or factions are seen to be vital to democracy because they divide up power, reducing the exclusive influence of any one group or class.

Some of the work on sport and leisure that emerged during the 1970s was closely linked to what might be termed conventional liberal pluralism.[2] One of the main features of this research was that sport and leisure involvement tended to be explained in terms of a sociology of competing interest groups. A rejection of class as the major basis for explaining social differentiation rested upon the acceptance of a capitalist economic framework as the natural setting for democracy. Societal demand and the market place were seen as major factors influencing tastes, fashions and developments in sport and leisure. That is to say that popular pastimes would emerge and fade according to the natural ebb and flow of societal demand. The emphasis was therefore placed upon the sovereignty of the consumer in exercising his or her leisure choices.

For example, as Plumb suggests, rather than view the destruction of village games as a sinister bourgeois intervention against the yeomanry of England, pluralists might argue that during the eighteenth century consumers in England had real choices for the first time.[3] Considered in this light sport and leisure was viewed as having become more democratic over time because a balance of power had been achieved between competing interest groups and individual choices. In support of this type of argument pluralist writers have tended to use historical and comparative methods to assert that some sort of democratisation process has developed over time. It is asserted that sport and leisure is more democratic in the 1990s than it was, for example, during the eighteenth century. In the first instance it might be insightful to consider some of the central tenets of conventional pluralism.

A sociology of competing interest groups

The looseness and lack of coherence in the concept of pluralism has allowed a wide variation in the nature of the analyses offered by those who have been classified as pluralists. None the less, some generalisations and underlying assumptions and values have tended to characterise the pluralist approach. The main features of conventional pluralism included: a sociology of competing interest groups; a rejection of Marxist class analysis; an advocacy of a theory of industrial society in which no homogeneous ruling class existed; a rejection of the idea of absolute sovereignty by viewing the state as not being the sole arbitrary player distributing power – that is to say that power was dispersed amongst all the associations and interests of civil society and not just concentrated in the state – and finally an empiricist or multi-factorial approach to sociology. Let us consider some of these ideas in more detail.

According to one writer the defining characteristic of an interest group was:

> that they articulate the claims and needs of society and transmit them into the political process. In the most developed political system the division of labour between interest groups, parties and government is one in which interest groups transmit pragmatic specific demands to parties; parties aggregate these

demands, integrate them into a general programme, and mobilise support for them; and parliaments and bureaucracies enact them as policies and laws and implement them.[4]

Just as no religious group possesses a monopoly of spiritual values, nor does any political group possess a monopoly of political values. No leisure group or sporting group, argued pluralists, should be in a position to define what leisure is or should be. The notion of a leisure class or even a dominant class determining leisure or sporting needs was a view that could not be sustained by the pluralist interpretation of society. A view which saw leisure tastes, needs, choices and demands as being relatively open, fluid, changing and relatively voluntary. The number of leisure interests and potential sporting tastes in principle was unlimited with no single set of interests (e.g. those of capital or the state) as being necessarily victorious or determining.

The aversion to taking class as a major basis of group differentiation was one possible source of pluralism's tendency to accept a capitalist economic framework as the natural setting for liberal democracy. Another reason was the pervasive inclination to see the jostling and bargaining of customers in the political market place as akin to the process of group interaction.[5] The train of thought being that since interest groups were perceived as spontaneous growths in modern or post-industrial society then they would emerge and fade, or ebb and flow, depending upon the level of societal demand. The prospect in terms of sporting choices, leisure styles and fashions was one in which such developments were seen to be mediated by social agents behaving as equalising forces. Leisure consumers and producers were seen to be bargaining for and exchanging preferences within the capitalist market.

When the state was brought into play it tended to be constructed as a neutral and rather passive switchboard of contending interests. Its agencies were simply one set of interest groups amongst all others. Pluralists tended to speak of the political system or governmental process as if it were a self-maintained system or as a neutral, evolving, balancing organism which responded to multiple interest groups. The polity was consequently viewed as being driven by a tendency to produce equilibrium and a consensual view of politics and government. The state was viewed as the honest broker which balanced out the respective interests and wishes of multiple groups in society. In other words one of the principal roles of both the national and local state was one of ensuring that all interest groups had a forum for expressing their views and tastes, regardless of the numerical force or lack of force behind a particular view. A notion which itself was supported in J. S. Mill's discussion of suffrage and representative democracy.[6]

The democratic pluralist argument implies a minor role for state intervention. The state is viewed as being essentially responsive as opposed to proactive. It is an analysis, suggests Henry, which is consistent with Roberts' 1970s account of leisure participlation.[7] An analysis which takes:

> account of leisure participation as reflecting a fragmented pattern of public tastes. The state should . . . avoid positive involvement in leisure provision, limiting itself to generating the conditions under which individuals and groups may meet their own needs. However, where a consensus supporting state involvement does exist . . . the state may step in. Nevertheless, such state involvement is insulated from the competition of interest groups by employing neutral technical experts to make decisions about the precise nature of resource allocation.[8]

It would be incorrect to label the work of Roberts as a singular case of pluralism or even conventional pluralism. His work over the years has reflected a more complex understanding of leisure development.[9] For instance during the late 1970s Roberts, while supporting a pluralist scenario, was critical enough to suggest that leisure itself was intrinsically anomic.[10] The nature and pace of industrialisation and changing degrees of pluralism all affected the nature and distribution of this anomie. A view of leisure in society which was relatively compatible with the views of Durkheim (see Chapter 1). Durkheim, like Marx, attributed certain types of mental condition to certain types of social condition. He pointed to greed, competitiveness, status-seeking, the sense of having rights without duties, an over-concentration on consumption and pleasure, a lack of a sense of community and of a feeling of limits to one's desires and aspirations. It is fairly obvious why Roberts' pluralist scenario allowed for an anomic view of leisure in society. Leisure could never fulfil the promise of being consistently satisfying in any social formation which was characterised by social disorganisation and the denial of human possibilities within an ordered and fulfilling life.[11]

Given that a central tenet of pluralism was a sociology of competing interest groups it is worth concluding this section by mentioning some general problems with this notion. One immediate problem is with the very concept of a social interest group since pluralists seldom make clear just exactly which agents constitute such groups. Without further specification of the people who form the various types of group allegiance we are left with a mosaic of leisure tastes and patterns of leisure consumption without really understanding the people behind such tastes and patterns.

Another source of criticism behind conventional pluralism has been the implied equality between interest groups. This thesis has been criticised for overlooking the massive concentration of power in the hands of those with structural economic advantages. Even within groups there often tends to be an iron law of oligarchy whereby certain individuals or pressure groups effectively wield power over rank and file members. Perhaps it is more illustrative to think of the following questions in relation to the way in which decisions are made and secured; what structural and economic advantages do the following have in common – David Murray at Glasgow Rangers Football Club, Bernard Tapie at Marseille Football Club and Alan Sugar at Tottenham Hotspur Football Club? How has this power influenced certain decisions that have been taken at the respective clubs? Does the pluralist model help us to explain how these decisions have been reached?[12]

In summary, it could be said that the conceptual seperation between the state and social structure which lies at the heart of pluralist theory is not matched by the actions or quasi neutrality of competing interest groups at a more concrete level. Inequalities between interest groups are not eradicated as a result of a series of balances and checks, at best they are tempered or defused. In answer to the question Who rules or Who decides, the truth is perhaps somewhere between the picture painted by pluralists and the view developed by C. Wright-Mills in *The Power Elite*.[13] John Scott's notion of intersecting circles of power is also a more attractive answer to the question of Who Rules Britain?[14]

Neo-liberals, democracy and the market place

The ideas of both Max Weber (see Chapter 2) and Joseph Schumpeter strongly influenced the pluralist approach to democracy.[15] For Schumpeter, as for Weber, democracy was more important as a method of generating effective and responsible government. Democracy, argued Schumpeter, was the rule of politicians and the means of choosing between sets of leaders. Politicians were viewed as dealers in votes in much the same way as brokers were dealers in shares on the stock exchange. The democratic process was to be viewed as a special kind of market – a market where votes are exchanged for policies. Thus, according to pluralists, government policies in a democracy are influenced by a continual process of bargaining between numerous groups of interests. A democratic polity in which there is, as mentioned earlier in this chapter, a balance between competing interest groups. In terms of sport or leisure policy all of these would be seen as having some impact on the policy process without actually dominating the actual mechanisms of government.[16]

Monopoly is, of course, the great dread within this liberal-democratic model. So long as there is no monopoly in buying and selling, so long as there is competition between individuals, it does not matter whether these individuals are single persons or huge corporations for each is conceived in law as an individual subject. Freedom within this understanding of society was only to be preserved by encouraging competition. One of the foremost duties of liberal democratic governments was to preserve competition. Such a rationale was seen to preserve the independence of government and thus leave it free to formulate the national interest which apparently emerged from the mêlée of sectional interests.

Within conventional pluralism the main protection against monopoly was the constitutional state. A liberal-democratic framework of law which was seen to establish and protect a market order by enforcing equality before the law. Every individual or corporation was entitled to legal protection within the pluralist framework. It is assumed that if individuals were free to pursue their interests in their own way, within the confines of a liberal-democracy, then all would have the opportunity to do well. Failure and poverty were viewed as personal or corporate responsibilities or misfortunes, since everyone in theory had the chance of mobility and success. In such a market order, it was argued, almost every conceivable kind of human want could be satisfied. Individuals were viewed as having a considerable degree of freedom as to how they spent their income and how they divided their time between work and leisure and within work and leisure.[17]

One of the great difficulties and objections to pigeon-holing pluralism is that it is hard to find one particular sport or leisure text which explicitly articulates or defends all of the points that we have been making about conventional pluralism.[18] Several writers owe allegiance to some but not necessarily all of the points that we have raised. In perhaps one of the most recent and concise attempts to summarise the role of pluralism in both sports policy and cultural policy in Britain, Henry provides the following vignettes of Liberalism (New Right) and Labourism (Utopian socialism).[19]

Free market pluralism, argues Henry, forms the core cultural values behind Liberalism's approach to both sports policy and cultural policy.[20] The individual is free to choose both sport and leisure forms through the market place. The state as a provider only acts where market imperfections occur. With regards to arts policy state subsidies are seen to foster poor taste. Aesthetic judgement is encapsulated by the judgement of the market place. In the same sense those leisure forms or sport experiences which are seen to be valuable are those which people pay for. Sport and leisure provision is therefore determined by the market place which in turn is open for business between competing sport and leisure tastes.

By comparison mixed market pluralism has at times formed the core cultural values behind a labourist approach to both sports policy and cultural policy in Britain.[21] Within this policy no sport or leisure forms are seen to be superior or inferior. A major goal is to reduce the inequalities in access to various sport and leisure forms. Inequalities are seen to deny individuals and groups broad access to a range of cultural opportunities. Some sport or leisure forms might be uneconomic but this, it is argued, should be supported because they contribute to either individual or group well-being. It is part of the state's role to protect minority leisure tastes and subsidise uneconomic leisure forms where possible.

Liberal pluralist theories have not been without their critics. We shall limit ourselves to commenting briefly upon certain observations concerning pluralism. Firstly, it is arguable that the pluralist concern with democracy is less about participative democratic values and more about stability or more specifically a stable liberal social system. For many pluralists stability is more important than participation.[22] A picture of a vibrant democratic culture often conceals the problem of low participation rates in the democratic process. Thus, under the guise of liberal democracy, pluralism in reality settles for something considerably less than the classical ideal of direct rule for and by the people themselves. The central dilemma here is that there must be a high level of involvement in

politics if there is to be any reasonable level of democratic participation and yet the involvement must not be so intense that it
endangers stability.

A second dilemma lies at the interface between doctrine and
reality. To put it simply, how long can a political order, based on the
assumption of equality through the market place, survive a long term
organic crisis such as high unemployment? For how long will a leisure
society that tolerates a high level of unemployment remain in any
useful sense of the word democratic? As Marquand suggests, it is hard
to imagine any advanced Western society experiencing a violent
revolt of the sort Marx foresaw a century or more ago.[23] But the
emergence of an alientated underclass, or even if we use Roberts'
notion of anomic leisure, effectively denied the right to full participation in sport, leisure or wider society, would be equally incom-
patible with the democratic ideal. Such groups even if not actively
hostile to pluralist values would have put a strain on the social
tolerances which make democracy possible.

Thirdly, it is questionable to what extent we can accept the
notion of the state as the neutral mediator which merely reacts to
the market place. The bureaucrats in government may argue that
they are serving the public good but they also have at stake their
own interests and careers. In reality just as entrepreneurs try to
maximise their profits bureaucrats try to enlarge their bureaux.
The bureaucratic equivalent of profit is size. Since civil servants
generally have a monopoly of expertise in their own spheres, it is
extremely difficult for nominal political chiefs to condemn the
interests or values or their advisers. Thus, the supposed freedom
which liberal democracy offers is hedged with limitations.[24]

A final related point is that liberal-democratic societies, like all
societies, are systems of power. Steven Lukes, amongst others, has
suggested that a central method behind conventional pluralist
analysis has been to adopt a one-dimensional view of power.[25] An
approach which he sees as limited because power relations are
determined not merely by what decisions are arrived at but also by
the efforts of groups and individuals to prevent certain outcomes
emerging or issues arising. For example, a dispute amongst
planners about the best place to locate a sport or leisure centre
does not raise issues about the legitimacy of the leisure centre
itself.[26] Indeed, it may be that sharp disagreements about the
location of the leisure centre may deflect critical attention away
from the question of whether the centre should be built in the first

place. In a two-dimensional theory of power, the legitimacy of the leisure centre itself and the social patterns of resource allocation which ground it would be open to debate.

Modernisation, industrialisation and social evolution

In a critique of those accounts of sport that have been related to a general theory of industrial society Gruneau has implied that at least four types of argument are usually involved.[27] Firstly, that the modernisation of sport has evolved from a pre-industrial or traditional stage of development to an industrial or modern change of development. Secondly, that one of the key consequences of this evolutionary process was that sport was increasingly democratised. Sport was viewed as an area of social life in which disadvantaged groups or dominated groups could gain upward mobility. Thirdly, the emergence of the modern sporting institution had to be seen as a functional, rational adaption to the needs of urban industrial society. Major social conflicts were merely explained away as part of this evolutionary process. Finally, Gruneau asserted that writers who adhered to this tradition generally viewed the characteristics of sport as being similar throughout all modern social formations.[28]

Pluralists have been supportive of the notion that the processes of industrialisation, democratisation and modernisation have all entailed similar patterns of evolution. Like history and society, sport and leisure development tended to be explained in terms of a progressive evolutionary movement from pre-industrial to industrial society. Despite on-going problems such as patriarchy, racism and social inequality, modern sport and leisure, it was often argued, should be viewed in terms of increasing democratisation and opportunity for all. Some or all of this thinking has been central to many sport and leisure texts such as: Adelman's detailed case study of the rise of modern athletics in New York City;[29] Cashman and McKernan's somewhat celebratory edited review of the development of sport in Australia;[30] Kirsch's narrative-based account of the creation of American team sports between 1838 and 1872 which fruitfully debunks the myth of Abner Doubleday and the invention of baseball;[31] Reiss's study of the relationship between urbanisation and sport between 1870 and 1960;[32] Mandell's general review of the development of sport based largely on a modernisation thesis;[33] Rader's textbook on the development of American sport – cited widely by North American scholars;[34] and

Walvin's case study of British soccer and his more general work on leisure, linking its emergence to the urbanisation and industrialisation of British society.[35] More specifically Walvin suggested that:

> (i) these complex, inter-related forces of urbanisation and industrialisation had produced a society which by the 1840s was qualitatively different from any previous human society. . . . Changes in recreations seen in their most acute form in the cities, were but one manifestation of deeper economic changes.[36]
>
> (ii) When economic conditions began to improve in the 1950s people turned eagerly to the consumer durables pouring from the new light industries, a process which reshaped many of the nation's leisure occupations. Most seminal of all these durables were the television and the car. In essence, however, it was but a reprise on a more massive and fundamental scale of a process already clearly defined in the last quarter of the nineteenth century, of leisure emerging in response to demands created by consumer power, and commercial interests taking advantages of new opportunities.[37]

It is not too difficult to see why general theories of modernisation, industrialisation and liberal pluralism have been viewed within a similar genre of writing on the sociology of sport and leisure. A genre which has: shared a similar view on the nature of democracy and its most appropriate setting; shared a similar explanation of social development which rejects class as a major basis for explaining social differentiation; shared a similar view on the role of the market place in responding to a consumer-led demand for sport and leisure tastes; and adopted an evolutionary approach to social change which views modern societies not only as evolving from the simple to the more complex but more importantly that the move towards understanding modernity should generally be viewed positively and progressively.

Several criticisms have been levelled at both the modernisation thesis and liberal-pluralist accounts of industrialisation. It is not our intention to outline these criticisms in detail, since many of them are relative in nature. Some of these criticisms have already been briefly mentioned. Many people have asserted that these traditions of social thought reflected less of a concern for participative democratic values than for a stable, liberal social formation. While an ideology of democratic sport and leisure may exist, others suggested that sport and leisure experiences were perhaps more divisive than allowed for by the classical modernisation thesis. The notion that all industrial societies have undergone a significant degree of convergence, and particularly, that the differences between capitalist and socialist countries no longer mattered has also been questioned. Many of these concerns were valuable not because they provided any answers but because they re-opened questions and debates to do with social change and social development. In similar fashion, postmodernism or postmodernity has brought into question the modernisation thesis (see Chapter 9).

Modernisation itself became a questionable concept from the point of view that it was thoroughly ethnocentric. That is to say that accounts of sport and leisure which relied upon both notions of modernisation and industrialisation have tended to look at other cultures through the eyes of the West. Writers such as Edward Said have constantly questioned the relevance of Western and post-colonial frames of reference for explaining developments within and between non-Western social formations.[38] By the 1970s it was clear that modernisation did not lead to automatic economic growth, particularly in Third World countries seeking to catch up with the developed West. Indeed, many radical critics of modernisation argued that low growth and social inequality resulted from precisely those processes of modernisation that were meant to be the harbingers of prosperity and plenty.

From conventional to critical pluralism

Since the 1980s many of the classical paradigms associated with industrialisation, pluralism and modernity have continued to be questioned. The critique of post-industrialism may have beaten off one assault, but the fundamental weakness of the structure remained, only to be attacked again under a new guise, namely postmodernism or radical modernity (see Chapter 9). Conventional pluralism with its emphasis on social interest groups, liberal democratic society, acceptance of the capitalist economic system, and conservative stability has also responded to changing world conditions and shifts of thinking within the sociology of knowledge. During the 1980s for example, pluralist paradigms in some respects shifted towards what McLennan has outlined as critical pluralism.[39]

One aspect of this critical pluralism was the development of an increased awareness of the distinctions within and between groups. During the early 1980s a greater sense of awareness of social division, competing interests, conflict and overlapping commonalities emerged. The very notion of social interests also appears to have been sharpened. For instance Dahl in his later work moved away from the temptation to label totally different entities under the label, interests group. Organised political lobbies constituted one group type while the notion of different subcultures also indicated a greater sensitivity to a more specific analysis of interests.[40] Furthermore critical pluralism has revised its thinking on the notion that all societal interest groups are relatively equal in terms of power. Revisionists have accepted the Marxist critique of conventional pluralism that business groups, for example, usually have a much greater sway over government politics than other less powerful interest groups. Robert Dahl has stressed the need to introduce programmes of economic democracy which would counterbalance the powerful interest of large corporate groups.[41]

The imperfect nature of democracy has also forced conventional pluralism to bury some of its idealism about the virtues of Western democratic social formations. The complacency of the pluralist suggestion that minority voices could be heard and represented without resorting to conflict has been shattered by various forms of social unrest and violence in major cities in both Britain and America throughout the 1980s and early 1990s. The re-emergence of millions of American and British people unemployed and living in poverty has dented pluralist idealism that democracy and affluence go hand in hand. Above all, critical pluralism recognised that a theoretical model which advocated a vision of all competing interest groups bargaining and being heard around the conference table was not well equipped to deal with too many turbulent actions which expressed a crisis within democracy itself. An institutional, political-party approach to politics was not always the best platform from which to respond to community pressure groups operating within the public realm.[42]

While conventional pluralism never lacked a sense of history, it tended to rest upon the premise that economic growth and evolution were necessary foundations of democracy. Critical pluralism has at least registered an awareness that underdevelopment in some social formations has resulted from Western greed and Western advancement. That is to say that chronic underdevelopment in some places has been a consequence of and not just a contingent accompaniment to Western development. This in itself is an acknowledgement that the ideals of the West are not necessarily the hopes of the rest of the world. There has also been a realisation that global resources are perhaps finite and that continual economic growth is itself a matter of careful moral consideration.

In short it may be suggested that a shift from conventional to critical pluralism has been made in the light of a realisation that American and Western dreams more generally have provided pluralists with a limited conceptualisation of democracy, power and social development. Whether some or all of these points have been addressed either by the critics of the variants of pluralism which have permeated the sociology of sport and leisure literature or by those who continue to adhere to the liberal pluralist model must remain an open-ended question.

Certainly during the late 1980s one advocate of pluralism was still suggesting that:

> In contrast to the Marxist view of society and leisure, with its basis of class division and conflict, analyses of leisure based on the pluralist defence of the liberal democratic market system seem to lack both a satisfactory classificatory system of society and an adequate sociological explanation of the dynamic forces shaping leisure and society. This leads in turn to an inadequate agenda for the study of leisure in its wider social context. This paper suggests that Weber's concept of status, status groups and lifestyle offer a way forward for pluralist analysis.[43]

The argument here appears to be that a variant of pluralism, which has at its core the concepts of status and lifestyles, provides an ideal way to understand and explain the complex nature of leisure in society. Drawing on Weber the writer suggests that a system for distinguishing between groups in society must take as its starting point the notion of status. Status groups appear to be the best classificatory system for a pluralist view of society. It is suggested that status groups have unique and specific ways of life and that such groups are consequently involved in constant struggles for control over the means of symbolic production. Such struggles are viewed as the essence of what the writer refers to as status politics. Add to this that such groups are concerned with the politics of lifestyle and the author draws an analysis of leisure which is capable of raising questions concerning status, prestige, lifestyle and social structure. The link with Veblen and the conspicuous consumption of leisure is perhaps obvious but, as the author points out, Veblen's focus was perhaps more concerned with an elite group during one particular period, while a concern with the politics of lifestyle has the potential for a much wider application.[44]

The pluralist would accept that economic inequalities between status groups would arise from the inevitable consequence of the economic system. Yet the pluralist could also draw attention to the variety of lifestyle/status groups at various levels. Similarities in lifestyle are seen to cut across economic classes and mobility between groups. Thus, argues Veal, the struggle over status is compatible with both revisionist Marxist and pluralist scenarios. The Marxist would view the struggle for status and bourgeois lifestyles as one of the means by which the ruling class undermines the unity of the working class, disguises class conflict and, by associating wealth with prestige and status, rather than class position, ensures that a Marxist position is consolidated. The general conclusion being that the concept of status groups and the politics of lifestyle offer a basis for a sociological framework for the analysis of leisure which is still consistent with pluralism in the late 1980s.

The overall tenor of Veal's pluralist account of leisure in society remains locked into the historic opposition between Marxism and pluralism – an antagonism which was already losing its momentum at the time when Veal was writing. It is an approach which is laced with orthodoxy and traditionalism and seems to be embracing change as mere novelty rather than assessing either the changing political climate of the times or some of the critical revisions to the then contemporary Marxist and pluralist traditions of social thought. We do not intend to outline all of the major responses to 'leisure, lifestyles and status: a pluralist framework for analysis', but merely mention but two principle criticisms of this piece of work.

Feminist writers have responded by suggesting that Veal's claim for pluralism totally neglects those feminist critiques which have influenced social theory (see Chapter 7).[45] They suggest that the influence of the sexual division of labour, patriarchal power relations, and the social construction of sexuality are all masked by the catch-all concept of lifestyle. This critique points out that Veal excludes from consideration the very real differences in the power of different people to make decisions regarding the use of time, money and other resources all of which influence leisure consumption and lifestyle. This feminist critique goes on to suggest that lifestyle as a construct can be of use to a pluralist-informed account of leisure but only when considered in relation to a whole range of social relations and social constructions such as femininity and masculinity. Clearly Veal fails to convince such feminists that the constructs of status and lifestyle provide an adequate agenda for the analysis of leisure.

Perhaps the sociology of sport and leisure might benefit if academics and populist writers put a moratorium on the use of such terms as status, lifestyle, feminism, and a whole collection of other concepts unless they are prepared to specify just exactly what they are referring to in any given instance. A book of this nature is perhaps not the best place to make this point but we generally believe that Veal would have done more for the pluralist cause if he had unpacked in a much more concrete and historical way just exactly what he meant by terms such as status, lifestyle and leisure. What is apparent to us is that such an approach needs not only to be fully informed by developments concerning pluralist theory itself, but perhaps more importantly, accept the notion that new demands in society and indeed people's choices cannot always be explained with old doctrine. Even if we were to accept that traditional orthodox sociology, which in Veal's case means Weber, in the last instance we would encourage a much closer integration of the original texts. As Chapter 2 in this book illustrates, Weber (and Simmel) had quite a lot to say about sport and leisure.

Concluding thoughts

This chapter has attempted to evaluate some of the central themes that have permeated many liberal-pluralist accounts of sport and leisure. It would be foolish not to recognise the pluralist exchange with Marxism during the late 1970s and early 1980s. On the one hand Marxism strived to provide a coherent materialist analysis of the systematic dynamics of modern society. On the other hand pluralism rejected Marxist class analysis in favour of a sociology of competing interest groups. Furthermore pluralism countered ideas of absolute sovereignty by viewing the state as one association amongst many. Pluralists thus argued that power was dispersed amongst all the associations and interests of civil society and not just concentrated within the state.

At the heart of this debate was a struggle to define the very nature of the term democracy. At least two assertions of democracy represented themselves. In the socialist tradition democracy generally referred to popular power, a state in which the interests of the majority of people were seen to be paramount. These interests were also seen to be practically exercised and controlled by the majority. Even a fully representative parliament was not a sufficient condition of a socialist democracy which ultimately had to involve the direct exercise of popular power. In the liberal-pluralist tradition of democracy the term simply referred to open election of representatives and certain conditions which maintained the openness of election and political argument. Thus general elections and freedom of speech were viewed as primary criteria, while other expressions of popular power, such as general strikes or player boycotts were viewed as being anti-democratic. The range of confusion over the term democracy still remains. To paraphrase C. B. MacPherson 'the real world of democracy has many variants' – with the liberal-pluralist model being but one of them.[46]

We have used the work of certain writers to illustrate how certain sport and leisure texts have been influenced by pluralist themes. The texts we have used are by no means exhaustive of the pluralist literature on sport and leisure. By way of summary it might be suggested that some or all of the following themes have been central to the problematic of pluralist thinking about sport and leisure: (i) that as sport and leisure have evolved they have become more open and democratic over time; (ii) that individuals are free to choose from those leisure tastes and sporting forms available through the market place; (iii) that the market place is the best determinant of what leisure and sporting goods are and should be popular; (iv) that capitalist economic societies provide the best setting for pluralist sport and leisure provision; (v) that class should be rejected as the sole basis for explaining social differentiation; and (vi) that an empiricist or multi-factorial approach to sport and leisure research provides the best defence against mono-causal explanations of sport and leisure behaviour.

It has been suggested that much of the pluralist research into sport and leisure has tended to fall within a conventional pluralist model. Several more critical pluralists attempted to respond to some of the shortcomings of conventional pluralist thinking. Even within the sociology of sport and leisure, writers in the late 1980s were still attempting to legitimate or give more status to pluralist leisure research. Pluralist and Marxist thinking was perhaps at its sharpest when it was in dialogue or confrontation with each other's doctrine. As the next chapter will indicate events of the late 1980s and early 1990s have meant that many critics have brought into question the relevance of Marxism *per se*. But what about pluralism?

Perhaps a common theme that runs through the precise failures of both models is the dwindling legitimacy of the institutions and conventions which support in particular Westminster style democracy. This lack of legitimacy has in part come about because the pluralist belief that democratic politics and the competitive struggle for people's votes rests upon an assumption that the victors in the struggle are entitled to make what they wish of the power placed in their hands – a view that in the 1990s is being continually eroded as the sole basis for a legitimate political order. The institutions, oligarchies or bureaucracies upon which both conventional pluralist and Marxist doctrines have depended are themselves losing authority. As Marquand suggests such an authority is being dwindled because those who operate such authority are no longer trusted.[47] Trust itself is ebbing because the assumptions and conventions of club government are no longer respected by the club members. Perhaps more importantly the public no longer believe that the pluralist democratic model provides an adequate safeguard against the abuse of power.

NOTES AND REFERENCES

1 There has been a debate between Marxism and pluralism for about one hundred years. This chapter attempts to elaborate upon some of these tensions but also reflect some of the key concerns raised by pluralist writers on sport and leisure. This task has been made considerably easier by the publication of G. McLennan, *Marxism, Pluralism and Beyond*, Cambridge, Polity Press, 1989, and A. Giddens, *Sociology*, Cambridge, Polity Press, 1993.

2 K. Roberts, *Contemporary Society and the Growth of Leisure*, London, Longman, 1978. For a critical discussion of this view see J. Clarke and C. Critcher, *The Devil Makes Work: Leisure in Capitalist Britain*, London, Macmillan, 1985, pp. 40–4.

3 J. Plumb, 'Sports of Fortune', *The Listener*, 19 October 1978, pp. 497–8.

4 S. Berger, *Organising Interests in Western Europe*, Cambridge, Cambridge University Press, 1981, p. 8. It is also suggested that pluralism in the 1980s might be a source of the increased ungovernability of advanced Western societies as rising expectations, conceived increasingly as entitlements, contribute to the overloading of state bureaucracies.

5 R. King, *The State in Modern Society: New Directions in Political Sociology*, London, Macmillan, pp. 115–20.

6 J. S. Mill, *Representative Government*, London, Routledge, 1861, p. 155.

7 K. Roberts, op. cit., 1978.

8 I. Henry, *The Politics of Leisure Policy*, London, Macmillan, 1993, p. 78.

9 The charge of singular pluralism is in this case made in J. Clarke and C. Critcher, op. cit., 1985, p. 42.

10 K. Roberts, op. cit., 1978, pp. 84–92.

11 This discussion is developed further in D. Marquand, *The Unprincipled Society, New Demands and Old Politics*, London, Cape, 1988.

12 Pluralism's focus on interest groups in civil society, we might suggest, also ignores the role of specific interest groups within the state itself.

13 C. Wright-Mills, *The Power Elite*, Oxford, Oxford University Press, 1980.

14 J. Scott, *Who Rules Britain?* Cambridge, Polity Press, 1991.

15 The pluralist ideas of Max Weber and Joseph Schumpeter have been evaluated by A. Giddens, op. cit., 1993, pp. 335–7.

16 On this issue see H. Wheeler, *Democracy in a Revolutionary Era*, Santa Barbara, Centre for the Study of Democratic Institutions, 1970.

17 A. Gamble, *An Introduction to Modern Social and Political Thought*, London, Macmillan, 1987, p. 160.

18 Perhaps one of the closest examples would be J. Goodger, 'Pluralism, Transmission and Change in Sport', *Quest*, no. 38, 1986, pp. 135–47.

19 I. Henry, op. cit., 1993, p. 48–51.

20 I. Henry, op. cit., 1993, p. 48, p. 50.

21 I. Henry, op. cit., 1993, p. 49, p. 51.

22 In this sense apathy may often be regarded as a constructive force in terms of stability. Democratic participation and revolutionary rebellion are viewed as forces which may upset the carefully evolved equilibrium of Western societies. In hindsight such views need qualifying given the nationalist tensions which have unhinged a stable European community during the early 1990s. Yet, in the 1980s several leading pluralist thinkers all promoted the functional role played by consensus in stable, liberal, social and political orders.

23 D. Marquand, op. cit., 1988, p. 88.

24 Writers such as Hayek suggest that if a market order is to survive people cannot be free to follow any purposes whatsoever. They can only be free to follow pathways and purposes that are compatable with the rules of the market. See F. Hayek, *The Constitution of Liberty*, London, Routledge, 1976.

25 Lukes makes the argument that such a one-dimensional view restricts attention to the way in which political decisions and outcomes come to a consensus. A three-dimensional view of power would at least provide a much closer sociological examination of the material and ideological conditions of participation in the decision-making process. See S. Lukes, *Power and Radical View*, London, Macmillan, 1974. For a further critical view of liberal democracy and power read C. B. MacPherson, *The Real World of Democracy*, Toronto, Canadian Broadcasting Corporation, 1979.

26 This is very similar to Knox's critique of the Sports Council's commissioned survey of community responses to leisure provision of Belfast. Knox is critical of the pluralist thinking within the report. See C. Knox 'Polity evaluation in leisure services – the Northern Ireland Case', *Leisure Studies*, no. 10(2), 1991., pp. 106–17. See also John Sugden and Alan Bairner, *Sport, Sectarianism and Society in a Divided Ireland*, London, Leicester University Press, 1993.

27 R. Gruneau, 'Modernisation or Hegemony: Two Views on Sport and Social Development', J. Harvey and H. Cantelon (eds) *Not Just a Game: Essays in Canadian Sport Sociology*, Ottawa, University of Ottawa Press, 1988, pp. 9–33.

28 R. Gruneau, op. cit., 1988, p. 15.

29 M. Adelman (ed.) *A Sporting Time: New York City and the Rise of Modern Athletics*, Urbana, University of Illinois Press, 1986.

30 R. Cashman and M. McKernan (eds) *Sport in History*, St Lucia, University of Queensland Press, 1979.

31 R. Kirsch, *The Creation of America Team Sports: Baseball and Cricket 1838–1872*, Urbana, University of Illinois Press, 1989.

32 A. Reiss, *City Games: The Evolution of American Urban Society and the Rise of Sports*, Urbana, University of Illinois Press, 1989.

33 R. D. Mandell, *Sport: A Cultural History*, New York, Columbia University Press, 1984.

34 B. Rader, *American Sports: From the Folk Games to the Age of Spectators*, Englewood Cliffs, Prentice Hall, 1989.

35 J. Walvin, *The People's Games: A Social History of British Football*, London, Allen & Unwin, 1975, and J. Walvin, *Leisure and Society, 1850–1930*, London, Longman, 1978.

36 J. Walvin, op. cit., 1978, p. 3.

37 J. Walvin, op. cit., 1978, p. 163.

38 E. Said, 'Intellectuals in the Post-Colonial World' *Salmagandi*, no. 71, Spring, 1986, pp. 44–81.

39 D. McLennan, op. cit., 1989, pp. 43–56.

40 D. McLennan, op. cit., 1989, p. 50.

41 For a discussion on this point read A. Giddens, op. cit., 1993, p. 336.

42 D. Marquand, op. cit., 1988, p. 207–47.

43 T. Veal, 'Leisure, Lifestyle and Status: a pluralist framework for analysis', *Leisure Studies*, no. 8, (2), 1989, pp. 141–53.

44 T. Veal, op. cit., 1989, p. 147.

45 S. Scraton and M. Talbot 'A Response to Leisure, Lifestyle and Status: a pluralist framework for analysis', *Leisure Studies*, no. 8, (2), 1982, pp. 155–9.

46 C. B. MacPherson, op. cit., 1976.

47 D. Marquand, op. cit., 1988, p. 241.

Chapter 4

Classical Marxism, political economy and beyond

There exists in the 1990s a widely held assumption that the revolutions in eastern Europe, during the late 1980s and early 1990s, have rendered Marxism obsolete and untenable. This belief is shared by some who in the past were strongly identified with the Marxist tradition.[1] Those who have questioned the continuing relevance of Marxism today have tended to do so by positing a number of assertions; some have argued that the people's revolutions of 1989 marked a rejection of the positive freedoms of Marxist ideology and an initial acceptance of the free market economy and the negative freedoms of consitutional democracy; others have argued that in a post-Marxist, postmodernist era it may not be only Marxism that is dying but all grand theories, all history and yet again the end of ideology; some have argued that while there will undoubtedly be academic shelf space for Marx the critic, or Marx the sociologist or philosopher, there remains an impending crisis for Marx the political organiser or Marx the socialist utopian; and still others have argued that in the 1970s and 1980s while it was possible to draw a line between Marxism's and other intellectual camps, it is increasingly difficult if not impossible to do so today.[2]

There are reasons for believing that the death of Marxism is both premature and exaggerated. First, as a nineteenth-century thinker Marx's academic future is secure in the same way as, for example, David Ricardo, Adam Smith, Hebert Spencer or Charles Darwin. The force of Darwinism as a pattern of thought is not fatally diminished by new advances in biology, nor is the work of Adam Smith, or other nineteenth-century Scottish philosophers, increasingly irrelevant as a result of changing attitudes towards political economy or global culture.

Second, as long as domination, exploitation, and subordination exist in the world, Marxism is likely to remain a form of explanation and praxis, although one has to be sceptical about any notions of a working-class vanguard in the late twentieth century. Class reductionism has for some time been questioned by Marxists themselves. In a classical Marxist sense the working class had at least four clear characteristics: it was a majority in society; and it comprised the people who did the producing, the people who were exploited and the people in the greatest need. It is doubtful today if such a group exists in the classical sense of the term working class and yet other forms of exploitation, an ever present gap between rich and poor and the relationship between the First World and the developing Third World, are still potential organic sources of tension and crises for Western capitalism in particular.[3]

Third, in Britain we began the 1980s with the Marxist left more influential in the main party of the left, the Labour party, than in any other Western state. Since then the 1984–5 miners' strike has destroyed many notions of working-class power. The 1987 election destroyed unilateralism, while the 1992 election defeat consolidated the treaty of Union and put paid to the constitutional challenge which was one of the few genuinely radical projects supported by the left. Yet, despite such events, it is likely that both politics and the academy will continue to find a place for the humanitarian, egalitarian social and political justice that is at the heart of Marxism. Many people will continue to believe in the possibility of transforming capitalism into a more progressive and better society. Marxist thought, although not Marxist dogma, will continue to have a part to play in this process. What label you put on such a process is perhaps irrelevant.

Finally, it might be suggested that perhaps the sharpest edge of working-class radicalism in the late twentieth century lies not within Europe but in the African Diaspora and the living legacy of the black radical tradition. Black Marxism has always questioned the ethnocentric nature of Western Marxism on the basis that various aspects of black consciousness are simply not accounted for within the official Marxist explanation of world development. Part of this intervention has been to assert that European Marxism articulated an inevitably Western experience of pre-capitalist and capitalist societies and assumed, incorrectly, the primacy of class consciousness over other forms of mass ideology, notably racism.[4]

As a German socialist and political economist Karl Marx (1818–83) was born in Germany but lived most of his adult life in England. He studied Hegelian philosophy in Berlin, became active as a political writer and edited a radical newspaper in the Rhineland for which he was expelled. He lived in Paris and Brussels, at first helping to organise with Friedrich Engels (1820–95) the Communist League. Eventually Marx settled in England where he relied on financial support from Engels. His major works, many of which were not completed in his lifetime were; *Economic and Philosophical Manuscripts* (1844); *German Ideology* (1846); *Poverty of Philosophy* (1847); *The Eighteenth Brumaire* (1851); *Grundrisse* (1858); *Capital* vols. I–III (1867); and *Theories of Surplus Value* (1862).

The classical Marxist tradition generally refers to those writers who were writing before the First World War.[5] The generation of classical Marxists who followed Marx and Engels were small in number. The four major figures within this second generation were Labriola (1843–1904); Mehring (1846–1919); Kautsky (1854–1938) and Plekanov (1856–1918). While this generation of classical Marxists had been introduced to historical materialism during a period of relative tranquillity the subsequent generation came of age within a much more turbulent environment which without exception was located east of Berlin. Lenin (1870–1924) was the son of a civil servant from Astrakhan; Luxemburg (1871–1919) the daughter of a timber merchant from Galicia; Trotsky (1879–1940) the son of a farmer from the Ukraine; Bauer (1881–1938) the son of a textile manufacturer in Austria, and Bukharin (1888–1938) the son of a teacher from Moscow. Nearly all of the major writings of these cohorts of classical Marxists had been completed before the end of the 1914–18 World War.

This whole ensemble of theorists who were writing before 1914 were in part replaced by those writing initially during the inter-war period but mainly after the 1939–45 World War. It is not necessary to provide a lengthy dialogue on the advent of Western Marxism but merely to note that the long and complex displacement of classical Marxism resulted not just from those who sought to reinterpret the work of Marx and others but also from the geographical, generational and political formal shifts.[6] If Marxist-Leninism proved to be one particular mis-interpretation of Marx's ideas then academic Western Marxism certainly proved to be another. In many cases the study of Marxism became an end in itself rather than a philosophy of practice. This is not to suggest that the works of Marx, or some Marxist writers, do not deserve to be studied in their own right, but that one cannot accept Marx the theorist and reject Marx the revolutionary. The two go together.

Marx, unlike Castro, neither played sport nor contributed directly to the sociological analysis of leisure. More generally, the Marxist body of literature on sport and leisure takes up more than an egalitarian amount of shelf space within those library sections that hold collections of books on the sociology of sport and leisure. While it is important not to overstate the case, various forms of political praxis have involved sport and leisure practices. The African National Congress and the Independent Labour Party are but two parties which recognised the transformative or revolutionary potential within sport. The black power demonstrations at the 1968 Mexico Olympic Games and the drive for a black Caribbean captain of the West Indian cricket team during the late 1950s and early 1960s were also influenced by a number of factors, not least of which was the influence of black Marxist thinkers such as Harry Edwards and C. L. R. James.[7]

A contribution to the critique of political economy

Marx never had a theory of political economy but he did have a critique of eighteenth- and nineteenth-century thinking about political economy. Scottish Enlightenment thinkers such as Adam Ferguson and Adam Smith wrote histories of civil society based upon analyses of social structures and social institutions.[8] Adam Ferguson, who was one of the earliest sociologists, anticipated the negative effects of a division of labour to be found in the later writings of Marx. Although Marx came to the notion of political economy through his critique of Hegel's philosophy of the state, his critique of political economy is rooted in a consideration of the work of Scottish Enlightenment thinkers, most notably, Adam Smith and David Ricardo.

Liberal political economy, as opposed to Marxist political economy, developed around several broad themes: (i) an economic theory of historical progress; (ii) the theory of accumulation and economic growth through the division of labour and spread of exchange; (iii) a redefinition of wealth as comprised of commodities, not just treasure; (iv) a theory of individual behaviour which reconciled pursuit of self-interest with the collective good; and (v) the labour theory of value which argued for labour as a measure and sometimes as a source of value.

One of the greatest weaknesses of liberal political economy, for Marx, was the conceptualisation of history inherent within this tradition of classical economics. The Scottish Enlightenment thinkers promoted the idea that human history could best be explained in terms of human growth. Each key stage of human development reflected the transition from one mode of obtaining subsistence to another mode of obtaining subsistence. Hunting, pastoralism, agriculture and commerce were identified as the principal modes of development. Liberal political economists viewed commerce, by which they meant capitalism, as the last stage in human history. Capitalism was the natural setting for commerce and therefore there would be no further changes in the key stages of human development.

This economic theory of progress through the work of Ricardo, and subsequently Marx's critique of Hegel, emerged as Marx's materialist conception of history, popularly known as historical materialism. Marx had at least two main problems with liberal political economy. First, Marx challenged the notion of naturalism and the idea that individuals existed in isolation from society. This view of individuals as isolated from the demands of capitalist society failed to take account of the social relations of production and what Classical Marxism viewed as the exploitative relationship between lord and serf or capitalist and worker. Marx called isolationist tendencies 'Robinsonades' because they viewed people as if they were like Robinson Crusoe on an island.[9]

Second, Marx was critical of those political economists who viewed capitalism or commerce as some fixed entity in which certain laws of development apply to every society. Such approaches, suggested Marx, do not take account of how production takes place or how the relations of production are produced at any given time. Economic categories, it was suggested, 'are only the abstractions of the social relations of production so these too will change as society changes'.[10] Thus Marx used the notion of historical materialism to demonstrate the historicity of capitalism. While liberal political economists tended to view the stage of commerce as an end in itself, Classical Marxists tended to view capitalism as but one stage in the development of the materialist conceptualisation of history and human progress.

As a critique of capitalism Marxist political economy deals with the following questions: What is wealth?; How is wealth produced?; How did the ownership of the means for producing wealth fall into the hands of the minority; What do we mean by class and how did classes come into being?; What are the causes of slumps and economic crises under capitalism?; What is the economic and political significance of the term imperialism? and what is the economic foundation of socialist and communist society?

In a similar sense political economies of sport and leisure have tended to highlight some or all of the following concerns: How has sport and leisure been organised under capitalism?; Who profits from professional sport and the leisure industry?; What is the basis of wage-labour relations in the world of sport and leisure?; To what extent are professional sports people and recreation workers exploited?; To what extent are the employee rights of the professional athlete recognised?; How do monopolies, corporations, and cartels influence decisions, profit and ideologies concerning sport and recreation practices?; How has imperialism affected world sporting development?; and how is sport and leisure in the periphery mediated by global, economic, political and cultural relations?

The work of Rob Beamish may be used as an example of a programme of research that is informed by classical Marxist political economy.[11] Beamish illustrates the close relationship between professional sport as work in Canada and America and other sectors of Canadian and American forms of capitalism. The very term professional sport implies an employee/employer relationship. Yet, as Beamish empirically illustrates, the monopoly position of owners of professional sports teams enables them not only the power to hire and release professional athletes but also establish such factors as the length of the season, the number of exhibition games, the timing and length of training camps and the structure of post-season play.

Central to this analysis of the political economy of sport is a discussion of the labour process. At its simplest level the labour process is the process whereby labour is objectified or materialised in use values. For Marx, the labour process consisted of two basic elements, human labour power and the means of production. The labour process is seen as a condition of human existence common to all forms of society. Sports workers and recreation professionals, with their labour power to sell, and be sold, are no different from other active agents in the labour market. But to see how different human participants relate to one another in the labour process requires consideration of the social relations within which the process occurs.

Within the capitalist labour process the means of production, teams, cartels, leisure organisations, are purchased in the market by the capitalist. So too is labour power. The athletes, the teams, the music star, and the box-office film hero/heroine perform the work under the supervision of the capitalist with the product of that labour remaining the property of the owner of the means of production. The purpose of the capitalist labour process is to produce profit, or at least produce commodities whose value exceeds the sum of the values of labour power and the means of production consumed in the process of production.

Thus, in a classical Marxist sense while players, film stars and recreation professionals are not powerless they are not as powerful as the owners of the means of production. The following are illustrative examples from the world of football: Jack Walker at Blackburn Rovers Football Club whose estimated wealth during 1992 was £360 million; David Thompson at Queen's Park Rangers Football Club whose estimated wealth during 1992 was £350 million; Alan Sugar of Amstrad and Tottenham Hotspur fame whose estimated wealth during 1992 was £80 million; David Murray of Murray International Metals and Glasgow Rangers fame whose estimated wealth during 1992 was £50 million and Leslie Silver of Leeds United whose estimated wealth during 1992 was a mere £40 million.[12]

While the classical notion of a capitalist class tended to consist of those whose wealth originated in traditional sources such as industry, banking and commerce a more traditional aristocracy or hereditary elite have also profited from the world of sport and recreation. Indeed some of Britain's wealthiest landowners have profited not only from the exploitation of local, and in some cases migrant labour forces, but also the management and selling of private sporting and recreation estates. Landowners such as Lord Kimball who placed Altnaharra's 47,000 sporting acres on the open market during 1992 with an asking price of more than £7 million. Captain Alwyn Farquharson is part of an elite group of traditional Scottish landowners which includes the Duke of Buccleuch, the Earl of Seafield, the Duke of Atholl, the Earl of Stair, the Duke of Westminster and the Duke of Roxburghe. All contribute to the upper circles of power within British and Scottish social structure, all are regarded as major sporting landlords and all negotiate wage-labour relationships with various groups of estate workers, tenants and crofters who, in a classical Marxist sense, have only their labour to sell.[13]

Alienation and the division of labour

Much of classical Marxism's meaning behind the concepts of alienation and the division of labour are derived from elsewhere. According to Adam Ferguson, those who labour with their hands lose control over the decisions which affect their labour and, being no longer required to think for themselves have difficulty in comprehending the system within which they are locked.[14] Those left performing manual labour are thus degraded, the object of the workers' labour is thus degraded and the object of the workers' labour and the means by which it is produced dehumanises and degrades workers. As Ferguson points out, the labourer who toils that he may eat, the mechanic whose art requires no exertion of genius, are degraded by the means they employ to attain it.[15]

If Ferguson were to have used the term alienation here, he would have anticipated two of the four senses Marx gave to the term in the *Economic and Philosophical Manuscripts*. Marx identified four main characteristics of alienation, namely, humanity's (Marx used the term man) alienation from nature, from humanity or the species, from him/herself and from others. In his critique of Feurbach Marx's notion of alienation took on many disguises and yet all forms of alienation were in the last instance one, namely different aspects of man/women's self-alienation. For both Hegel and Feurbach, alienation was purely an intellectual phenomenon, an attitude of mind which resulted in seeing the world in a certain mistaken way. Marx considered alienation to be a material and social process. A condition which arose out of the division of labour.

Discussions of sport and leisure have incorporated the notions of alienation and the division of labour in several ways. Although sport is potentially a creative, expressive, meaningful avenue of human self-development, professional sport and the business world of leisure are highly regimented, restrictive and controlled not least by management. Capitalist sport and leisure is characterised as alienating athletes, artists and recreation professionals from the activity of sport and leisure as work.

Sometimes this type of argument is used to explain why so many promising athletes or young people drop out of sport, physical education or a healthy recreational lifestyle. Alternatively it has been argued that when a professional sports player sells his or her labour to an employer the opportunity for creative self-actualisation becomes restricted. It becomes secondary to the performance of the team, work is subordinated to the instrumental demand for profit with the result of some or all of this being alienation.

A further dimension of alienation deals with how players or athletes help to create the structure which actually works against them or their interests. Players rarely own the stadia, the teams, or the leagues in which they play and therefore rarely promote their own labour, unless they are up for sale. In terms of objective alienation the players produce a product which they do not own, a product which has the potential for returning high profits for the owners while at the same time involving minimal risk to the owners. This lack of control over the product of one's own labour, argue Classical Marxists, leads to alienation.[16]

The unmasking of different forms of self-alienation was, for Marx and other Classical Marxists, not an end in itself but rather a step towards radical revolution, a realisation of communism and de-alienation. Closely connected with this praxis was the abolition of the classical division of labour and the distinction between manual and mental labour. Although Marx never posited a theory of leisure it is perhaps surprising that those who do posit such theories have not made more of the famous passage in *The German Ideology* in which Marx writes;

> In communist society where nobody has no one exclusive sphere of activity but each can become accomplished in any branches he/she wishes, society regulates the general production and thus makes it possible for me to do one thing today and another tomorrow, to hunt in the morning, to fish in the afternoon, rear cattle in the evening, criticise after dinner, just as I have a mind, without ever becoming hunter, fisherman, shepherd or critic.[17]

Even before the people's revolutions of 1989 such a view was often denounced as utopian. For Marxists the problem of de-alienation is inextricably linked to social transformation which itself is inextricably linked to the abolition of the division of labour and private property. Some Marxists reject the notion of absolute de-alienation, others suggest that only relative de-alienation is possible. Many critics have posited the idea that it might be possible to create a social system that would be favourable to the development of de-alienated individuals, but it is not possible to produce a society that would automatically produce such individuals. Marx and Ferguson may have disagreed over the concept of alienation, but undoubtedly they both agreed that in the division of labour lay one of the keys to understanding subordination and inequality.[18]

Ideology, political consciousness and class formation

The longer capitalism managed to survive many of its own internal contradictions the more important it became for Western Marxists to explain such questions as: How does society continue to reproduce itself in the same format?; How has capitalism survived and responded to its own internal contradiction?; and despite chronic experiences of poverty, unemployment, and deep-rooted organic crisis, how has the status quo been maintained in advanced capitalist societies? One particular response was to place a greater emphasis on such notions as ideology and other aspects of the infra-structure that helped to maintain the relations of production.

One of the most influential post-war expositions of ideology was to be found in the work of the French philosopher Louis Althusser. In this respect his essay 'Ideology and Ideological State Apparatuses' formed but one cornerstone of a structural Marxist analysis which viewed Marxism as the science of social formations, the study of the inner objective logic of various structures.[19] Within the modern state Althusser identified two particular forms of oppression which helped not only to maintain the status quo, but also what he referred to as the 'structure in dominance'. The first form of oppression was predominantly violent and was to be found in the practices of the army, the police, the judiciary and other forms of the Repressive State Apparatus (RSA). The second form of oppression was predominantly ideological and manifested itself in schools, families, churches, communication networks and other forms of the Ideological State Apparatus (ISA). The assertion made by Althusser that what seemed to take place outside ideology did, in fact, take place inside ideology, may seem pessimistic but what academic Marxism latched on to was the notion that the ISA had some form of relative autonomy. For many this meant that you could retreat from the real political arena, carry out small scale micro studies, and pass off elitist intellectualism in the name of revolutionary theoretical practice.[20]

Althusserian Marxist philosophy has been singled out here not so much because of its lasting influence but because it informed one of the clearest, if somewhat idealistic, statements on sport, leisure and ideology in the 1970s.

While we will concentrate here upon the work of Jean-Marie Brohm, it should not be forgotten that by the 1970s a number of writers, such as Paul Hoch, had already contributed to a critical Marxist body of literature on sport.[21] Hoch, amongst others, argued that modern sport was but a microcosm of modern capitalist society and an integral facet of cultural domination and exploitation. Hoch's work claimed to be influenced by European social and political theory – the works of Antonio Gramsci in particular – and yet the immediate problem with this work is a suspicious absence of Gramscian theory. While Hoch's discussion of American sport goes beyond simple descriptions of American sporting ills and must be credited for its influence in the early 1970s, ironically it borders upon a Marxist version of functionalist theory and fails to get to the roots of the problems within a society which he so mightily condemns. Like the work of Jean-Marie Brohm, it might be suggested that the work of Hoch is strong on moral indignation and a commitment to progressive change, but weak on objective reasoning and even factual accuracy.

For Jean-Marie Brohm in *Sport a Prison of Measured Time* the neutrality of sport and leisure was brought into question by locating sport and leisure firmly within a discussion of the ideological and repressive state apparatus. Sport and recreation practices were viewed as part of the process through which a structure in dominance was secured or reproduced. In this sense sport: provided a stabilising factor for the existing social order; provided a basis for reinforcing the commodity spectacle; provided a basis for reproducing patriarchy; provided a basis for regimenting and militarising youth and reproducing a set of hierarchical, elitist, authoritarian values. If competitive sport is condemned to the dustbin then forms of recreation fare no better since they were viewed as ideological ways of running away from reality. That is, leisure practices were viewed as false techniques of escapism.[22]

Both Althusser and Brohm were at pains to distinguish between a general theory of ideology from the theory of particular ideologies. On the one hand a general theory of ideology may have served to represent an imaginary relationship between individuals and their real conditions of existence but on the other hand Althusser also affirmed the existence of dominated ideologies which expressed the protest of exploited classes. Perhaps one of the difficulties with this approach is that it is almost impossible to reconcile the existence of any potential revolutionary ideology with the assertion that all ideology in the end subjects individuals to a structure of dominance. Still others have argued that the rigidity of Althusser's Marxism places too great an emphasis on the power of ideology to structure people's lives, in other words too great an emphasis on the object without the subject.[23]

For all its inadequacies it remains one of the few attempts to reconcile the two major conceptions of ideology found within the Classical Marxist tradition. Despite the fact that the word ideology is often used loosely to refer simply to any set of beliefs, the concept itself, in its strict classical usage, involves two definite assertions; (i) that beliefs and ideas, or more generally the way people perceive the world, are socially determined and (ii) that beliefs and ideas are necessarily flawed or distorted in specific ways, and consequently the ways in which people perceive the world are normally false. The first of these claims can be found within both Classical Marxism and non-Marxist sociological traditions while the second claim, although having parallels in other traditions of thought, is more specifically rooted in the work of Marx.[24]

The concept of ideology as a distorted false consciousness is developed in great detail with *The German Ideology.*[25] Here Marx affirms that the real problems of humanity are not mistaken ideas but real social contradictions which in turn give rise to forms of false consciousness about material reality. This theory of ideology simply assumes a corresponding relationship between social structure and systems of thought. Ideas are merely viewed as the passive reflections of an external economic base. Throughout the work of Marx and Engels, ideology maintains its critical negative connotation and is used only in explaining those distortions which are connected only with the concealment of reality.

The notion of false consciousness is an aspect of Classical Marxism that few writers, if any, are happy with and yet it has parallels in other traditions of social thought, most notably positivism. Here distortion is treated as a matter of error to which normal thought is subjected because of the limitations of everyday life. But whereas with positivism the only escape from the normal realm of errors and illusions is through adherence to the cannons of scientific method, for Classical Marxism the only escape from false consciousness is through a practical critique of the conditions producing such consciousness.

The idea that forms of sport and leisure have contributed to a state of false consciousness is an assertion that has been made by several Marxist and non-Marxist scholars. Writing in the late 1970s Ralph Miliband not only asserted the need for a Marxist sociology of sport, but also went on to argue that working-class involvement in sport was not necessarily conducive to the development of class consciousness.[26] In the early 1990s this was a theme that was echoed by his Marxist team-mate, Eric Hobsbawm, who suggested that the imagined community of many nation states seemed more real in the form of a team of eleven named people.[27] Non-Marxists have also commented upon the gulf between nationalist fervour at international matches and the lack of nationalist fervour at the polling booths. Most notably, Jim Sillars, former deputy leader of the Scottish Nationalist Party, following his defeat in the 1992 general election, asserted that 'the great problem is that Scotland has too many ninety-minute patriots whose nationalist out-pourings are expressed only at major sporting events'.[28]

At a more general level the notion of ideology has been used to legitimate some or all of the following beliefs and ideas about sport and leisure: (i) the idea that sport and leisure interests help to mask a number of competing social, economic and political ideologies is a common critique of statements which tend to suggest that people's experiences of sport and leisure are universal, natural, and harmonious; (ii) the idea that sport and leisure forms are themselves sites of ideological struggle not just about sport and leisure but about the type of world we should live in; (iii) the idea that the ability of consumer orientated capitalism to produce a range of leisure goods and experiences carries a range of ideological implications when compared with the poorer sections of the world; (iv) the idea that sport and leisure can help to distort and constrain social reality and progress; and (v) the idea that sport and leisure practices contribute to a process through which particular interests are represented as universal interests that should be adopted by society or humanity as a whole.

Yet if the work of Marx tended to reflect a negative attitude towards the notion of ideology it received a more positive treatment from other Classical Marxist writers such as Lenin. For Lenin, ideology strictly referred to the political consciousness of various classes which were in a state of tension or confrontation. Ideology for Lenin did not entail a state of false consciousness nor any distortion of reality. Lenin's approach to ideology also influenced subsequent Marxist writers such as Gramsci and Lukacs. Gramsci, like Lenin, explicitly rejected a negative conception of ideology, but unlike Lenin he rejected any theory of ideology by articulating different levels of ideological practice, namely philosophy, religion, common sense and folklore. Yet despite various modifications to the way in which the notion of ideology has operated within Classical Marxism, early debates within Western Marxism tended to emanate from either the work of Marx or Lenin. While some tried to reconcile the negative and positive approaches towards ideology others have argued that only one of these versions can be truly Marxist.

Marxism after Marx

The various attempts to re-interpret and synthesise the ideas of Marx have been many, too many to provide a comprehensive study here.[29] In any case, only certain schools of thought have mediated the sociology of sport and leisure literature. Within Marxist economics the central question remained how and when would captialism collapse? The resilience of capitalism in the West certainly led to a decline of interest in Marxist economics as capitalism prospered. During the 1970s structural Marxism expended a lot of energy trying to explain the continuing survival of captialism. Like the Frankfurt school, structuralism placed relatively little faith in the revolutionary potential of the working class. Others such as Kautsky, Luxemburg and Gramsci all contributed to an on-going debate concerning the relationship of the party to the proletariat. It is perhaps an indication of just how far Marxism travelled after Marx when one considers that some of the most vibrant contributions to Marxist thought have either developed outside of the former Western and Eastern bloc or been critical of the forms of Marxism which developed within it.

For instance, the Frankfurt school, whose genesis emerged from within Germany during the 1920 and 1930s, came to be associated with an anti-Bolshovik radicalism and an open-ended or critical Marxism. Horkheimer, Adorno, Marcuse and Habermas were all key contributors to a continuing refinement of Marxist critical theory. Some of these intellectual journeys are still being developed in the 1990s. Hostile to both capitalism and Soviet socialism, the Frankfurt school sought to keep alive the possibility of alternative paths for social development. The growth of technology and the 'culture industry' was seen as a threat to the very nature of the existing social order. The mass media and mass culture transfixed an anesthetised public into a mass of passive consumers of pre-packaged information and entertainment. By raising issues concerning the division of Labour, bureaucracy, leisure, popular culture, family structure and ownership and control, the Frankfurt school sought to broaden the terms of reference of Neo-Marxist debate decisively.

Although significant differences existed within the Frankfurt school, they maintained that most cultural entitites such as sport, art and other leisure forms had become commodities. The term culture industry was simply used to refer to the 'standardisation' of many cultural artefacts in the West (for example, television Westerns or film music). For from creating relaxation leisure and the culture industry were seen to distract people from the basic pressures of their lives and yet they produced no genuine escape since they simply duplicated or reinforced the structure of the world people attempted to avoid.

Outside of the former Western and Eastern bloc other traditions of social thought continued to a refinement and critique of Marxism after Marx. While accepting that the dependency approach, in so far as it constitutes the application of historical materialism to the analysis of peripheral or marginal capitalist countries has been heavily critiqued by Marxists such as Leys, Warren and Bernstein, it is not dead. While Leys correctly criticises dependency theory and its simplistic pairings of developed/underdeveloped, dominant/dependent and centre/periphery it is important not to throw away the baby with the bathwater. The critics of dependency theory hardly ever post an alternative and hence one is left with the impression that either they find nothing specific in the situation of the Third World or peripheral nations. In either case one is left with a vacuum that neo-liberal theories are only too happy to fill.

Nationalism as the natural reaction to processes of dependency and uneven economic development, even in Marxist terms, still has some explanatory power in the 1990s. (See Chapter 10 for a further discussion of dependency theory.) The concept of marginality and the revolutionary potential of marginal underclasses may also have been grossly overestimated but it still draws attention to a recurrent problem of dependent capitalist development, namely poverty and a continuing gap between rich and poor.[30]

If the dependency and underdevelopment debate of the 1970s and 1980s helps to serve as a reminder of the ethnocentrism

inherent within Western Marxism then Black Marxism and the
writers of the black radical tradition provides but one further
source of criticism.[31] At least three concerns are flushed out in the
work of such writers as William Dubois, C. L. R. James, Richard
Wright, Angela Davis and many other black radical writers: (i) that
the whole basis of Marxism as a Western construction is a conceptualisation of human affairs and human development which has
been drawn from the experiences of European peoples and as
such it loses much of its explanatory power when faced with
non-Western evidence; (ii) even allowing for Marxist-Leninist
terms such as imperialism and colonialism or even a view of world
development based upon a materialist understanding of history,
Marxism fails to consider or question the existence of modern
slavery or specific forms of exploitation born out of, for example,
black poverty in America or black reserve armies of labour in
South Africa. It has also been suggested that Classical Marxism
itself paid insignificant attention to slavery as a key phase in the
materialist analysis of history; and (iii) that Marxism has paid little
attention to the way in which racism mediates the organisation of
labour, or racism itself as an expression of alienation, or the
specific contribution to revolutionary or reformist change born
out of the struggle of African peoples.

It is not necessary to view all this as irrelevant to the analysis of sport
and leisure. Alan Klein's political economy of sport in the Dominican
republic tends to view the history of baseball as an expression of
underdevelopment and American exploitation.[32] The 'Black Power'
demonstrations by American athletes at the 1968 Mexico Olympic
Games were explained in the following terms;

> For years we have participated in the Olympic Games carrying the
> USA on our backs with our victories and race relations are worse
> then ever. We are not trying to lose the Olmpics for America, what
> happens is immaterial. But it is time for the black people of the
> world to stand up as men and women and refuse to be utilised as
> performance animals in return for a little extra dog food.
>
> *The New York Times*, 12 May 1968

Certainly some or all of the following questions would be central
to developing a political economy of black sport: How has wealth
been produced from the exploitation of black athletes? How have
black sporting struggles affected the emancipation of black
people? Who profits from the play and display of black athletic

talent? How are black people represented within positions of power and influence in the world sport or leisure? To what extent are terms such as alienation, racial capitalism, imperialism and colonialism useful in explaining the development of black sporting or leisure experiences?

Of the Black Marxist/black radical writers who have commented upon sport, pride of place belongs to C. L. R. James. *Beyond a Boundary* (1963) remains a classic statement on the relationship between cricket and Caribbean society during the 1950s and early 1960s.[33] It recognised that an almost fanatical obsession with organised games was not merely an innocent social activity but also a potential signifier of oppression and liberation. It provided a statement not only about an expanded conception of humanity but also the necessity to break from the colonial legacy which had affected the development of the West Indies. In placing the cricketer centre stage James attempted to transcend the division between high and popular art. The cricketer, in the 1960s, was seen as a modern expression of the individual personality pushing against the limits imposed upon his/her full development by society (class/colonial/nationhood/periphery). Non-white cricketers came first to challenge then overthrow the domination of West Indian cricket by members of the white plantocracy. By the 1980s some have argued that the transformation of West Indian cricket had come full circle – from being a symbol of cultural imperialism to being a symbol of Creole nationalism.[34]

If Black Marxism and the writings of the Black Radical tradition provided one significant source of criticism of Western Marxism, then Marxist feminist analysis provided another.[35] Like many other fields of knowledge and practice, Marxism was viewed as being male-centred, silent on the question of the domestic mode of production, and to a certain extent dependent upon an abstract bourgeois notion of equality. There are arguably many ways in which Marxism might have proved extremely useful in analysing the position of women but at the same time Marxism itself was being challenged, in the 1980s, by both feminism and the women's movement. Classical Marxists would argue that both Marx and Engels learned a great deal from the utopian socialists and in *The Origins of the Family, Private Property and the State* (1884) sought to show that the oppression of women was bound up with the emergence of the monogamous family, of classes, and that the emancipation of women was inseparable from that of the working class.[36]

Yet there are many important gaps in the way that both Marx and Engels posed issues regarding women. For instance Marxist feminist analysis raised the whole question of production, the belief in production for production's sake, as relegating the whole sphere of reproduction to that of secondary importance. Furthermore it was argued that unless institutions are created that would transform the division of labour between men and women then why should women believe that life on earth would be any better under socialism? Still others asserted that any feminism worthy of the name had to be both methodologically and politically post-Marxist.[37]

While a great deal of feminist literature on sport and leisure has emerged, very few Marxist feminist accounts of sport and leisure have attempted to consider the inter-dependence of capitalism and patriarchal systems of oppression in terms of trans-historical analysis and not just at the level of theory. We need more work which analyses precisely the mechanisms by which women's oppression, including black women's oppression, has been historically procured and challenged within the contexts of sport and leisure.

In general Marxist-feminist accounts of sport and leisure have relied heavily upon the notions of patriarchy, ideology, and a re-conceptualisation of the various modes of production. The patriarchal system is viewed as subordinating women to men in contemporary society through the economic relations of the domestic mode of production.[38] Sport and leisure as sets of social practices are viewed as both reproducing and challenging the premises upon which male bourgeois domination rests. The struggle to remove discrimination in sport and leisure is seen to contribute to the broader struggle to remove the practical and symbolic means of perpetuating relations of domination and subordination. As Jenny Hargreaves insists, this concerns the social and economic constraints on women's sport and leisure (what is possible), the connection with ideology and symbolic forms of control (what is permissible) and self-determination and the articulation and fulfilment of desire (what is pleasurable).[39]

More specifically Marxist-feminist traditions have generally been clear about the starting points for considering historical sociological work on sport and leisure, to highlight sport and leisure practices and their contribution to the reproduction of patriarchal social relations, to promote the revolutionary or emancipatory potential of women's sport and leisure, and to adopt a critical perspective towards dominant intellectual traditions which have ignored or justified women's oppression. Whatever the theory, argues Hall, the starting point must be an emancipatory one.[40]

Concluding thoughts

This chapter has attempted to evaluate some of the central themes that have permeated many Marxist accounts of sport and leisure. It is by no means exhaustive but, by way of summary, it might be suggested that some or all of the following concerns have been central to both Classical Marxist accounts of sport and the political economy of leisure: (i) to provide a materialist understanding of the development of sport and leisure; (ii) to provide a general critique of capitalism and more specifically the development of sport and leisure under capitalism; (iii) to determine if the reproduction of wage-labour relations in the world of sport and leisure have contributed to problems of alienation, a changing division of labour, social control, and the maintenance of capitalism; and (iv) to consider if specific struggles over sport and leisure have contributed to any form of reformist or revolutionary politics.

It would be foolish not to recognise the contribution which academic Marxism has made to the sociology of sport and leisure. Some of the central ideas of Classical Marxism, political economy and Marxism after Marx have been covered in this chapter (other aspects such as Marxist cultural analysis are covered in more depth in Chapter 5). Yet it would also be foolish not to recognise that academic Marxism has also been responsible for a certain violence of abstraction that has at times drifted from a central point of Classical Marxist focus namely, the labour movement and praxis. Any account of Marx's ideas is bound to be controversial but, when all is said and done, one cannot accept Marx's scientific theory and reject his revolutionary politics; the two always went together.

NOTES AND REFERENCES

1 The historian Eric Hobsbawm declared in *Marxism Today* that those of us who believed that the October Revolution was the gate to the future of world history have been shown to be wrong. Fred Halliday wrote in *New Left Review* that the collapse of the Stalinist regimes amounted to nothing less than the defeat of the communist project as it was known in the twentieth century and the triumph of the capitalist. See A. Callinicos and D. Walker, 'Marxism Dead or Alive', in *The Times Higher Educational Supplement*, 1991, 12 July, pp. 13–17.

2 More specifically the point that is being made is that throughout the late 1970s and 1980s various epistemological and ontological positions tended to use Marxism as a control model or a straw person against which to compare one's preferred position. The same statement cannot be made with the same conviction in the early 1990s.

3 For a concrete exposition of the continuing influence of social class on both life chances and life styles refer to I. Reid, *Social Class Differences in Britain*, Glasgow, Fontana Press, 1989. There has been a lot of evidence to suggest that since 1979, in Britain alone, the rich have become increasingly richer while the poor have become increasingly poorer. Yet living standards of the poor in Britain are high compared to many developing countries such as India and Ethiopia. Marx's classical conceptualisation of class formation was rooted not in terms of class as a category but in the relationship between classes brought about by the division of labour which in turn secured relations of domination, subordination and exploitation.

4 See C. Robinson, *Black Marxism and the Making of the Black Radical Tradition*, London, Zed Press, 1991 and A. Grimshaw (ed.) *The C. L. R. James Reader*, Oxford, Blackwell, 1991.

5 For a useful short summary of the classical tradition, see P. Anderson, *Considerations on Western Marxism*, London, Verso, 1979, pp. 1–23. See also A. Swingewood, *A Short History of Sociological Thought*, London, Macmillan, 1984, pp. 59–88.

6 P. Anderson, op. cit., 1979, pp. 24–74.

7 In this context two essential readings are H. Edwards, *The Revolt of the Black Athlete*, New York, Free Press, 1969 and C. L. R. James, *Beyond a Boundary*, London, Stanley Paul, 1963.

8 Adam Smith was not the most materialist of the Scottish Enlightenment thinkers but he was certainly one of the most influential. For a discussion of the Scottish contribution to Marxist Sociology, see R. L. Meek, *Economics and Ideology*, London, Chapman & Hall, 1967. Adam Ferguson is often unthinkingly categorised along with the Scottish political economists such as Smith, Hume and Miller, but unlike classical Marxism there was no blind belief in social progress in Ferguson's work. Although his discussions on the division of labour are often quoted in a classical Marxist sense of the term Ferguson actually argued that the division of labour actually enhanced social solidarity rather than class conflict or class struggle.

9 See K. Marx, *Preface and Introduction to a Contribution to the Critique of Political Economy*, Peking, Foreign Language Press, 1976, p. 9.

10 See K. Marx and F. Engels, *Collected Works Vol VI*, Moscow, Progress Publishers, 1975, p. 165.

11 We have commented here specifically on R. Beamish, 'Political Economy of Professional Sport' in J. Harvey and H. Cantelon (eds) *Not Just a Game: Essays in Canadian Sport Sociology*, Ottawa, University of Ottawa Press, 1988, pp. 141–57. For a more theoretically grounded exposition of sport and classical Marxism, read R. Beamish, 'Sport and the Logic of Capitalism' in H. Cantelon and R. Gruneau (eds) *Sport, Culture and the Modern State*, Toronto, University of Toronto Press, 1982, pp. 141–97.

12 For a discussion on the ten richest individual backers of British football teams during the 1991–92 season, see C. Blackhurst, 'Chequebook Football', in *The Independent on Sunday*, 3 May 1992, p. 6.

13 For a recent Marxist discussion of Britain's social elites, see J. Scott, *Who Rules Britain?*, Oxford, Polity Press, 1991. See in particular the discussion on landownership and sport in the British social calendar.

14 A. Ferguson, *An Essay on the History of Civil Society*, Edinburgh, Edinburgh University Press, 1966.

15 John Brewer provides a summary and critique of Adam Ferguson's notion of the division of labour in D. McCrone, Stephen Kendrick and Pat Straw (eds) *The Making of Scotland, Nation, Culture and Social Change*, Edinburgh, Edinburgh University Press, 1989.

16 For an excellent summary of the relationship between labour, alienation and political economy refer to Alex Callinicos, *The Revolutionary Ideas of Karl Marx*, London, Bookmarks, 1983, pp. 64–77.

17 K. Marx and F. Engels, *Collected Works Vol 47*, Moscow, Progress Publishers, 1980, p. 78.

18 A. Ferguson, op. cit., 1966.

19 L. Althusser, *Lenin and Philosophy and Other Essays*, London, New Left Books, 1971, pp. 162–8. For a very readable summary of the work of Althusser, see A. Callinicos, *Althusser's Marxism*, London, Pluto Press, 1976.

20 This point is made more forcibly by Martin Bright in the light of a renewed interest in the work of Althusser in the early 1990s. See M. Bright, 'Sane Marxists Cry in a World of Madness' in *The Guardian*, 27 June 1992, pp. 29–31.

21 J. M Brohm, *Sport, a Prison of Measured Time*, London, Ink Links Ltd, 1978; and P. Hoch, *Rip Off the Big Game*, New York, Doubleday, 1972.

22 This view is developed further in R. Gruneau, *Class, Sports and Social Development*, Amherst, University of Massachussetts Press, 1983, pp. 34–9.

23 The classical critique of Althusser's earlier work is to be found in E. P. Thompson's *The Poverty of Theory*, London, Merlin Press, 1978. Thompson's appeal to agency and the need to recognise the autonomous logic of Althusser's rigid objective structures is a direct critique of Althusser's structuralism which is seen to separate both the human subject and human action from the very structures which make up social reality. A good summary of this exchange can be found in P. Anderson, *Arguments Within Western Marxism*, London, Verso, 1980, pp. 16–58.

24 For example, Durkheim also advanced the argument that beliefs were shaped by society. Ideology was the reflection of society itself. More specifically collective representations often equated with projections of social structure in their symbolic or ritualistic form.

25 K. Marx and F. Engels, *The German Ideology*, London, Lawrence & Wishart, 1964, p. 37–8.

26 R. Miliband, *Marxism and Politics*, Oxford, Oxford University Press, 1977, p. 52.

27 E. Hobsbawm, *Nations and Nationalism since 1780: Programme Myth and Reality*, Cambridge, Cambridge University Press, 1990, p. 143.

28 *Glasgow Herald*, 24 April 1992, p. 1.

29 A useful summary can be found in T. Bottomore, L. Harris, V. Kiernan and R. Miliband (eds) *A Dictionary of Marxist Thought*, Massachussetts, Harvard University Press, 1985. See also D. McLellan (ed.) *Marxism After Marx*, London, Macmillan, 1980.

30 One of the classic Marxist statements on the relationship between nationalism and Marxism can be found in T. Nairn, *The Break Up of Britain*, London, Verso, 1979. For Nairn, nationalism is viewed as a natural reaction to the pressures of dependency and uneven development. Nationalism itself has often been viewed as the gravedigger of the Nation-State. These two apparent contradictions are discussed fully in D. McCrone, *Understanding Scotland: Towards The Sociology of a Stateless Nation*, London, Routledge, 1992.

31 See C. Robinson, op. cit., 1991 and A. Grimshaw (ed.) op. cit., 1991.

32 A. Klein, 'Baseball as Underdevelopment: The Political Economy of Sport in the Dominican Republic', in *Sociology of Sport Journal*, vol. 6, no. 1, 1989, pp. 95–112.

33 The game of cricket to some extent mirrored life in West Indian society. Whites were represented in the top echelons of West Indian society, out of all proportion to their number in the population. They led and non-white West Indians were expected to follow. Decisions with respect to who should play, on which grounds Test matches in the West Indies should be played, amount of entrance fee for games and hence profits, continued to be made by whites. C. L. R. James, op. cit., 1963.

34 M. St. Pierre 'West Indian Cricket – A Socio-Historical Appraisal' in *Caribbean Quarterly*, vol. 19, no. 2, 1973, pp. 8-17. See also R. Burton, 'Cricket, Carnival and Street Culture in the Caribbean' in G. Jarvie (ed.) *Sport, Racism and Ethnicity*, London, Falmer Press, 1991, pp. 7–29.

35 For an excellent overview of British feminist traditions of social and political thought, see T. Lovell, *British Feminist Theory*, Oxford, Oxford University Press, 1990. The work of Michelle Barrett in *Women's Oppression Today* (London, Verso, 1980) remains one of the outstanding attempts to critically associate Marxism with feminism.

36 K. Marx and F. Engels, op. cit., 1975, pp. 455–576.

37 C. Mackinnon, 'Desire and Power: A Feminist Perspective' in C. Nelson and L. Grossberg (eds) *Marxism and the Interpretation of Culture*, London, Macmillan, 1988, pp. 105–17.

38 Jenny Hargreaves, 'Where's the Virtue? Where's the Grace? A Discussion of the Social Production of Gender through Sport' in *Theory, Culture and Society*, vol. 3, no. 1, 1986, pp. 109–23. See also F. Devine, *Affluent Workers Revisited, Privatism and the Working Class*, Edinburgh, Edinburgh University Press, 1992, pp. 134–52. For a summary of the relationship between women and class, see N. Charles, 'Women and Class – A Problematic Relationship?' in *Sociological Review*, vol. 38, no. 1, 1990, pp. 43–90.

39 Jenny Hargreaves, 'The Promise and Problems of Women's Leisure and Sport' in C. Rojek (ed.) *Leisure for Leisure*, London, Macmillan Press, 1989, pp. 130–49.

40 A. Hall, 'The Discourse of Gender and Sport: From Femininity to Feminism' in *Sociology of Sport Journal*, no. 5, 1988, pp. 330–40.

Chapter 5

Culture as a war of position and a way of life

The Gramscian influence within the sociology of sport and leisure reflected a widespread recovery and rehabilitation of Gramsci's ideas throughout Western societies during the 1970s. Gramsci's work is characterised by a concern with problems of culture and the relation of cultural formations to political domination; the central concept of hegemony became widely recognised as the most significant concept for a cultural studies which condensed and crystallised the processes of cultural resistance and domination. The whole tenor of Gramsci's Marxism was a rejection of reductionism of any kind albeit class, economic or biological. One of the most revealing contributions made by the Gramscian intervention in attempting to understand the development of sport and leisure was to reveal the inadequacy of such static ahistorical definitions such as mass sport, leisure for the masses, and the people's game.[1]

Talking about the social and historical construction of leisure in Britain, Clarke and Critcher insist that leisure has been integral to the struggle for hegemony in British society in a number of ways.[2] As an area of social life leisure may be viewed as an arena through which cultural conflict over meanings, views of the world and social habits have been fought. Struggles over time and spaces for leisure have been part of the continuous development of leisure in Britain. Thus the very idea of leisure may be seen as central to the struggle for hegemony in Britain. The struggle to define what leisure is and what leisure should be was part of that struggle for many cultural Marxists.

The analysis of the relationship between sport, power and culture, in Britain, by John Hargreaves and in America by George Sage, is also premised upon the notion that hegemony is central to understanding the ways in which a class or class fractions achieve leadership over the rest of society.[3] The central thesis in the work of John Hargreaves, in relation to class power and sport, was that sport was significantly implicated in the process whereby the growing economic and political power of the bourgeoisie in nineteenth-century Britain was eventually transformed into that class's hegemony in the later part of the century. To thematise sport as an object of struggle, control and resistance necessitated viewing sport as an arena for the play of power relations. Although the works of Clarke and Critcher and Hargreaves are in some cases different they both imply that the development of sport and leisure in Britain was at best comprehended by viewing sport and leisure as cultural formation.

Gramsci would have been the first to admit that we need modalities of historical and cultural situations to bring out the relevance of his theory and yet Gramsci's theory was much broader than that which is often expressed in the cultural genre on sport and leisure. Shortly after Gramsci began his twenty-year prison sentence, in 1926, he stressed in a letter to his sister-in-law Tatiana his eagerness to create something which would last forever, an integral framework for understanding not only the complex way in which capital maintains its rule but also new paths towards socialism.[4] Yet it is precisely this integral framework which was often missing from cultural writings on sport and leisure. The Gramscian notion of hegemony cannot be fully understood beyond the totality of Gramsci's integral framework, a framework which involved a series of key concepts such as economism, hegemony and counter-hegemony, organic and conjunctural, coercion and consent, war of position and war of movement, the integral state, intellectual and moral reform to name but a few. In the same sense that we argued in Chapter 4 that one cannot accept Marx's scientific theory and reject his revolutionary politics, similarly one cannot accept Gramsci's notion of hegemony and jettison other aspects of what was a total framework.

Gramsci's Italy, economism and a rejection of Marxism

Gramsci's notion of hegemony was totally at variance with any economic reductionist view of capital domination; that is, the interpretation of political developments as being reducible to economic developments. This perspective was adhered to by

socialist parties at the time of the Second International, particularly the German Social Democratic Party before the First World
War, but was still entrenched in Italian Socialist Party thinking
during the period when Gramsci was writing (1914–1930). Variations of this theme remained embedded within the British labour
movement of the 1970s and early 1980s. A view that was totally
focused upon wages, conditions of employment and the antagonistic relationship between capital and labour (see Chapter 4
for a broader discussion of the origin of this point of view). Equally
important were the Gramsican critiques of class essentialist views
of culture and ideology. More specifically the Gramscian framework allowed the cultural politics of socialist movements to be
debated without the respective politics of feminist, nationalist or
racial liberation struggles totally engulfing one another. It provided an integrating framework within which different sets of
socialist issues could be worked through in relation to one another.[5]

The rise of fascism in Italy demonstrated for Gramsci that there
was nothing inevitable about the emergence of socialism from
periods of economic or organic crisis. It was only through consciously developing political initiatives, encompassing a broad
social terrain and not just the working class, that a shift in the
balance of class forces could be effected. Thus Gramsci over-
whelmingly rejected the model of an economic base giving rise to
a political and ideological superstructure. If the forces that were
active within any historical period were to be correctly analysed
two principles, suggested Gramsci, must be:

(i) that no society sets itself tasks for whose accomplishment the
necessary and sufficient conditions do not either already exist
or are not at least beginning to emerge and develop;
(ii) that no society breaks down and can be replaced until it has
first developed all the forms of life which are implicit in internal
relations.[6]

In studying any structure Gramsci was emphatic on one point,
namely, that it was necessary to distinguish between organic movements (those which were relatively permanent) from movements
that were essentially conjunctural (those which were occasional,
immediate, almost accidental or unintended). Conjunctural
phenomena tended to depend on organic movements but they did
not have as far reaching a significance as organic or deep-rooted
forces. Conjunctural phenomena gave rise to political criticism of

a minor day to day character while organic phenomena gave rise
to a wider socio-historical criticism which was beyond day to day
public figures or leaders. A common error in historical political
analysis, argued Gramsci, was the inability to find the correct
relation between what was essentially organic and that which was
conjunctural.[7]

Such an analysis has not been overlooked by those sociologists
and cultural critics who have commented upon sport. Some writers
have for some time now asserted that prior to the reforms introduced by F. W. de Klerk in the early 1990s it was perfectly plausible
to explain the development of sport in South Africa in terms of
Gramsci's organic and conjunctural dimensions of crisis.[8] The
continuing development of class, national and racial consciousness in the 1980s turned an initial economic crisis facing South
Africa into a more deep-rooted organic crisis. The conjunctural
terrain organised by those attempting to hold onto the structure
of apartheid implicated sport in at least two main senses. In the
first sense sport was used to suggest to the outside world that sport
in South Africa was, in the 1980s, open to all when in fact a number
of social, political, economic, religious and historical factors miti-
gated against any form of democratic sporting structure.

In a second sense sport was also implicated in those forces that
were struggling to dismantle apartheid or see through the conjunctural response to South Africa's organic crisis. According to
Gramsci if the forces of opposition at any given moment were
going to benefit from any organic movement then it was precisely
the conjunctural response to such a crisis that had to be dis-
mantled or deconstructed. During the 1980s the African National
Congress (ANC) in alliance with the non-racial sports movement
insisted that there could be no normal sport in an abnormal
society. Even after the end of apartheid policy, sport continued to
play a role in the reform process and in particular the ANC used
sport to convince whites of the bona fides of its non-racial policy.
In a post-apartheid South Africa co-operation between the ANC
and the government over sports issues have provided a positive
model of what might be achieved.[9] Critics of this view tend to
suggest that until the establishment of one person one vote in
South Africa becomes a reality then a question mark must remain
against the extent to which reforms in South Africa have been
merely conjunctural or whether a deep-rooted organic transformation has occurred.

A question must also remain over whether one can in fact adapt Gramsci's ideas in a simplistic comparative sense. Gramsci's Marxism was in its original sense developed in Italy between the First and Second World Wars. Yet Gramsci's ideas became popular in a post-war Britain that differed markedly from the Italy of Gramsci.[10] First, Italy's history was one of early rise and decline of merchant capitalism, political partitioning, late unification and late industrialisation. As a nation-state it remained loosely integrated. Britain's history during this period was virtually the opposite. Second, Gramsci's Italy was a mass of agricultural smallholders and proletarians with a relatively small industrial proletariat, predominantly although not exclusively, based in the South. Britain had a large industrial working class with a small crofting proletariat on the periphery, most notably in the Highlands of Scotland. Third, Italy had a culturally powerful Catholic Church while Britain practised a strongly anti-Catholic prejudice (the situation still exists in Great Britain where no Catholic can become king or queen). Fourth, in Italy the dominant Labour movement traditions were Marxist and syndicalist while in Britain they were invariably, although not completely, labourist. Finally, in Italy, the dominant cultural traditions were idealist and historicist (Hegel, Croce) while in early twentieth-century Britain they were empiricist, and quite often anti-historicist.

The consequence of not recognising such differences has often meant that aspects of Gramsci's work have been selected both out of context and outside the integral totality of the Gramscian philosophy. The same is true of both the cultural studies work on sport and leisure and the sociology of sport and leisure literature. To some extent, a violence of abstraction has occurred in the sense that some writers have been quick to highlight the importance of hegemony at the expense of other aspects of Gramsci's thinking or worse an abstraction of hegemony has been exercised at the expense of concrete modalities of historical and cultural situations.[11] Perhaps the first lesson to be learned from Gramsci's own writings is that if one wants to adapt Gramscian insights and concepts to relatively new fields of enquiry then one has to carry out more specific theoretically integral and historically concrete accounts of sport and leisure.

Hegemony and the forces of coercion and consent

Marxists and non-Marxists alike have used the Gramscian concept of hegemony in an extremely subtle and sophisticated way, stressing that contestation between dominant and subordinate groups over, say, recreational or sporting activities was itself a dialectical process by which the ruling elite had to make concessions and search for new forms of alliance in order to maintain a position of dominance. At a concrete level one of the most insightful uses of the Gramscian notion of hegemony can be found in the work of the late Stephen Jones.[12] At a concrete level Jones explains the extent to which British working-class leisure practices figured within various political struggles between about 1918 and 1939. As Jones argues:

> Although the hegemony of Capitalist leisure remained and the great majority of people actually preferred commercially provided for activities, Marxist inspired leisure never exerted a total control over the spare-time interests of any worker.[13]

In contrast to many of the cultural forms of Labour socialism, Marxist cultural formation was essentially the antithesis of the commercialised product. The main reason for Marxist cultural activity was political – to further the class struggle and to disseminate the principles of British Communism. Although many Marxist-influenced cultural organisations responded to different political forces, they were united in their opposition to capitalism. In the case of the British Workers Sports Federation simple sports festivals in the 1920s were both a demonstration against war and fascism and a fight against the capitalist system for more adequate recreational facilities as well as opportunities to take part in healthy vigorous physical recreation.[14]

At an abstract level the Gramscian analysis of sport and leisure served as a useful critique of crude notions of leisure or sport as social control. Viewing sport and leisure as part of civil society permitted sport and leisure to be part of an overall war of position in establishing a level of hegemony or counterhegemony. Several explanations of sporting development in different social formations have tended to allow for complex abstract formulations of hegemony often at the expense of concrete historical examples. Not only do the agencies of hegemony have to be made clear but detailed historical work on sport and leisure needs to be done before we can be more sure about which sports and forms of leisure contributed to different wars of position and when. The abstract has to be unpacked at a concrete level in order to make sense of what is going on.

Gramsci saw the integral nature of state activity as crucial to the maintenance of a dominant group and a range of allies. A distinction between the judicial or coercive apparatuses of the state and the state's role as educator or organiser of consent was central to Gramsci's analysis of state power. Thus he redefined the state as force plus consent to hegemony armoured by coercion in which political society organised force and civil society provided consent. The state is viewed in Gramsci's writings as the entire complex of activities with which the ruling class not only maintains its dominance but manages to win consent from those over whom it rules.[15] The state, therefore is the sum of 'political society plus civil society' or what Gramsci more rigidly referred to as the integral state. In Gramsci's own words:

> For it should be remarked that the general notion of State includes elements which need to be referred back to the notion of civil society (in the sense that one might say that State = political society + civil society, in other words hegemony protected by the armour of coercion). In a doctrine of the State which conceives the latter as tendentially capable of withering away and of being subsumed into regulated society, the argument is a fundamental one. It is possible to imagine the coercive element of the State withering away by degrees, as ever-more conspicuous elements of regulated society (or ethical State of civil society) make their appearance.[16]

The importance of this distinction lies in terms of Gramsci's emphasis on the nature of power. Power for Gramsci was seen to be embodied within the state, since it had a monopoly over coercion; but power should also be seen in a relational sense within the social institutions of civil society. The task for the working class therefore, was not only to seek control of the state in order to achieve socialism, but also to strive through political struggle in order to win hegemony in the sphere of civil society.

As Sugden and Bairner's work on the development of sport and leisure in Northern Ireland clearly illustrates, the Gramscian distinction between political and civil society can be insightful.[17] The manner through which the state influences sport and leisure in

Northern Ireland provides a good illustration of the process of diffusion and redirection. A unique constellation of the forces of coercion and consent. Sugden and Bairner allude to the fact that the state in its many disguises in Northern Ireland deals with the Gaelic Athletic Association in a dramatically contradictory fashion. Central government provides financial support for sport, local government does its best to block such support while the judiciary penalises local government for being sectarian. As an element of civil society the GAA is encouraged by the state in its educative policy to try to achieve the acquiesence of Northern Irish Catholics. At the same time it is also the object of considerable attention on the part of the coercive elements of political society (the security forces) which, suggest Sugden and Bairner, deem the role of the GAA to be essentially counterhegemonic.[18] The most obvious conclusion to draw from this scenario being that sport and leisure as aspects of civil society may only reveal themselves clearly as foci for political hegemonic struggle during times of protracted civil unrest. Sport and leisure in Northern Ireland can neither be explained in terms of crude notions of social control or as a form of soft policing through certain ideological practices. The development of sport and leisure in Northern Ireland has been caught up in a constellation of forces which have been aimed at exercising control through striking a balance between coercion and consent.

There were three major aspects of Gramsci's philosophy of praxis which are worth briefly mentioning. First, the concept of national-popular struggle which was central to Gramsci's thinking on socialist transformation. Gramsci stressed the absurdity of a class or group attempting to situate itself within a position of hegemony, of national leadership, whilst hermetically bound within the precincts of sectionalist struggles based on class. He maintained that it was necessary for a class trying to achieve hegemony to form linkages with other popular democratic struggles that were not solely confined to the antagonisms between capital and labour. For Gramsci it was crucial for both socialist transformation and democracy to take into account the specific national context and national traditions, to create a new historic bloc driven by a national popular collective will.[19] Thus the crucial problem of the national-popular, in a practical sense, lies in broadening the often narrow distinction that is made between class alliances that are effectively counterhegemonic for the working class, and class alliances or federative groupings that are more short term, and arranged around particular issues, in order to tip the balance of power away from the hegemony of the bourgeoisie.

Second, one of the most significant parts of Gramsci's total theory was his writings on intellectual and moral reform. For Gramsci intellectuals exercised a critical role in the formation of both ideologies and consent. Gramsci analysed the unification of Italy, in particular the role of intellectuals and the way in which the mass of the peasantry gave at most passive consent to a new political order. Everybody in society was viewed as an intellectual although not everybody had the opportunity to function as an intellectual. Gramsci divided intellectuals into two broad groups, organic intellectuals who were charged with generating new progressive paths to a new social order and traditional intellectuals who drew upon traditional methods from earlier historical periods. Organic intellectuals produced ideas which marked a sharp break from the past. Traditional intellectuals maintained continuity between one social formation and another.

In relation to his ideas on intellectuals Gramsci suggested that whereas professional philosophers developed the skill of abstract thought, all human beings engaged in philosophical practice in the sense that they interpret the world albeit in an unsystematic and uncritical way. As Gramsci put it, it is necessary to

> work out consciously and critically one's conception of the world and thus, in connection with the labours of one's own brain, choose one's sphere of activity, take an active part in the creation of the history of the world, be one's own guide, refusing to accept passively and supinely from the outside the moulding of one's personality.[20]

Such a critique, however, must be part of a collective activity in order that it may become part of a social force generating a philosophy of praxis. This implied linkages between the political practice of the working class, social movements, and increasingly wider sections of the population. A praxis that would engage in a war of movement and war of position is the third aspect of Gramsci's thinking which will be briefly mentioned here.

Because of the complex nature of state power Gramsci saw it necessary to wage a political battle on a broad terrain encompassing every area in which capitalist power was exerted. Such a strategy was deemed necessary because capitalist authority relied to a large extent upon mass consent and thus diminished the possibility of a war of movement or spontaneous dramatic struggle. A war of position was necessary to win a political leadership that was based upon a mass movement against capitalism. Such a strategy did not stop with the transformation of state power but continued within the context of developing a socialist society. Clearly Gramsci saw the necessity for a plurality of parties and alliances within the transformative process but he also emphasised that the party which linked the various interests and movements together must have a national character.

The working class on two wheels

At one level it might be argued that sport and leisure activity were irrelevant to the politics of Gramsci's Italy. However, the work of Pivato tends to indicate that both Italian nationalists and socialists saw sport as a vehicle for encouraging fractions of the Italian working class.[21] There is good reason to believe that bicycling in Italy, at the beginning of the twentieth century, represented what football was in Great Britain, in the words of Hobsbawm 'almost a laic religion'.[22] Football in Italy at the beginning of the twentieth century tended to be regarded as a snobbish pastime with aristocratic or bourgeois associations, (A C Milan was both a football and cricket club) while the bicycle, in contrast was widely used among the working class. The propaganda that nationalists disseminated by means of the bicycle had a great influence on the relationship of the Italian working class with sport. Opposition to sport among young Italian socialists was often premised upon the belief that activists might be distracted by non-political associations and this would reduce their commitment to the Socialist Party. Clearly the bicycle was not an innocent bystander in the struggle for hegemony within Gramsci's Italy.

In 1910 an artice in Avanti attacked young socialists for not being aware that the passion for sport and the bicycle in particular was an influential factor in struggling for the hearts and the minds of the mass of workers.[23] By 1913 the launching of the Ciclisti Rossi Association (Red Cyclists) represented a more generalised interest shown by Italian Socialists in sport. The Red Cyclists' opposition to nationalism was typical of the preoccupations that dominated the anti-militarist meetings of many young socialists. On one occasion the Italian Home Office reported that:

young subversives must act together and provide effective anti-militarist propaganda especially in those areas, such as Rimini, where battalions of volunteer cyclists may be found encouraging young people, who would be militant in subversive parties, to join in the ranks of the conservatives.[24]

Soon afterwards teams of Ciclisti Rossi were founded in towns such as Turin, Milan, Venice, Pesaro, Rimini and Florence. This awareness that sport was part of the struggle for hegemony was certainly a basic impulse that lay behind the Ciclisti Rossi initiative. In the context of a long-standing opposition to sport such a stance was a remarkable step forward. Yet class and national factions were not alone in struggling over the bicycle since Italian Catholic clerics also recognised the political force of sport. There was some opposition from certain Catholic groups who not only cited gymnastics in schools as more or less the eighth sacrament but also warned against the terrible crime of pederasty.[25] More than once prohibition of the bicycle for the clergy was enforced with strict steps against the transgressors.

Eventually the Catholic movement overcame early suspicions and strongly endorsed the use of the bicycle by mythologising one of the people's most popular cycling champions; Gino Bartali. The Catholic promotional apparatus symbolised the magnificent Christian athlete, the Catholic champion who stood out in defiance against the Communist cycling champion Fausto Coppi.[26] Bartali illustrated that sport had become part of a broad scheme of Catholic hegemony. As Pivato explains the canonisation of the Tuscan cyclist cannot be understood outwith the political context of Italy in the 1940s.[27] For instance Bartali's 1948 victory in the Tour de France took place in the days following the attempt by the Communist leader Togliatti to seize power in Italy. Bartali's victory was given front page coverage in the Catholic press who assigned to him the role of saver of the mother country. The newspaper *Azione Cattolica* attributed to the cyclist the merit of averting the danger of a revolution by just pressing on the pedals.[28]

The political symbolism of the bicycle in Italy has been used here to illustrate that sport itself has often been proactive as well as reactive in the struggle for hegemony. The bicycle symbolised a constellation of forces which were active in the struggle for power in the first half of the twentieth century. Sport contributed to a war of movement and to a lesser extent a war of position. The Red

Cyclists are but one example of a range of cultural practices which have not only contributed to socialist strategies but also questioned the left's initial long-standing myopia about the analysis of play, pleasure and the politics of popular culture. Whether it be Gramsci's Italy of the 1920s or Britain of the 1970s Gramsci's philosophy served as a critique of long-standing set positions and a growing awareness of the politics of the popular.

Beyond the border country

If Gramsci's writings on hegemony provided an impetus for an emerging Cultural Studies in the 1960s and early 1970s it was in particular the work of Richard Hoggart, Raymond Williams, E. P. Thompson, Terry Eagleton, Stuart Hall, Richard Johnson and Jorge Larrain, and others, that helped to shape a number of distinctive features of British Cultural Studies. Williams in effect expanded his idea of culture by critically adapting Gramsci's concept of hegemony to:

> a whole body of practices and expectations, the whole of living; our sense and assignments of energy, our shaping perceptions of ourselves and our world. It is a lived system of meanings and values – constitutive and constituting – which as they are expressed as practices appear as reciprocally conforming.[29]

When Raymond Williams died in 1988, he was considered to be one of the most authoritive, consistent and original socialist thinkers in the English speaking world.[30] The fact that Williams did not belong to the Left alone does not detract from the fact that his writing was consistantly grounded in working towards a vision of a more democratic social order. His work has influenced a plethora of texts on sport and leisure although Williams himself always struggled with the notion of leisure and rarely mentioned the word sport.[31] It is somewhat ironic that while many writers such as Donnelly and Ingham and Loy are quick to highlight the relevance of such themes as dominant, residual and emergent cultural practices, hegemony and lived experience in examining and interpreting sport and leisure practices, such writers rarely, if at all, mention William's own struggle with the notion of leisure. Nowhere is this more evident than in Williams' discussions on art.[32]

The cornerstone of much of the early work of Raymond Williams lies in the idea that culture is ordinary and that culture does not sit comfortably in the chair of high culture or mass culture. Having dismissed the claims of art as high culture or art as mass culture Williams argues for greater access to art so that it may become common. In taking art to new audiences, art itself in many respects would change. Thus Williams views the relationship between art, democratisation and the culture of the ordinary as inextricably linked. Yet in attempting to locate art in the ordinary Williams reinforces a split between that which is ordinary and that which is creative. Art in the ordinary may redeem the creativity in living but creativity itself must be separated from the habit of leisure consumption which Williams can only view as mundane. The problem here is that Williams remains unwilling to recognise that leisure consumption constitutes an integral part of daily life and hence of popular culture in contemporary society and so cannot be dismissed as mundane, degrading or even trivial. People might experience both the consumption of leisure and art as creativity and as part of the ordinary processes of their lives.

Williams clearly resists the minority's claim to represent common culture but he shares their resistance to the common character of mass culture.[33] His attachment to art as creativity in all our living is rooted in a desire to separate creativity in all our living from what he sees as a secondary reaction to leisure consumption. In other words he joins the conservative cultural critics in rejecting the idea that the leisure pursuits of the ordinary might amount to a common pursuit of culture. The search for such a common culture is a notion that divided many influential thinkers who contributed to British Cultural Studies. Unlike Williams and Hoggart, Hall and Johnson remained sceptical of any notion of an inclusive culture held in common by all people. Instead they argued that contemporary culture was marked by conflicting and overlapping cultural practices competing for a legitimate defini-tion of common culture. For Hall and Johnson the predominance of one kind of culture does not make it common culture but rather indicates its hegemony. Against this hegemony contemporary cul-tural studies raised the flag of popular culture and difference as a juxtaposition to any idea of common culture. More forcibly Stuart Hall declared:

> Popular culture is one of the sites where this struggle for and against a culture of the powerful is engaged: it is also the stake to be won or lost in that struggle. It is the area of consent and

resistance. It is partly where hegemony arises, and where it is secured. It is not a sphere where socialism, a socialist culture – already fully formed – might be simply expressed. But it is one of the places where socialism might be constituted. That is why popular culture matters.[34]

With one or two exceptions it is fair to say that much of the nitty gritty ground-clearing work on sport, leisure and popular culture was undertaken by many social historians. As Holt and others have correctly argued much of the cultural studies writing about sport, leisure and popular culture remained tightly packed with abstract formulation at the expense of concrete historical examples of when, how and which sport and leisure practices helped to consolidate and divide popular culture.[35] Stedman Jones, while critical of what he saw as a poorly grounded project on popular culture, provided his own solutions to the danger of studying leisure in isolation by locating leisure as part of a culture of consolation in his influential study of the London working class, 1870–1900.[36] The early 1970s body of work on young women's leisure by McIntosh, Griffin, Trisca McCabe and Dorothy Hobson has subsequently been added to by, for instance, the Glasgow Women's Study Group project on unchartered lives and Sheila Scraton's analysis of young girls experiences of physical education.[37] Football as an aspect of working-class culture was touched upon by a number of writers most notably by Mason, Holt, Critcher and Moorhouse, while Malcolmson, Cunningham, Bailey, Metcalfe and Ross McKibben all provided insights into the role and place of leisure within working class communities.[38]

The function of culture for Williams was invariably linked to the possibility of community, a sense of neighbourhood, and a sense of place which is expressed most clearly in his feelings and thinking about Wales and the relationship between local and national, urban and rural, and city and country.[39] People construct community differently – it becomes a symbolic depository for meanings associated with different territory. Yet as Williams points out the word community is a word which is generally agreed upon as being a term that everyone likes, a notion that everyone is in favour of. At first instance it conveys a common ground, a common project which, argues Williams, if reflected into reality would mean that we were living in a very different world from the one in which we live today.[40] In trying to come to terms with the notion of community

Williams in the last instance draws upon his own experiences. Three lengthy but important extracts from his writings may convey a tension and struggle over the term.

(i) I happened to grow up in a very small rural community right on the Welsh–English border. That original experience was in a way, so special and, in other ways, so marginal. What it meant for me was, first, the experience of a relatively stable community, which had acquired a certain specific identity in opposition to certain external forces, mainly on the land issue, and which practised within that kind of scattered rural society certain habits that, as I came to recognise when I moved away from it, could certainly not be taken for granted.

(ii) When I went to Cambridge I heard a lecture on the meaning of the word neighbour. The Professor said that the word indicated something that no twentieth-century person can understand, because it signified a whole series of obligations and recognitions over and above the mere fact of physical proximity. . . . Well, I got up and said I knew perfectly well what neighbour in that full sense meant. Now this was not to idealise my own place. I did not mean that people didn't play dirty tricks on each other sometimes. I meant that there was, nevertheless, a level of social obligation that was conferred by the fact of seeming to live in the same place and, in that sense seeming to have a common identity.

(iii) This was entirely within my sense of neighbour and community. But it was still – as I soon realised when I moved out – so marginal a case that I had to learn a whole range of other possible meanings. And it did come to seem to me that there was a different kind of community, physically quite close to where I'd grown up, but which I'd known so well. A community that had been hammered out in very fierce conflict, the kind of community that was the eventual positive creation of struggles within the industrialisation of South Wales.[41]

Such extracts are important because they not only indicate that Williams is sensitive to the fact that the rhetoric within the term community is fraught with dangers but that a distinct shift in his thinking is evident when one compares his earlier and later writings. There is an explicit recognition and acceptance of the fact that most people are required to live across culture, move between borders and as such conceive of community at a series of levels. For instance people may know that a certain feeling of community may exist; may understand what that feeling involves; may allow that feeling to effect behaviour; may make a particular community a basis of identity or shift between borders as the structures of feeling change. Thus Williams recognises the limitations of his earlier work and in particular he seems to accept the criticism that the notion of common culture cannot have its sole focus on working-class culture or even popular culture.

Significantly for Williams recent social movements have tended to emerge outside organised class interests and institutions. Old socialism dictated a unilinear view of social relations, one that relied on abstract class determinations. If socialism is to survive in some renewed form then its practical politics must acknowledge diversity. Williams thus insists that since there are many peoples and cultures there must be many socialisms. Socialisms must emerge for the actual struggle for social identities and effective communities.[42] Communities of many different kinds which are interlinked around the socialist value of sharing must be seen as a key resource for the future.

In the last instance community to Williams is related to the principle of maximum self-management, new forms of self-determination and the basic right of people to govern themselves.[43] Decision-making powers should, as far as possible, reside amongst those most directly affected, in their work, localities and other associations. Community is thus, in part, a normative notion referring to social relationships of a certain type and quality, counterposed against various forms of centralist control and international corporate capitalism. Such a view was echoed by Raymond Williams, himself a man of the border country but who moved between cultures.

> It is clear that if people are to defend and promote their real interests on the basis of lived and worked and placeable social identities, a large part of the now alienated and centralised powers and resources must be actively regained, by new actual societies which in their own terms, and nobody else's, define themselves.[44]

Concluding thoughts

In seeking to develop answers to unanswered questions and to provide alternative codes for understanding the past and the present, the Gramscian concept of hegemony gained a lot of credence within Marxist Cultural accounts of sport and leisure during the 1980s and early 1990s. To paraphrase Clarke and Critcher, hegemony became a significant concept for cultural studies, because it condensed a number of major themes concerning the process of cultural domination and conflict.[45] It helped to emphasize that the field of culture, including sport and leisure practices, was made up of different cultures and sub-cultures. The use of the term also implied that a degree of cultural struggle was needed to unite different cultures under the leadership of a dominant culture. The term also implied that cultural conflict was a process that did not simply happen at the level of political ideology but that it also involved common sense experiences and struggles over patterns of everyday thinking. Thus the term hegemony opened up the field of popular culture, and sport and leisure as facets of popular culture, to a number of limits and possibilities. In particular the term highlighted the relationship between power and culture and a rejection of reductionist thinking in whatever manner it appeared.

In general cultural studies work on sport and leisure has been undertaken for some or all of the following reasons: (i) to consider the relationship between power and culture; (ii) to demonstrate how a particular form of sport or leisure has been consolidated, contested, maintained or reproduced, within the context of society as a whole; and (iii) to highlight the role of sport and leisure as a site of popular struggle. A central question for many Marxist Cultural research agendas on sport and leisure has been what exactly is the reproductive or transformative capacity of sport and leisure. This simply means to what extent does sport and leisure challenge, reproduce or contribute to patterns of social organisation or political struggle. Obviously cultural studies work on sport and leisure has changed over time but a certain emphasis has been placed on the media, analysis of subcultures; sport and leisure as text; and sport and leisure as part of popular culture.

While the authors recognise that a vast number of thinkers have contributed to what is termed cultural studies, which itself is a contested terrain, we have concentrated our efforts around the work of Antonio Gramsci and Raymond Williams since arguably all roads in cultural studies during the 1980s and early 1990s tended to lead back to one of these two writers. We might even be tempted to say all roads lead back to Gramsci but unfortunately much of the

Cultural Studies research into sport and leisure has been extremely selective when considering Gramsci's praxis. If anything was to be taken from Gramsci's work then surely two non-negotiable starting points would have been (i) the totality of Gramsci's philosophy of praxis and (ii) a testing of Gramsci's philosophy against specific historical modalities of the way in which sport and leisure has contributed directly to socialist politics. For all the complexities in Gramsci's philosophy the work of Pivato, Jones and Sugden and Bairner are but three examples of work on sport and leisure located in different national-popular contexts which clearly illustrate the spirit of Gramsci's thinking.

As Radhakrishnan concedes it is unfortunate that we do not have Raymond Williams' insights into the changing nature of the left, socialism and changing world conditions in the mid 1990s.[46] Since there is no distinct Williams school of thought it is difficult to see how the driving force behind his ideas will last or even develop. Yet there is much in Williams' writings that is both relevant and worth holding on to. Undoubtedly there is a need to move beyond hegemony theory and at an historical and empirical level there is much that could be done in terms of considering sport and leisure within local, regional and national cultures, or to use Williams' own terms, the cultural politics of location. What part has sport played within the local and regional areas of Scotland, England, Ireland and Wales?

Apart from the popular sports of football, rugby, cricket, athletics, etc., what less well known local pastimes and sporting customs have contributed to a sense of community within different neighbourhoods?

The strongest single demand in Williams' theory of democracy was for the self-management of communities and work places. People, he argued, should have the power and resources to manage their own affairs. The terms decentralisation, devolution, and local participation apply as much to the world of sport and leisure as they do to education, water privatisation, and increasing demands for popular sovereignty within Great Britain. Yet such democracy has the danger of remaining on the shelf of academic rhetoric unless a distaste for authoritarianism, bureaucratic intransigence and the excesses of the centralist state are transformed into a 'common sense' approach to political issues affecting sport and leisure.

Effective power means getting the political or social conditions right, but in the meantime we could find out a little bit more about who, what and why sport and leisure is what it is today. Yes, community, neighbourhood and sociability but not at the expense of the rights of women, Catholics, and ethnic minority communities. Surely any socialism that neglects the liberties of others either destroys itself or shoots itself in the foot.[46] We could expose many of the taken-for-granted assumptions and myths about sport and leisure before considering the way in which sport contributes to nationalism or regionality or even identity. However, each of these terms have to be unpacked in relationship to specific contexts, communities and local histories. The production of public information and dialogue about how sport works, who makes decisions about sport and leisure, what is going on, who is involved and why, are all important ever changing questions which differ from territory to territory or community to community. Yet they are part and parcel of understanding the overall anatomy of sport and leisure in a changing contemporary world.

NOTES AND REFERENCES

1 Antonio Gramsci was born in Sardinia on 22 January 1891 and died from cerebral haemorrhage in Rome on 27 April 1937. His experience of Italy influenced his view that any socialist revolution in Italy required national-popular struggle which was to be brought about, in part, through an alliance between the Italian working class and the peasantry. For a useful introduction to the work of Gramsci, see C. Boggs, *Gramsci's Marxism*, London, Pluto Press, 1976 and R. Simon, *Gramsci's Poltical Thought* (second edition) London, Lawrence & Wishart, 1991. For a short review of Gramsci's influence in British politics, see D. Forgacs 'Gramsi and Marxism in Britain' *New Left Review*, no. 176, 1989, pp. 70–91.

2 J. Clarke and C. Critcher, *The Devil Makes Work: Leisure in Capitalist Britain*, London, Macmillan, 1985, pp. 225–9.

3 J. Hargreaves, *Sport, Power and Culture*, Cambridge, Polity Press, 1986 and G. Sage, *Power and Ideology in American Sport*, Illinois, Human Kinetics, 1990.

4 Lettere dal Carcere (Gramsci's Letters From Prison) were translated by Hamish Henderson and appear in a special issue of *New Edinburgh Review*, no. 1, 1972. Tatiana (Tania) Schucht did not meet Gramsci until 1925. She soon became a close friend and after Gramsci's imprisonment she was his closest confidante and helper. She moved to Milan when Gramsci was transfered there and helped to preserve Gramsci's prison notebooks after his death. She returned to the Soviet Union in 1939 where she died in 1941.

5 P. Tritschler 'Gramsci', *Radical Scotland*, no. 20, 1986, pp. 29–31.

6 A. Gramsci, *Selections from Prison Notebooks*, New York, International Publishers, 1971, p. 177.

7 ibid, p. 178.

8 G. Jarvie, *Class, Race and Sport in South Africa's Political Economy*, London, Routledge & Kegan Paul, 1985, and G. Jarvie, 'Sport, power and dependency in Southern Africa' in E. Dunning and C. Rojek (ed.) *Sport and Leisure in the Civilising Process*, London, Macmillan, 1992, pp. 183–200.

9 A. Guelke, 'Sport and the end of Apartheid' in L. Allison (ed.) *The Changing Politics of Sport*, Manchester, Manchester University Press, 1993, pp. 151–71.

10 This point is developed by D. Forgacs, op. cit., 1989.

11 P. Calvalcanti and P. Piccone, *History, Philosophy and Culture in Young Gramsci*, St Louis, Telos Press, 1975, pp. 69–88. For a discussion of the relationship between historicism and the philosophy of praxis see A. Gramsci, op. cit., 1971, pp. 404–7.

12 S. Jones, *Workers at Play: a Social and Economic History of Leisure 1918–1939*, London, Routledge & Kegan Paul, 1986.

13 ibid, p.153.

14 ibid, p.153.

15 A. Gramsci, op. cit. 1971, p.244.

16 ibid, p. 263.

17 The general argument here is that the political crisis in Northern Ireland has been met with a wide range of responses from the British state, responses that range from naked repressive social control to more subtle forms of soft policing. Because of the close relationship between sport, leisure and the separate cultural traditions that underpin the political conflict, this area of popular culture has proven to be a highly contested terrain. These authors have provided several Gramscian influenced accounts of sport and leisure in Northern Ireland. A contemporary account of this research can be found in J. Sugden and A. Bairner, *Sport, Sectarianism and Society in a Divided Ireland*, London, Leicester University Press, 1993.

18 J. Sugden and A. Bairner, 'Ma, There's a Helicopter on the Pitch! Sport, Leisure and the State in Northern Ireland', *Sociology of Sport Journal*, vol. 9, no. 2, 1992, pp. 154–66.

19 See Gramsci section in the Prison Notebooks on the problems of Marxism where he spells out clearly the relationship between intellectuals and the people and the role of the people as a social force in establishing a historic bloc. A. Gramsci, op. cit., 1971, pp. 378–472 and in particular pp. 418–22.

20 ibid, p. 323.

21 In this particular section we have drawn heavily upon the work of Stefano Pivato 'The Bicycle as a Political Symbol: Italy 1885–1955', *International Journal of the History of Sport*, vol. 7, no. 2, 1990, pp. 173–87.

22 E. Hobsbawm, *Lavaro, Cultura e mentalita nella societa industriale*, Rome, Raenza, 1986, p. 188. For Hobsbawm's view on the general relation-

ship between sport and nationalism, see E. Hobsbawm, *Nations and Nationalism since 1789: Programme, Myth and Reality*, Cambridge, Cambridge University Press, 1990, pp. 140–2.

23 S. Pivato, op. cit., 1990, p. 179. The aims of the Red Cyclists included promoting tours in town and regions never reached by socialism, and preparing work for public demonstrations or strikes during election time.

24 ibid, p. 180.

25 ibid, p. 182.

26 ibid, p. 182.

27 ibid, p. 182.

28 ibid, p. 183.

29 Raymond Williams, *Marxism and Literature*, Oxford, Oxford University Press, 1977, p. 110.

30 For an excellent review of Williams' contribution to socialist thinking and cultural studies, see D. Dworkin and L. Roman *Views Beyond the Border Country*, London, Routledge, 1993.

31 Indeed whole books on sport have been designed around the work of Raymond Williams. For example, see A. Ingham and J. Loy (eds) *Sport in Social Development: Traditions, Transitions and Transformations*, Leeds, Human Kinetics, 1993. See also P. Donnelly, 'Sport as a Site for Popular Resistance' in R. Gruneau (ed.) *Popular Culture and Political Practices*, Toronto, Garamond Press, 1988, pp. 69–82.

32 Raymond Williams, *The Long Revolution*, Harmondsworth, Penguin, 1984 and Raymond Williams, op. cit., 1977, pp. 149–57.

33 For a discussion on Williams' views on common culture, see D. Dworkin and L. Roman, op. cit., 1993, pp. 21–72.

34 S. Hall, 'Notes on deconstructing the popular' in R. Samuel (ed.) *People's History and Socialist Theory*, London, Routledge, 1981, p. 239.

35 R. Holt, *Sport and the British: a Modern History*, Oxford, Oxford University Press, 1989, pp. 355–67.

36 Stedman Jones, 'Working-class culture and working-class politics in London, 1870–1900: notes on the re-making of a working class', *Journal of Social History*, 7, 1974, pp. 179–238. See also Stedman Jones, 'Class expression versus social control? A critique of recent trends in the social-history of leisure', *History Workshop*, no. 4, 1977, pp. 162–70.

37 S. Scraton, *Shaping up to Womanhood: Gender and Girls' Physical Education*, Milton Keynes, Open University Press, 1992.

38 For a review of this literature, see P. Bailey, 'Leisure, Culture and the Historian: Reviewing the First Generation of Leisure Historiography in Britain' in *Leisure Studies*, vol. 8, no. 2, 1989, pp. 107–28.

39 R. Williams, 'Homespun Philosophy' in Channel 4, *Borderlands*, London, Channel 4, 1992, pp. 8–12.

40 ibid, p. 9.

41 ibid, p. 9.

42 This discussion of new social movements has benefited from the reading of D. McCrone, *Understanding Scotland: The Sociology of a Stateless Nation*, London, Routledge, 1992, pp. 197–222.

43 Raymond Williams, *Towards 2000*, London, Chatto & Windus, 1983.

44 ibid, p. 197.
45 J. Clarke and C. Critcher, op. cit., 1985, p. 228.
46 R. Radhakrishnan, 'Cultural Theory and the Politics of Location' in
    D. Dworkin and L. Roman, op. cit., 1993, pp. 275–95.

Chapter 6

Figurations, power and civilising processes

When people first encounter figurational sociology they tend to view it in relation to already existing frames of reference. Hence, at various times, the perspective has been associated with functionalism and Marxism and has even been seen as a variant of symbolic interactionism. Figurational sociology thus appears difficult to pigeon-hole. The intention here is to pull together several seemingly disparate strands into one general discussion and thereby present this tradition of social thought in its own terms. The promise and vision of figurational sociology for the study of social life in general, and sport and leisure in particular, will then become more accessible to those who encounter it.

Stemming from the pioneering work of Norbert Elias, he, and several sociologists working within this tradition, have arguably conducted a radical ground-clearing exercise in our way of seeing the social world.[1] Given the sociology that Elias was trying to promote, the difficulty that people have when they encounter this approach is perhaps understandable. For Elias's project entailed a synthesis of elements of Comte, Durkheim, Marx, Simmel, Weber and Freud. Though he did not want to develop another competing school of thought, he was attempting nothing less than the overhaul of sociological thinking, teaching and research.[2] Within this overall project, Elias took the study of sport and leisure as a serious area of investigation.

For Elias, sociology involved the study of how people cope with the problems of interdependence.[3] This deceptively simple statement rests on several key sensitising concepts that characterise figurational sociology. These are: that human beings are interdependent; that their lives evolve in the figurations that they form with each other; that these figurations are continually in flux,

undergoing changes of different orders, some quick and superficial, others slower but perhaps more enduring; and that the
long-term developments taking place in figurations have been and
continue to be largely unplanned and unforeseen.[4] These sensitising concepts are closely interconnected to what advocates of this
approach maintain is a crucial building block or guiding theory,
namely, the theory of civilising processes.[5]

Each of these sensitising concepts is designed to overcome the
dichotomies that have been seen at times to plague sociological
research. These include: the individual and society, agency and
structure, freedom and determinism, the micro and the macro
and the synchronic and the diachronic. Several of these dichotomies centre around the puzzle of human agency. For Elias, this
puzzle cannot be solved if these dichotomies are maintained.[6] In
developing an alternative form of thinking about human relations,
he made reference to 'game models'. In *What is Sociology?*, he
makes clear his reasons for this:

> With their help it is possible to bring out more graphically the
> processual character of relationships between interdependent
> people. At the same time, they show how the web of human
> relations changes when the distribution of power changes.[7]

Designated to facilitate a 'reorientation of our powers of imagination and conceptualisation in order to understand the nature of
the tasks confronting sociology', these game models highlight how
people are enmeshed in relations with each other.[8] The character
of this interdependence can be as allies and/or opponents.
Locked into the networks that individuals or social groups themselves form, the pattern of these relations is not the direct outcome
of intentional acts alone. The implication of this observation needs
to be made clear. While 'action' theories do take into account the
fact that intentional interactions have unintended consequences,
they conceal a circumstance that Elias maintained was central to
sociological theory. This is, that unintentional interdependencies
lie at the root of every intentional interaction. Referring to the
twelfth move in a two-person game (a game of chess between
Kasparov and Short) where both players are equally strong, Elias
made an observation that illuminates this issue:

> For the twelfth move in such a game can no longer be ade-
> quately explained in terms of short, unilinear causal sequences.

Nor can an explanation be based on the individual character of one or other player. This move can only be interpreted in the light of the way the preceding moves of both players have intertwined, and of the specific figuration which has resulted from this intertwining. Any attempt to ascribe this intertwining to one or other player alone, or even to a mere accumulation of both as originator or cause, is doomed to inadequacy. Only the progressive interweaving of moves during the game process, and its result – the figuration of the game prior to the twelfth move – can be of service in explaining the twelfth move.[9]

Clearly, the emphasis here is placed on the study of people in the plural. That is, how human beings are interdependent. People are born into, develop within, help create, and finally die, in networks of interdependencies with fellow human beings. These chains of interdependencies are formed by the plans and intentions of individuals out of which something emerges which was neither planned nor intended by any one individual or social group. Johan Goudsblom, one of the advocates of this type of sociology, expressed this issue in a succinct form when he observed that 'in the development of human societies, yesterday's unintended social consequences are today's unintended social conditions of intentional human actions'.[10]

Figurational sociologists focus attention on structured processes that occur over time and space. Emphasis is placed on probing how the present has emerged out of the past. It is suggested that there are non-intentional interconnections between intentional acts. These non-intentional interconnections prevail over the intentional, meaningful connections made by people. In reality, intentions and individual acts are themselves constituted by non-intentional interconnections. One further point needs to be stated: interconnections between intentions can have a non-intentional character.

Several implications flow from these insights. In order to capture these interconnections, a change in one's thinking and use of language is required. Thoughts and words which are rooted in *homo clausus* and process-reduction models that isolate individuals from 'society' and involve reducing processes to monocausal, static and non-relational variables, have to be avoided. The search for 'prime movers' is not only a doomed enterprise, it is not worth embarking upon. Instead people are viewed as *homines aperti* or 'open human beings' living out their lives in interdependence with others. In order to capture the dynamics of this existence, there is a need to think processually. This is striven for by the deployment of thinking and language that probe the emergent and contingent yet structured or patterned nature of social relations.[11]

The concept of figuration helps to assist in this task. It refers to the webs of interdependence which link and both constrain and enable the actions of individuals. Though produced and reproduced by acting individuals, the long-term structure and dynamics of figurations cannot be explained solely in terms of the properties of individuals.[12] By figuration is meant the totality of the relationships which, created by interdependent people as a whole, undergo different magnitudes of development over time. Referring again to games and the actions of players, Elias states:

> By figuration we mean the changing pattern created by the players as a whole – not only by their intellects but by their whole selves, the totality of their dealings in their relationships with each other. It can be seen that this figuration forms a flexible lattice-work of tensions. The interdependence of the players, which is a prerequisite of their forming a figuration, may be an interdependence of allies or of opponents.[13]

Figurations are not artificial structures imposed by the investigator on the people being observed. Figurations are just as real as the people forming them. A related concept also designed to promote process thinking is that of development. This concept is used in contrast to the term change because it more adequately captures the complexity of figurations in flux.[14] A developmental approach allows the possibility of capturing both the processes which involve movements towards higher or lower levels of differentiation and integration and the connections between stages in such processes. Use of this concept allows scope for probing an issue which is essential for developmental and figurational sociologists, namely, that of tracing 'movements' over time and of explaining how later social formations arise out of earlier ones. Sequences of interdependencies do not happen without rhyme or reason. There is a structured pattern to these processes. While the occurrence of this structured change is inevitable, there is nothing inevitable about the specific course taken by any figurational sequence. That is, it is important to distinguish between the proposition that event A must be followed by event B, and that event A was a necessary forerunner of B. This applies whether the course of a specific game or that of a long-term social process, such as the emergence and global diffusion of sport, are being charted.

These figurations that stretch over time and place are marked by a series of tension balances. The study of game dynamics also reveals these tensions at work. In fact, these tensions, or power relations, are a structural feature of all human interdependencies. Understood in this sense, power is a relational and dynamic phenomenon.[15] Networks of allies and opponents are marked by a series of power balances that contain elements of co-operation and conflict. Addressing this issue with reference to football, Elias noted:

> Taking football as an example, it can be seen that a figuration is a game-structure which may have a hierarchy of several 'I' and 'he' or 'we' and 'they' relationships. It becomes quite apparent that two groups of opponents, who have a 'we' and 'they' relationship to each other, form one single figuration. We can only understand the constant flux in the grouping of players on one side if we see that the grouping of players on the other side is also in constant flux. . . . At the core of changing figurations – indeed the very hub of the figuration process – is a fluctuating, tensile equilibrium, a balance of power moving to and fro, inclining first to one side and then to the other. This kind of fluctuating balance of power is a structural characteristic of the flow of every figuration.[16]

Power then is seen as an enabling and constraining feature of human relations. Focusing on games can reveal how power relations work in practice. Elias proposed a series of questions that could guide such enquiries. He discussed a variety of games – the 'primal contest', two-person games and multi-person games at different levels. Here we will focus on multi-person games. In examining the dynamics of a sport form, the question arises of whose potential for withholding what the other requires is greatest. Closely related to this is the question of who, accordingly, is more or less dependent on the other? The question of who has to submit or adapt him or herself more to the other's demands can thus be answered. On this basis, an assessment of the relative power balance can also be undertaken. No one individual or group can determine the outcome on the game. Only with reference to their own past moves and the counter-moves undertaken by their opponents can a team begin to co-ordinate their tasks and execute further moves. Both teams are interlocked in a series of reciprocal moves out of which will emerge the specific game dynamic that was neither planned nor intended by any one individual or team. As Elias and Dunning observe, 'if one watches a game of football one can understand that it is the fluctuating figuration of the players itself on which, at a given moment, the decisions and moves of individual players depend'.[17] Understanding games in this way not only reveals features of group dynamics more generally, but also highlights the *raison d'être* of these sport and leisure forms. A series of interdependent polarities are 'built into' the game-pattern. It is these that not only help to explain the dynamics of the game form but also its appeal to human beings. Let us spell this out.

Elias and Dunning identify a series of interconnected polarities that assist in the production and reproduction of the tension balance of a game. These polarities include those between: the opposing teams and their attack and defence formations; the co-operation, competition and tension within and between the teams involved; the balance between internal and external controls that regulate the contest. Other polarities include the polarity between the elasticity and fixity of the rules and the balance between affectionate identification with and hostile rivalry towards the opponents.[18] Elias and Dunning discuss the significance of these polarities in the following way:

> Such polarities operate in close connection with each other. In fact, a complex of interdependent polarities built into the game pattern provides the main motive force for the group dynamics of a football game. In one way or another they all contribute towards maintaining the 'tone', the tension-balance of the game.[19]

Identification of the importance of these tension balances connects to how Elias and Dunning explain people's 'quest for excitement' in sport encounters and how the tonal qualities of a game assist in the controlled decontrolling of the emotions. This will be discussed in greater detail shortly.

The study of games is seen then to serve three main functions. First, it highlights in stark relief how the pattern of a game, and social life in general, is not the direct outcome of the plans and intentions of any one individual or social group. Seeking to understand these dynamics within the framework of the patterns of dichotomous thinking that typify much of conventional sociology and philosophy is inherently flawed. The figurations formed by social actors – in a sport setting or elsewhere – are the unintended outcome of the interweaving of a myriad of intended actions. Second, the polymorphous, relational and dynamic nature of power can be revealed in the study of games. Power is not something that one side possesses and another side lacks. Rather, power in sport, leisure and broader social encounters is to be understood as a structural characteristic that enables and constrains the reciprocal cut and thrust of interdependent human interaction. Third, the study of games serves a didactic function. That is, steeping oneself in the intermeshing of different types of game dynamics can lead to the emergence of a processual, relational and comparative type of thinking that Elias sees as essential in sociological research. But Elias and Dunning were also careful to weigh up the advantages and disadvantages of such a study. In the concluding remarks to their essay on 'the dynamics of sport groups', they addressed this very issue:

> But if it is a limitation of the study of sport-games – compared with that of social units concerned with the serious business of life – that they have no purpose except perhaps that of providing enjoyment, and are often pursued as ends in themselves, it is also an advantage. It may serve as a corrective to the teleological fallacy still fairly widespread in sociological thinking. In a simplified manner, this can be described as a confusion between the individual level and the group level. With regard to games of football this distinction is fairly clear. Individual players and teams have aims, scoring goals is one of them. The enjoyment of playing, the excitement of spectators, the hope of rewards may be others. But the concentration of purposeful actions results in figurational dynamics – in a game – which is purposeless. One can determine it as such and to some extent that has been done here. But this could not have been done if one had attributed the aims of individual players to the changing figuration which the players form with each other.[20]

The tension-balances to which Elias and Dunning are drawing attention to here are also closely connected to the socially conditioned psychological need to experience a kind of spontaneous, elementary, unreflective yet pleasurable excitement. The 'quality' of the tension-balance, the ebb and flow of the game dynamics, influences the nature of the participants' emotional experience. The question as to why it is that sport and leisure encounters have come to serve the function of providing enjoyment and excitement for large sections of humanity thus arises. It is to this that we now direct our attention.

Sportisation and the making of modern sport and leisure

Derived from the work of Elias and Dunning, the research agenda of figurational sociology on sport and leisure was initially structured around three deceptively simple questions: (i) What kind of society must it be, for people to enjoy so much the excitement and tensions engendered by physical contests of skill and strength that are called sport? (ii) Why has sport increased in terms of its cultural centrality? (iii) What accounts for the relatively quick reception of British sport models by other countries?[21] These questions were closely connected with the desire to test and develop ideas regarding the civilising process. Given that this theory is a 'cornerstone' of the figurational/process-sociological approach, let us first spell out what it entails before proceeding to examine the substantive evidence relating to the questions concerning the development of sport and leisure.

In examining what he termed the civilising process, Elias was concerned to trace the development of both the personality structure of individuals and the social standards that have been formed in European societies since the Middle Ages. Changes in etiquette and manners revealed a trend towards greater control over the expression of effect and towards greater emotional evenness, less of a tendency to fluctuate between emotional extremes. The key features of this long-term ongoing process are the gradual acquisition of stricter and more all-embracing and more even forms of emotional restraint and instinctual renunciation. Closely interwoven with this process on the level of social structure have been a lengthening of interdependency chains and state formation. A central aspect of this was the monopolisation of violence and taxation by the state and a concomitant process of internal pacification.

The European civilising process thus marks an increase in the degree of control which people are expected to exercise over their emotions and the expression of their impulses. This increasingly stricter control of impulses was first developed in court circles, more particularly in the courts of the absolute monarchs. Later, as the lengthening of these interdependency chains and the process of state formation percolated down the social scale, the majority of individuals in urban industrial societies gradually came to exercise relatively automatic self-restraint. In considering how this civilising process was marked by what he termed 'diminishing contrasts and increasing varieties' of habitus, of manners, emotions and bodily deportment, Elias makes a number of observations that centre on the issues of taste and distinction. What Elias had to say is worthy of quoting at some length:

> The habituation to foresight, and the stricter control of behaviour and the affects to which the upper classes are inclined through their situation and functions, are important instruments of their domination . . . they serve as marks of distinction and prestige. For this reason such a society regards offences against the prevailing pattern of drive and affect control, any 'letting go' by their members, with greater or lesser disapproval. This disapproval increases when the social power and size of the lower, rising group increase, and concomitantly, the competition for the same opportunities between the upper and lower groups becomes more intense.[22]

The European civilising process was marked not only by the habitual reproduction of distinctive conduct, but also by diminishing contrasts and increasing varieties of forms of body habitus. That is, while the secular upper classes were driven to maintain at all costs their special conduct and drive control as marks of distinction, the structure of the general movement carrying them along forced them in the long-term to reduce more and more of these differences in standards of behaviour.[23]

If we return to the substantive detail of his study of the civilising process we can observe that one of the issues which Elias focused on was bodily functions. This was a deliberate choice designed to highlight that the relationship between personality, the structure of society and the body was not random. The bodily functions examined include table manners, 'natural' functions such as urination and defecation, blowing your nose, spitting, and behaviour in the bedroom. In each of these areas, Elias details changes in a specific direction which point to a heightened sensitivity towards the indulging in and witnessing of such bodily acts. During the development of several European societies (Britain, France and Germany) and repeated in countless personal lives, a number of decisive changes gradually occurred. These included: a progressive refinement of outward manners; a strengthening of the thresholds of shame, embarrassment and repugnance; a hiding or pushing behind the scenes of what was felt to be embarrassing and a gradual internalisation of self-restraint and feelings of guilt and remorse. Increasingly, certain bodily acts were regarded with disgust and repugnance.

This structured directional change involved not simply a growth in self-restraint, but rather a move towards a more even and less fluctuating balance between external and internal restraints in the individual and society as a whole. It was also apparent in other aspects of people's bodily existence. Again over a long time period, Elias traces changing attitudes towards death and dying. The prospect and actual episode of death is shunned, pushed behind the scenes, repressed, and for those in the twilight of their lives there develops an increasing tendency to live a lonely and isolated existence. The act of procreation also underwent profound change. The open display of sexual encounters increasingly became taboo and there was a tightening of external and internal thresholds of shame and embarrassment attached to sexual intercourse.

Dunning also points to a gradual shift in the balance between affective and instrumental forms of aggressiveness and violence. In the European Middle Ages the secular elite were leaders of armed bands to whom war was normal, closely connected to their social function and which they participated in with relish. Burning heretics alive, committing acts of torture, participating in ritual executions and cruelty to animals were sources of pleasure. But as part of the civilising process there occurred a gradual long-term moulding and taming of aggressiveness and impulses towards cruelty and a ready resort to violence. These facets of bodily practices also came to be impeded by shame and repugnance. In addition, one significant feature of this transformation of the bodily impulses of aggressiveness and cruelty is the transfer of emotions from direct action to mimetic activities and the visual pleasures of spectating. It is here that sport, the body and civilising processes interweave.

Drawing on this line of enquiry, exponents argue that a central aspect of the development of modern sport has been a 'civilising process' regarding the expression and control of physical violence. A crucial aspect of this process, and one which is of particular significance for the study of sport violence, was a long-term decline in people's propensity for obtaining pleasure from directly engaging in and witnessing violent acts. There has been both an advance in people's 'threshold of repugnance' regarding bloodshed and other manifestations of physical violence and a tendency to push violence increasingly 'behind the scenes'. Let us look at this in more detail.

The term sportisation is used to describe the transformation of British pastimes into sports and the export of some of them on an almost global scale. Though the British term 'sport' has a long history, dating back as far as 1440, only in the eighteenth century did it begin to acquire its specific modern connotations. Did its emergence and subsequent spread correspond to some human social requirement by then more widespread? Why did these highly regulated contests requiring physical exertion and skill first appear among the landed aristocracy and gentry? According to this perspective, answers to these questions require linking sportisation processes to 'parliamentarisation'. In turn, this requires a probing of the power structure and cultural relations in, for example, eighteenth-century England.

Briefly, Elias and advocates of this approach argue that the emergence of sport as a form of physical combat of a relatively non-violent type was connected with a period when the cycle of violence between different political factions (Whigs and Tories) 'calmed down'. Groups increasingly settled differences by non-violent means. Parliament became the battleground where interests and conflicts were resolved and defused. Military skills gave way to verbal skills of debate. Crucial in both these parliamentarisation and sportisation processes was the involvement of the landed aristocracy and gentry. But this perspective does not argue that parliamentarisation caused sportisation, still less that the sportisation of pastimes caused the parliamentarisation of politics. Rather, the same people, the landed aristocracy and gentry, were caught up in two aspects of a broad process of development in which there occurred a 'civilising spurt'. According to Elias:

> The same class of people who participated in the pacification and greater regularisation of factional contests in Parliament were instrumental in the greater pacification and regularisation of their pastimes. . . . Sport and Parliament as they emerged in the eighteenth century were both characteristic of the same change in the power structure of England and in the social habitus of that class of people which emerged from the antecedent struggles as the ruling group.[24]

In essence then the more civilised habitus deployed by aristocrats and gentlemen to deal with the political aspects of their lives also led them to develop less violent, more civilised ways of enjoying themselves in their leisure time. One facet of this process was the formation of voluntary associations known as 'clubs'. Dunning neatly captures the processual nature of sportisation when he observes:

> It is useful to think of this initial sportisation of pastimes as occurring in two main waves: an eighteenth-century wave in which the principal pastimes that began to emerge as modern sports were cricket, fox hunting, horse racing and boxing; and a second, nineteenth-century wave in which soccer, rugby, tennis and athletics began to take on modern forms.[25]

Several studies have been conducted that bear out this general picture and show how this 'calming down' of violence manifested itself in the development of sport.[26] Stressing the role of clubs and the impact of the enclosure movement in which the free British peasantry were 'broken', thus allowing the landed aristocracy and gentry to patronise, adopt and modify folk pastimes, this perspective has examined a range of sports. These include the development of cricket, Highland games, boxing, folk football, fox hunting, Association football (soccer) and rugby (league and union).[27] But the figurational sociological perspective is not only concerned with tracing the emergence of modern sport and leisure forms but also with examining their role, function and significance in the lives of people.

Embodied emotions, pleasure and leisure in the spare-time spectrum

Figurational sociologists' concern with human emotions centres on both the emotional characteristics which humans share with non-human species and on others which are uniquely human and which have no equivalent in other species. On this basis, figurational sociology proposes three interconnected hypotheses regarding a theory of human beings and their emotions.[28] These hypotheses have to be located within the discussion of how the fact that the human species has certain unique characteristics can be reconciled with the continuity of the evolutionary process. First, human beings as a species represent an evolutionary breakthrough. That is, the balance between learned and unlearned conduct tilted decisively in favour of the former as the human species evolved. Second, human beings not only can learn far more than any other species, they also have to learn. The repertoire of unlearned ways of behaviour has become so softened and weakened in Homo Sapiens that human beings cannot orientate themselves or communicate with others without acquiring a great deal of knowledge through learning. Third, no emotion of a grown-up human person is ever an entirely unlearned, genetically fixed reaction pattern. Human emotions result from a merger of an unlearned and a learned process. On the basis of these hypotheses, Elias argues that the steering of human conduct is always the result of an intimate interweaving of learned and unlearned processes. This raises the problem of 'the hinge', that is, the need to explore the 'connectedness' or interweaving of learned and unlearned processes.[29]

As with most attributes and properties of a human being, emotions must be understood in relation to people's relationships with existences other than themselves. While noting that emotions contain three component aspects, a physiological, a behavioural and a feeling component, Elias emphasizes the need to recognise the importance of the latter, but not to the preclusion of the other components. Noting that the 'feeling vocabulary' may be more differentiated in one country than another, Elias argues that such differences in the vocabularies of different peoples also confirm the hypothesis that learning plays a part in the feeling component of emotions. For Elias emotions and the related movements or 'expressions' are, in short, one of the indications that human beings are by nature constituted for life in the company of others, for life in society.[30] Elias's work on the emotions is complemented by research he conducted with Eric Dunning. What, in essence, they are arguing is that it is not possible to work out an adequate theory of leisure, or indeed, of the emotions, within the framework of any single human science, whether it be human physiology, psychology or sociology.[31]

Reference to the European civilising process enabled Elias and Dunning, as noted, to formulate an answer to the question of why the early stages of the sportisation process set the tone of future sporting and leisure developments. In examining the sports of circket, fox hunting and the early forms of modern football, Elias and Dunning conclude that all of these cultural forms mark attempts to prolong the point-like emotional pleasure of victory in the mock-battle of a sport and are symptomatic of a far-reaching change in the personality structure of human beings. This in turn was closely connected with specific changes in the power structure of society at large. It is here that the function of sport and leisure forms becomes more evident.[32] The essential propositions of this approach to sport and leisure can thus be identified. Firstly, modern sport is not, according to Elias, Dunning and their followers, synonymous with freedom. Rather it obeys a historically specific affect economy of balances and restraints. Secondly, the expression of spontaneous, violent and intense emotions or bursts of excitement in modern society is moulded by higher thresholds of 'civilised' bodily restraint than tended to be the case in the European Middle Ages. Thirdly, modern sport increasingly corresponds to 'mimetic' forms of bodily practices.

For Elias and Dunning, a principal function of leisure is the 'arousal of pleasurable forms of excitement'.[33] One feature of the civilising of British society in the eighteenth and nineteenth centuries was a marked narrowing of what was acceptable in public life. As a direct corollary of this, the need for a social enclave in which socially approved moderate pleasurable excitement could be aroused and expressed increased. That is, the function of leisure activities has to be assessed in relation to the ubiquity and steadiness of excitement control. What is the significance of this? The function which leisure serves, according to Elias and Dunning, is based on a view of people whereby they have a socially conditioned psychological need to experience a kind of spontaneous, elementary, unreflective yet pleasurable excitement.

The precise function of leisure activities is assessed in relation to a number of interrelated criteria. These include: the degree of controlled decontrolling of emotions that is evident; the degree to which emotions flow freely; the degree of eliciting or imitating excitement akin to that which is generated in 'real' life situations; the nature of the tension balances created; and the degree to which the activity serves to counteract stress tensions. Here we are dealing with tension-balances of varying blends. But the perpetual tension between routinisation and deroutinisation within leisure activities is the principal source of their dynamics: this is the 'shift to risk' which is integral to the activity being experienced. Indeed, as society grows 'more serious', the cultural centrality of leisure sport increases. In rejecting conventional work-leisure analyses,

Elias and Dunning map out what they term the spare-time spec-trum.[34] This holds that leisure activities fall into three overlapping forms: purely or mainly sociable activities; activities involving motility; and 'mimetic' activities. While sociable activities have the potential to serve important *gemeinschaft* functions, and motility is important as far as sport is concerned, we will focus here on mimetic activities. 'Mimetic' activities vary considerably in terms of both their intensity and style but have basic structural charac-teristics in common. That is, they provide a 'make-believe' setting which allows emotions to flow more easily, and which elicits excite-ment of some kind imitating that produced by 'real-life situations', yet without their dangers or risks. 'Mimetic' activities thus allow, within certain limits, for socially permitted self-centredness. Excitement is elicited by the creation of tensions: this can involve imaginary or controlled 'real' danger, mimetic fear and/or pleasure, sadness and/or joy. This controlled decontrolling of excitement lies, for Elias and Dunning at 'the heart of leisure sport'. The different moods evoked in this 'make-believe' setting are the 'siblings' of those aroused in 'real-life' situations. This applies whether the setting is a Broadway play, a pleasure ride at EuroDisney or a closely contested sudden-death play off in a golf tournament. They involve the experience of pleasurable excite-ment which is at the core of most play needs. But whereas both involve pleasurable excitement, in sport, but especially in 'achieve-ment sport', motility and struggles between human beings play a central part. Indeed, some sport forms resemble real battles between hostile groups. Addressing the issue that is common across leisure activities, Elias and Dunning observe:

> The specific functions of sport, theatre, racing, parties and all other activities and events usually associated with the term 'leisure', especially of all mimetic activities and events, have to be assessed in relation to this ubiquity and steadiness of excite-ment control. . . . In the form of leisure events . . . our society provides for the need to experience the upsurge of strong emotions in public.[35]

Other key features of the Eliasian perspective on leisure, sport and embodied emotions need noting. The 'mimetic' sphere, though creating imaginary settings, forms a distinct and integral part of social reality. It is no less real than any other part of social life. The manner in which this quest for enjoyable excitement finds expression in social institutions and customs also varies greatly over time and space. Nevertheless, the 'mimetic' sphere does contain elements which are integral to all leisure forms, namely sociability, motility and imagination. There is no leisure activity where all of these elements are absent and more usually two or three elements combine with varying intensity. In studying the problems of leisure, pleasure and the emotions therefore, attention must focus on two interdependent questions: what are the characteristics of the personal leisure needs developed in the more complex societies of our time and what are the characterisitics of the specific types of leisure events developed in societies of this type for the satisfaction of these needs?

Exponents of an Eliasian approach argue that it provides an essential foundation on which to construct a synthesis or typology of sporting bodies, cultures and societies. Several reasons are offered for this judgement. Elias refuses to separate society and the individual. His substantive work attempts to show how even large-scale, 'macro' social processes, stretching back over long time periods, are connected to the actions and intentions of human beings. Elias looks at the civilising process in the West, in order to understand the sociogenesis of our societies, as well the psychogenesis of the individual persons who are formed in this process.[36] Elias also avoids the trap of over-emphasizing either the 'natural' or the 'cultural'. He does not separate the formation of rational consciousness from that of the emotions. He sees the personality structure as a totality, each part of which changes in unison with the others. A transformation in one aspect of the personality causes all its other aspects to change as well. In his work on the emotions Elias was centrally concerned with probing what he termed the 'hinge'. That is, the interconnectedness of the learned and unlearned aspects of human behaviour. For example, Elias shows how smiling is an unlearned sign employed by humans all over the world to signify friendly intent. And yet the learning of the more expanded system of signs and language, which is culturally specific, actually allows humans greater control over, and elaboration of, their natural repertoire.[37] Put simply, we can now control the pleasurable act of smiling so that it is not a 'reaction', but rather it is an intentionally deployed symbol which can convey a range of messages. The smile is also open to a more complex range of embodied interpretations. It becomes part of our 'second nature'. Leisure practices in the pleasure dome of the spare-time spectrum seemingly provide an ideal place to explore these embodied emotions.

Sport, leisure and globalisation processes: Diminishing contrasts and increasing varieties

It has been noted that figurational sociologists suggest that, up to the mid to late nineteenth century, there had been two main waves of sportisation. During the late nineteenth and early twentieth century a third wave began to unfold. This entailed the diffusion of modern sporting forms on a global scale, and was, or so exponents of this approach argue, closely connected to broader globalisation processes.[38] (For a more detailed discussion on globalisation see Chapter 10.) Let us look at these issues in broad outline.

Globalisation processes have no zero starting point. It is clear that they gathered momentum between the fifteenth and eighteenth centuries and that they have continued apace since the turn of the present century. Several of the more recent features of them can be identified. These include: an increase in the number of international agencies; the growth of increasing global forms of communication; the development of global competitions and prizes mainly but not solely in sport; and the development of notions of 'rights' and citizenship that are increasingly standardised internationally. The emergence and diffusion of sport has been clearly interwoven with this overall process. The development of national teams, the world-wide acceptance of rules governing specific, that is 'Western', 'sport' forms, and the establishment of global competitions such as the Olympic Games and soccer's World Cup tournament are all indicative of the occurrence of globalisation in the sports world.

The speed, scale and volume of sports development is interwoven with the broader global flow of people, technology, finance, images and ideologies. Global migration of both professional and college sports personnel was a pronounced feature of sports development in the 1980s. The flow from country to country of sports goods, equipment and 'landscapes' has grown by such a scale and volume that it is currently a multi-billion pound business. At the level of economics stands the fact that the flow of finance in the global sports arena has come to centre not only on the international trade in sports personnel, prize money and endorsements, but on the marketing of sport along specific lines. Crucial in all these regards, or so exponents of this perspective claim, has been the development of a 'media-sport production complex' which projects images to large global audiences. Global sports festivals, such as the Olympics, are seen to serve as vehicles for the expression of ideologies that are not only international in character but are also transnational in their consequences.[39]

For figurational sociologists several issues related to the globalisation of sport require attention. Both the intended and unintended aspects of global sport/leisure development need probing. That is, while the intended acts of representatives of transnational agencies or the transnational capitalist class are potentially more significant in the short term, over the longer term the unintended, relatively autonomous transnational practices predominate. These practices 'structure' the subsequent plans and actions of transnational agencies and the transnational capitalist class. Globalisation processes involve a blend between intended and unintended practices. While people have to cope with the problems of interdependency which globalisation engenders, the fact that these processes are relatively autonomous ensures that people can intervene. Global (sport/leisure) practices still lie within the province of human actions.

Several other points are worthy of note. Although elite sports/leisure migrants, officials and consumers are no less caught up in these unfolding globalisation processes, they do have the capacity to reinterpret cultural products and experiences into something distinct. Furthermore, the consumption of non-indigenous cultural wares by different national groups can be both active and heterogeneous. Sociologists working within this perspective do not overlook, however, that there is a political economy at work in the production and consumption of global sport/leisure products. They conclude that globalisation is best understood as a balance and blend between diminishing contrasts and increasing varieties, a commingling of cultures and attempts by more established groups to control and regulate access to global flows. Global sport/leisure development can be understood in the same terms: that is, in the late twentieth century we are witnessing the globalisation of sports/leisure packages and an increase in the diversity of sports/leisure cultures.[40] The analysis of global sport and leisure networks undertaken by Dunning, Featherstone and others is part of the broader investigation conceived of by Elias. Elias argued that an important peculiarity of the European civilising process is that there occurred a reduction in the contrasts within societies as well as within individuals. Despite the tendency of more powerful groups to use social customs and conduct to distinguish themselves from their social inferiors, a gradual commingling of patterns of conduct deriving from initially very different social strata gradually took place.

Examining the dynamics at work within and between Western societies, Elias highlights, as noted in the discussion of the incipient wave of sportisation processes, how the upper classes were and are involved in a process of 'reciprocal supervision' of their and others' behaviour. Throughout the course of these civilising processes there was a double-bind tendency at work. In what Elias termed a 'phase of colonisation', members of the established upper class, intentionally or otherwise, interact with and colonise the culture of others. They permeate the lower or outsider class with their own pattern of conduct. As this process of colonisation gains momentum, 'phases of repulsion' occur. That is, the upper classes build social barriers between themselves and the groups they colonise and whom they consider their inferiors. This strict regulation of their established conduct and that of the outsider class is especially intense when the former feel threatened as the latter gain in power. Despite building social barriers and being constantly vigilant, the upper classes cannot prevent a gradual seepage of distinguishing models of conduct into other strata. Indeed, the act of colonisation ensures that a degree of seepage occurs. Sooner or later, this process leads to a reduction in differences of social power and conduct.

Markedly similar processes are seen to be at work in relations between Western societies and non-Western societies. In world terms Western societies were (and still are?) the equivalent of the established upper class – as within particular European nations. The spread of their 'civilised' patterns of conduct occurred through the settlement of occidentals or through the assimilation of the upper strata of other nations. Crucially, the same doublebind tendencies that marked the upper classes colonisation of outsiders within the West is also evident in the West's dealings with outsider nations and peoples. With this spread came a particular view of civilisation – of humanity as a whole. Elias describes this process in the following way:

> The expansion of Western civilization shows this double tendency clearly enough. This civilization is the characteristic

conferring distinction and superiority on occidentals. But at the same time the Western people, under the pressure of their own competitive struggle, bring about in large areas of the world a change in human relations and functions in line with their own standards. They make large parts of the world dependent on them and at the same time . . . become themselves dependent on them.[41]

For figurational sociologists several points need stressing in this connection. Western societies were acting, as it were, as a form of upper class or established group on a world level. Their tastes and conduct, including their sports and leisure pastimes, were part of this, and these practices acted in similar ways to the elite cultural activities within Western societies. They were signs of distinction, prestige and power. Just as the established groups within Western societies found that their distinguishing conduct seeped, intentionally or unintentionally, across social strata, so the occidentals of the colonies also discovered that a similar process occurred in their dealings with their colonial social inferiors. Indeed, as a result of this cultural interchange, outsider, non-Western codes and customs began to permeate back into Western societies.

Here, too, according to Elias, these processes were characterised by intentional and unintentional features. But the manner and form of these processes of commingling were dependent on several factors. These included the form of colonisation, the position of the area in the large network of political, economic and military interdependencies and the particular region's own history and structure. Elias was pointing out that processes of commingling were (and are) characterised by unequal power relations. One means by which the established Western elites maintained their status and distinction was through the exercise of specific forms of conduct. Nevertheless, the social barriers that they built between themselves and the native outsiders proved semi-permeable. The contrast between Western and non-Western societies did indeed begin to diminish.[42] However, the form and extent to which Western values spread through specific regions reflect the history and structure of the area in question. This also applies in the diffusion of non-Western conduct back to specific Western nations. Established and outsider groups were and are active in the interpretation of Western and non-Western conduct and cultural forms. This creates the possibility that new varieties of 'civilised' conduct may emerge. Writing about these processes in 1939, Elias observed:

> In colonial regions too, according to the position and social strength of the various groups, Western standards are spreading downwards and occasionally even upwards from below, if we may adhere to this spatial image, and fusing to form new unique entities, new varieties of civilized conduct. The contrasts in conduct between the upper and lower groups are reduced with the spread of civilization; the varieties or nuances of civilized conduct are increased.[43]

Rejecting the idea that the spread or diffusion of styles of behaviour depends solely on the activities of established groups, exponents argue that a two-way process of cultural interaction criss-crosses the semi-permeable barriers that established groups – both within Western societies and between them and non-Western societies, – deploy to maintain their distinctiveness, power and prestige. The more they become interconnected with outsider groups, the more they depend on them for social tasks. In so doing, the contrasts between them diminish. The power ratio between these groups moves in an equalising direction. Concomitantly, new styles of conduct emerge.[44]

As 'civilised' forms of conduct spread across both the rising lower classes of Western society and the different classes of the colonies, an amalgamation of the Western and the indigenous patterns is seen to have occurred. Each time this happens, 'upper-class conduct and that of the rising groups interpenetrate'.[45] People placed within this situation attempt to reconcile and fuse the pattern of 'occidentally civilized societies with the habits and traditions of their own society'. In this they achieve a 'higher or lesser degree of success'.[46] The processes identified within the West and in the dealings between the West and non-Western countries, also occur within former colonial nations. As the rising classes of these nations shake off the shackles of their colonial overlords, they do attempt to distinguish their behaviour. This attempt again reflects not only the history and structure of the region in question but also the specific dynamics of the new amalgam that emerged between themselves and the former masters. Just as their former masters became bound to them, they become bound to the rising class situated below them in the social stratification hierarchy.

Four key insights are seen to cast important light onto the debate regarding national cultures, identities and globalisation. These are the concepts of diminishing contrasts and increasing varieties, the idea of the commingling of Western and non-Western cultures, the subsequent emergence of a new amalgam, and the ongoing attempts by established groups to integrate outsider people(s) as workers and/or consumers.[47] Several points need stressing in this connection. Aspects of globalisation are powered by Western notions of 'civilisation'. Cultural industries do provide a staple diet of Western products and the cult of consumerism has spread around the globe. In some respects, the media-sport production complex ensures that the marketing of the same sport forms, products and images does occur.[48] Given that there is a political economy at work regulating global flows, it is no surprise that the 'local' does not freely choose which cultural products are consumed. An over-emphasis on the marketing of sameness, however, leads the analysis to overlook that global marketing strategies also celebrate difference. That is, the cultural industries constantly seek out new varieties of ethnic wares. These ethnic wares are targeted at specific 'niches' within a local culture. This targeting can lead to a strengthening of 'local' ethnic identities. The spread of the South Asian 'sport' form of kabbadi and Japanese sumo wrestling to Britain are examples of this. In Featherstone's analysis of globalisation processes and consumer culture similar issues are raised. Drawing on elements of Elias's work, what Featherstone has to say is worthy of quoting at some length:

> The manners books examined by Norbert Elias, and his discussions of the taming of the medieval knights and the emergence of a court society in which the nobility became specialists in the art of consumption, point to the care individuals had to take with fashion, demeanour, style of presentation, as well as in developing the skills to read the appearance of others in order to survive in the fluctuating power balances of the court figuration. While these types of status games . . . led to an emphasis upon distinctions and differences which has been adopted within consumer culture . . . this should not blind us to the existence of the counter tendency which mass consumption and democratisation favoured, the tendency towards equalisation and the diminishing of contrasts. . . . Consumer culture here seen as part of a process of functional democratisation offered the transcendence of sumptuary laws and was accompanied by a levelling-out of balances of power . . .

as the less powerful were for the first time able to emulate, within the limitations of mass fashion, the consumption practices and styles of the more powerful.[49]

For figurational sociologists, sport also plays a similarly seemingly contradictory role in globalisation processes and the formation of national identities. Sport development is seen as being contoured by the interlocking processes of diminishing contrasts and increasing varieties. The emergence of modern sport out of its European, and particularly British heartland, was, as noted, closely tied to globalisation processes. Its standardisation, organisational development and global diffusion both reflected and reinforced the global processes that were then being powered by the West. During the twentieth century sport was to become a 'global idiom'. Its laws were the first to be voluntarily embraced across the globe.[50]

Sports are also seen as acting as 'anchors of meaning' at a time when national cultures and identities are experiencing the effects of global time-space compression. The settlement of people in different regions has led to the formation of ethnic enclaves within the total national culture of particular nation-states. The movement of elite sport labour within and between continents is also viewed in this light.[51] The development of Empire for example, resulted in a diverse commingling of 'British' national culture and identity with other cultures. While the spread of British 'civilisation' – included within this are its sport forms – ensured that contrasts were diminished, the process of cultural interchange, though unequal, was not all one way. Even with the spread of British sport forms throughout the Empire, some 'sports' such as polo, were diffused to the mother country. This process continues today: the emergence of revamped versions of British sport forms including American football and Australian rules football in the former mother country are examples of these processes at work. Further, the spread of sport from the British to their colonial subjects has proved to be a double-edged sword. While this indicates the success of the British in penetrating other cultures, over time people from former colonies have not only won their independence, but they now beat the British/English at 'their own games'. English sporting success restores, however superficially, a symbolic sense of stability. In contrast, losing to former colonies, who may regard victory over the British/English as a form of rite of passage, compounds the general sense of dislocation.

The association of sport with a specific place and season also provides a sense of *heimat,* a sense of invented 'permanence'. Sport occasions are viewed as counterpoints to change. The formation of sport was closely connected to the invention of traditions that attempt to bind the past and present together. Yet, paradoxically, the media-sport production complex is seen to erode this sense of stability. Through satellite broadcasting, consumers can 'be at' any sport venue across the globe. Bringing novel varieties of sport subcultures to national cultures, new sport and leisure identities can be forged.[52] Though sport has reinforced and reflected a diminishing of contrasts between nations, the close association of sport with national cultures and identities also means that moves towards integration of regions at a political level are undermined by the role of sport. Sport, being inherently competitive and based on a hierarchical valuing of worth, binds people to the dominant invented traditions associated with the nation. Yet, there may be also the first signs of countervailing trends. The tentative emergence of a European sports identity is a case in point. Referring to this issue Dunning notes:

> Three or four years ago, some members of the European parliament mooted the idea of entering an EC team in the Barcelona Olympics. It received short shift because, under present conditions, such identification with Europe as there is could not possibly hope to compete with the deep and powerful national sentiments of the British, the French the Germans, etc.[53]

As with European integration more generally, the sports process occupies contested terrain in which the defensive response of strengthened ethnic identities may yet win out over broader pluralising global flows.

Concluding thoughts

The figurational sociological approach has not been without its critics. Some observers suggest that this tradition is open to the criticisms made of the modernisation/industrial society thesis. Others have asserted that the Eliasian approach is neo-functionalist, evolutionary, and ethnocentric. By emphasizing the concept of detachment, it is alleged that this tradition lays claims to an implicit sense of superiority. This tendency is allegedly reinforced by caricaturing other traditions and thereby failing to engage in substantive debate. The tradition is also said to have little predictive value and, in practice, lacks a critical account of the existing status quo. Finally, several key areas of the sport–society relationship, in particular gender, political economy, and the state, are said to have been neglected.[54] Yet more recently, writers working within this tradition have sought to examine a range of issues connected to political economy, sport development, gender, the media-sport production complex, commercialisation and the transformation of rules.[55] Other observers have sought to assess the relative overlap with different traditions and provide a more sober assessment of the contribution that this tradition makes to sociological enquiry. In a recent review of a book examining these critiques and counter-critiques, Nicos Mouzelis highlighted the importance of this debate when he concluded that it would be of interest not only to 'those interested in the sociology of sport and leisure but also by all those interested in the present state and future prospects of sociological theory' more generally.[56] This chapter has sought to capture this relevance by probing how these concerns are interrelated, thereby allowing readers to make a judgement for themselves.

NOTES AND REFERENCES

1 Some of the key texts are N. Elias, *The Civilizing Process: The History of Manners*, Urizen, New York, 1939/1978; N. Elias, *The Civilizing Process: State Formation and Civilization*, Blackwell, Oxford, 1939/1982; N. Elias (1970) *What is Sociology?* Hutchinson, London; N. Elias, *The Court Society*, Oxford, Blackwell, 1983; N. Elias, *The Symbol Theory*, London, Sage, 1991; N. Elias, *Involvement and Detachment*, Oxford, Blackwell, 1987; N. Elias, *The Society of Individuals*, Oxford, Blackwell, 1991; N. Elias and E. Dunning, *Quest for Excitement: Sport and Leisure in the Civilizing Process*, Blackwell, Oxford, 1986. For a general discussion of Elias's work and his biographical details, see S. Mennell, *Norbert Elias: an Introduction*, Oxford, Blackwell, 1992 and an excellent interpretation of Elias is provided by J. Goudsblom, *Sociology in the Balance*, Blackwell, Oxford, 1977. See also the special edition of *Theory, Culture and Society*, no. 4, 1987 devoted to the work of Norbert Elias. For discussion of the sociology of sport see E. Dunning, 'Figurational sociology and the sociology of sport: some concluding remarks' in E. Dunning and C. Rojek (eds) *Sport and Leisure in the Civilizing Process*, Routledge, London, 1992.
2 It is debatable whether what has been developed, however adequate it may be, is another competing school of thought. Perhaps it is too early to tell!

3 See N. Elias, op. cit., 1970. Viewed in this light, sociology is about people in the plural, about people who are interdependent with each other in a variety of ways and whose lives develop in and are significantly shaped by the figurations they form with each other.

4 For an excellent discussion of these sensitising concepts see J. Goudsblom, 1977, pp. 6–8.

5 This 'central' theory will be discussed in the context of the analysis of sportisation processes.

6 Elias rejects the conceptualisation of these pairings in terms of opposites. He also eschews a *homo clausus* model of social life that places the individual at the centre of the analysis. Inherited from Western, particularly Anglo-Saxon philosophy, it is little wonder that individuals view society as 'out there' and understand the world in terms of 'what does it mean to me', and 'what impact can I have on others?'

7 N. Elias, op. cit., 1970, p. 80. In fact, Elias devotes a chapter to the issue of game models. Using them in a didactic sense, Elias was trying to promote a way of thinking about human relations. The study of games in the context of sport and leisure can fulfil a similar function.

8 N. Elias, op. cit., 1970, p. 92.

9 ibid, p. 97.

10 J. Goudsblom, op. cit., 1977, p 149.

11 Both in the formulation and the execution of the research task, the researcher is confronted with the relationship between theory and evidence. Simply put, figurational/process sociology rejects both the imposition of 'grand theory' onto evidence and 'abstracted empiricism' uninformed by theoretical insight. Rather, the processes of theory formation and empirical enquiry are seen as interwoven and indivisible. A constant interplay between mental operations directed at theoretical synthesis and empirical particulars is advocated. This is seen as recognition of the mutual 'contamination' of theory and evidence. As such, it commits researchers to a rather agile intellectual life in which they must both work on the empirical without dominating it with theory and, at the same time, develop theoretical insights firmly informed by evidence. An uninterrupted two-way traffic takes place. See Elias, op. cit., 1987; Goudsblom, op. cit., 1977. For discussion of how Elias relates to work on historical sociology, see P. Abrams, *Historical Sociology*, London, Open Books, 1982; D. Smith, *The Rise of Historical Sociology*, Cambridge, Polity, 1991.

12 Given that Elias's work is theoretical-empirical, the best exemplification of this method at work is his research on the European civilising process. Examining the knight–page–priest–bondsman figuration, Elias shows that while each individual making the network was unique and unrepeatable, the figuration itself was preserved unchanging over many generations. The figuration was, by and large, unchanged yet was formed by different, 'quickly' changing individuals. See N. Elias, op. cit., 1978, 1982, 1983.

13 N. Elias, op. cit., 1970, p. 130.

14 For an excellent discussion on the interrelationship between sociology and history see Elias's introduction to *The Court Society*, pp. 1-34.

Equally, the more common analytical approach in which societies are broken down into sets of 'factors' or 'spheres', e.g. the economic, the political, etc., is eschewed. No universal generalisations regarding the primacy of these 'factors' or 'spheres' is advocated. The question of the relative importance of particular features and the 'immanent dynamics' of figurations, though an empirical one, is investigated in a developmental manner and with an interweaving of theory and evidence. See also E. Dunning, 'The sociology of sport in Europe and the United States: critical observations from an "Eliasian" perspective', 1986, in C. R. Rees and A. W. Miracle (eds) *Sport and Social Theory*, Champaign, Ill: Human Kinetics, pp. 29-56 for further discussion of this.

15 Given that sociologists are, of course, part of the patterns they seek to investigate, it is more difficult for them to perform the mental operation of detaching themselves from the role of immediate participant and from the limited vista that it offers. For figurational/process sociology it is not a question of discarding an involved position for a completely detached role. As social actors, sociologists cannot cease to take part. In fact, their very participation and involvement is itself one of the conditions for comprehending the problems they try to solve as scientists. Sociologists must, if they are to understand the figurations which bind people together, probe from the inside how human beings experience such an existence. Sociologists must, therefore, be both relatively involved and detached in order to grasp the basic experience of social life. It is a question of balance. The sociologist as participant must be able to stand back and become the sociologist as observer and interpreter. See Elias, op. cit., 1987.

16 N. Elias, op. cit., 1970, pp. 130–1.

17 N. Elias and E. Dunning, 'Dynamics of sport groups with special reference to football' in N. Elias and E. Dunning, op. cit., 1986, p. 200. The assessment of the relative adequacy of evidence regarding figurations is dependent on establishing the precise pattern of interdependency between the groups involved. Central in this regard is the balance of power between them. Hence the analysis should focus on both the level of participation by the observers and on the pattern of tension and conflict evident in the relationship between observers and observed. The forms of distortion which permeate evidence are dependent on particular circumstances. The 'insider's' account will give you, sometimes inadvertently, the minutiae and emotional resonance of what you seek to examine: the 'outsider's' account is likely to give you a more detached view but may be distorted as a result of, e.g. class bias or lack of detailed knowledge. An analysis, therefore, ideally needs both but when one cannot get them, *verstehen* analysis based on the relative positions of groups in a figuration and a more detached knowledge of the balance of power and of tensions within that figuration can be used to work out an hypothesis. This applies with respect to both short-term, small-scale interation and more long-term, large-scale developments. See E. Dunning and K. Sheard, *Barbarians, Gentlemen and Players*, Oxford, Martin Robertson, 1979, pp. 44–9.

18 This does not exhaust the range of polarities identified by Elias and Dunning (1986) 'Dynamics of sport groups with special reference to football', op. cit., see pp. 201–04. See also F. Kew, 'The development of games: an endogenous explanation', 1990, in *International Review for the Sociology of Sport*, no. 25, pp. 251–68. For discussion of the dynamics involved in rule changes see E. Dunning, 'The dynamics of modern sport: notes on achievement-striving and the social significance of sport', op. cit., 1986.

19 N. Elias and E. Dunning, 'Dynamics of sport groups with special reference to football', op. cit., 1986, p. 201.

20 ibid, p. 204.

21 For further discussion of these questions see N. Elias and E. Dunning, op. cit., 1986 and E. Dunning, op. cit., 1992.

22 N. Elias, op. cit., 1982, p. 254.

23 ibid. See the synopsis to volume two of *The Civilizing Process* for discussion of this.

24 N. Elias, Introduction, 1986, in N. Elias and E. Dunning, op. cit., p.40.

25 E. Dunning, 'Culture, "Civilization" and the sociology of sport', *Innovation*, no. 5, 1992, pp. 7–18 and p. 13.

26 C. Brookes, *English Cricket*, London, Weidenfeld & Nicolson, 1978. E. Dunning, 'Social bonding and violence in sport', 1986. In N. Elias and E. Dunning, op. cit., pp. 224–44, E. Dunning and K. Sheard, op. cit., 1979. This approach has also been extensively deployed to study the roots of football hooliganism. Three key points of the Leicester group's position can be identified: far from being relatively recent, the roots of football hooliganism can be traced back to the formation of the Football League in the 1880s; football hooligan encounters are not exclusively an English disease, examples exist across continents of similar outbursts of spectator misconduct; the most serious confrontations between rival groups of supporters appear to be closely connected to the testing of a violent masculine style. See E. Dunning, P. Murphy and J. Williams, *The Roots of Football Hooliganism*, London, Routledge, 1988.

27 See C. Brookes, op. cit., 1978, E. Dunning, 'Social bonding and violence in sport', 1986, in N. Elias and E. Dunning, op. cit., 1986, pp. 224–44, E. Dunning and K. Sheard, op. cit., 1979, J. Maguire, 'The emergence of football spectating as a social problem 1880–1985: a figurational and developmental perspective', *Sociology of Sport Journal*, no. 3, 1986, pp. 217–44; K. Sheard, 'Aspects of the civilizing of boxing', 1992, unpublished PhD thesis, Anglia Polytechnic, Cambridge.

28 N. Elias, 'On human beings and their emotions: a process sociological essay', *Theory, Culture and Society*, 1987, no. 4, pp. 339–61 and p. 339. See also C. Wouters, 'The Sociology of Emotions and Flight Attendants: Hochschild's Managed Heart', *Theory, Culture and Society*, no. 6, pp. 95–123.

29 N. Elias, ibid, p. 347.

30 ibid, pp. 360–61.

31 N. Elias and E. Dunning, op. cit., 1986, p. 110.

32 N. Elias and E. Dunning, 'The quest for excitement in leisure' in N. Elias and E. Dunning, op. cit., 1986, pp. 63–90.

33 ibid. See also J. Maguire, 'Towards a sociological theory of sport and the emotions: a process-sociological perspective', 1992, in E. Dunning and C. Rojek (eds) *Sport and Leisure in the Civilizing Process*, Routledge, London, pp. 96–120.

34 N. Elias and E. Dunning, 'Leisure in the spare-time spectrum', 1986, in N. Elias and E. Dunning, op. cit., pp. 91–125. Elias and Dunning reject conventional work-leisure analyses due to the tendency to conceive of the relationship in dichotomous terms. For discussion of the 'shift to risk', see J. Maguire, 'Towards a sociological theory of sport and the emotions: a process-sociological perspective', 1992, op. cit.

35 N. Elias and E. Dunning, 'The quest for excitement in leisure', 1986, in N. Elias and E. Dunning, op. cit., p. 71.

36 For a recent appraisal of Elias's work see I. Burkitt, 'Social selves: theories of the social formation of personality', 1991, *Current Sociology*, no. 39, pp. 1–226. For its application to sport and the body see J. Maguire, (1993) 'Bodies, sports cultures and societies' in *International Review for the Sociology of Sport*, no. 28, pp. 33–52.

37 Burkitt, op. cit., pp. 184–5. For its application to the area of sports sciences see J. Maguire, 'Human sciences, sports sciences, and the need to study people "in the round', 1991, *Quest*, no. 43, pp. 190-206.

38 S. Mennell, 'The globalisation of human society as a very long-term social process: Elias's theory', 1990, *Theory, Culture and Society*, no. 7, pp. 359–73; E. Dunning, 'Sport and European Integration' unpublished paper, 1992, delivered at the Conference *Macht und Ohnmacht im neuen Europa*, Vienna, May 1992, pp. 29–30. See also J. Maguire, 'Globalisation, Sport and National Identities: the Empires Strike Back?' 1993, *Leisure and Society* 16, 2 pp. 293–322.

39 See J. Maguire, 'Globalisation, sport development and the media/sport production complex', 1993, *Sport Sciences Review*, no. 2, pp. 29–47 and E. Dunning, 'Sport and European Integration', 1992, op. cit. For a discussion of the broader application of Eliasian thinking to global cultural flows see M. Featherstone, *Consumer Culture and Postmodernism*, London, Sage, 1991. For a more critical acceptance of its contribution see R. Robertson, *Globalisation: Social Theory and Global Change*, London, Sage, 1992.

40 E. Dunning, 'Sport and European Integration', op. cit., and J. Maguire, 'Globalisation, sport development and the media/sport production complex', 1993, op. cit.

41 See the synopsis to volume two of *The Civilizing Process* for discussion of this issue. Elias, op. cit., 1982, p. 255.

42 See the synopsis to volume two of *The Civilizing Process* for discussion of this issue.

43 Elias, op. cit., 1982, p. 255 (italics in original).

44 ibid, p. 256.

45 ibid, p. 309.

46 ibid, p. 314.

47 For the application of these ideas to sport see E. Dunning, 'Sport and European Integration', 1992, unpublished paper delivered at the Conference *Macht und Ohnmacht im neuen Europa*, Vienna, May 1992 and J. Maguire, 'Globalisation, sport and national identities: the empires strike back?' 1993, *Leisure and Society* 16, 2, pp. 293–322.

48 See J. Maguire, 'Globalisation, sport development and the media/ sport production complex', *Sport Science Review*, no. 2, pp. 29–47. An unresolved question is whether this political economy is shaped by the concerns of global capitalism *per se* or the concerns of the elites of Western societies more generally.

49 M. Featherstone, *Consumer Culture and Postmodernism*, London, Sage, 1991, p. 115. In addition to Featherstone's work on consumer culture, reference could also be made to the work of Mennell on food and cultural taste choices; S. Mennell, *All Manners of Food: Eating and Taste in England and France from the Middle Ages to the Present*, Oxford, Blackwell, 1985.

50 A. Mazrui, *A World Federation of Cultures: An African Perspective*, New York, 1976, p. 411. For further discussion see M. Van Bottenburg, 'The popularity of sports in continental Europe', 1992, *The Netherlands Journal of Social Sciences*, no. 28, pp. 3–30; R. Stokvis, 'The international and national expansion of sports', 1989, in E. Wagner, (ed.) *Sport in Asia and Africa: A Comparative Handbook*, Westport, Greenwood Press, 1989, pp. 13–24.

51 J. Bale and J. Maguire (eds) *The Global Sports Arena, Athletic Talent Migration in an Interdependent World*, London, Frank Cass, 1994.

52 See J. Maguire, 'More than a sporting touchdown: the making of American football in England 1982–1990', 1990, *Sociology of Sport Journal*, no. 7, pp. 213–37; J. Maguire, 'The media-sport production complex: the emergence of American sports in European culture', 1991, in *European Journal of Communication*, no. 6, pp. 315–36.

53 E. Dunning, 'Sport and European Integration', 1992, unpublished paper delivered at the *Macht und Ohnmacht im neuen Europa*, Vienna, May 1992, pp. 29–30. See also J. Maguire, 'Globalisation, sport and national identities: the empires strike back?' 1993, *Leisure and Society*, (op. cit.). The jubilation expressed by those groups over the Danish 'No' in their national referendum on the Maastricht Agreement regarding European integration was uncannily paralleled by the joy expressed over the Danish victory in the European Nations soccer championships in which they defeated the favourites, Germany. Yet the incipient stages of the formation of 'European' teams is also under way in certain sports, notably in the men's Ryder Cup and women's Solheim Cup golf competitions where Europe play the United States of America.

54 See J. Horne and D. Jary, 'The figurational sociology of sport and leisure of Elias and Dunning: an exposition and a critique', 1987, in J. Horne, D. Jary and A. Tomlinson, *Sport, Leisure and Social Relations*, Routledge & Kegan Paul, London, pp. 86–112.

55 E. Dunning, 'Uber die Dynamik des Sportkonsums: Eine figurative Analyse' (Aspects of the Dynamics of Sports Consumption: a

Figurational/Developmental Analysis) 1992, in R. Horak and O. Penz (eds) *Sport: Kult and Kommerz*, Vienna: Verlag fur Gesellschaftkritik, pp. 203–23; E. Dunning, 'Sport as a male preserve', 1986, *Theory, Culture and Society*, no. 3, pp. 79–90; E. Waddington and P. Murphy, 'Drugs, sports and ideologies', 1992, in Dunning and Rojek, op. cit., pp. 36–64; J. Maguire, 'The Commercialisation of English Elite Basketball, 1988. A Figurational Perspective' *International Review for the Sociology of Sport*, no. 23, pp. 305–24.
56 N. Mouzelis, 'On Figurational Sociology', 1993, *Theory, Culture and Society*, no. 10, pp. 239–53, p. 252. See also Rojek's assessment in C. Rojek, 'The field of play in Sport and Leisure Studies', 1992, in E. Dunning and C. Rojek, op. cit., pp. 1–35.

Chapter 7

Feminist thought and the boundaries of sisterhood

From consciousness-raising, to political campaigns, to self-help groups, to theoretical analysis, to concerns about the very nature of sport and leisure, women have increasingly placed their own experiences centre stage. The nature and degree of impact that the women's movement has had within particular disciplines, cultural spheres and institutions has varied widely. The first two decades of the twentieth century witnessed an early wave of feminism which secured suffrage, forced access into the universities and academic life and made inroads into the male controlled world of sport. Sporting successes themselves were uneven. Although there was Olympic competition for women in golf and tennis as early as 1900 it was not until 1928 that the Olympic Games admitted female track and field athletes. In 1921 at the first international women's athletic meeting staged in Monte Carlo, Britain along with France, Czechoslovakia, Italy, Spain and the United States of America formed the Federation Sportive Feminine Internationale. This body staged a Women's Olympic Games in Paris, in 1922, an act that was in defiance of the International Olympic Committee's decision not to allow women athletes to compete in the Paris Olympic Games of 1924.[1]

Women's struggle for equality in the 1920s resulted not so much from collective action but from diverse individual struggles. This followed a general pattern that was self-consciously altered by a second wave of feminism from the 1970s onwards. Conceiving women's liberation as a collective goal the women's movement set up a network of groups and organisations in various towns, cities and nations. This served not only as a social movement but what is more important allowed women to secure space, be heard and no longer remain the hiddden shadow of history. This is not a claim that equality has been achieved but that, in comparison to the 1920s, collective action through the women's movement has procured, for example, an explosion of women's culture in various forms such as women's studies and the reassertion of a relevant identity. Feminism itself, although unevenly, has mediated the sociology of knowledge – if not all disciplines and traditions of social thought.

There is no question that both feminism and the women's movement have made a major impact within many social formations and yet like all good working myths the myth of equality and empowerment have farthings of truth buried in the Christmas pudding of self-service rhetoric. Despite a sexual revolution a few facts might indicate that a gender underclass of women still remains. When interviewed before the 1992 General Election Mr Major defined his famous classless society as 'a society in which people have the same choices and opportunities wherever they start from and wherever they come from' (*Glasgow Herald*, 6 April 1992). Presumably this vision includes women and yet if one takes Scotland as but one example then one finds that: in 1992 fewer than 20 per cent of local councillors were women; out of seventy-two Scottish MPs only five were women; during 1990 women on average earned only 67.7 per cent of that earned by Scottish men despite women contributing to nearly 50 per cent (48.6) of the labour force (*Herald*, 22 October 1992). One of the many barometers of the status of women in Scottish society is the role that women play in public life and yet the further you look up the ladder of public office the fewer women you find.[2]

There is no reason to believe that sport or leisure is any different from any other aspect of society or culture in terms of gender inequality. It has not been uncommon for some feminists to suggest that, due to the conservative nature of sport, it is an arena of public life that has been resistent to change in comparison to other spheres. At a specific level one might consider the following examples: during 1990 only seven out of 167 National Olympic Committee presidents were women; only two out of thirty-three Directors of Leisure in London boroughs were women; there were no women directors on the Sports Council and with the exception of the National Coaching Foundation all regional directors and national directors in England and Wales were male; and no women sports editors were to be found on the national or Sunday newspapers.[3] At a general level it seems to hold true that whatever sphere of employment one might consider, the further up the bureaucracy of public or private office you look the fewer women you will find. As long as such a situation exists it seems a bit premature to herald the death of feminism. Some feminists argue that it is only when patriarchy ends that post-feminism begins.

In the worlds of both sport and leisure several concrete reasons have been posited to explain this under-representation of women in positions of power. The following are but some of the many explanations that women themselves have voiced: unless women have access to training they get left in the job market's bargain basement; women face stereotypical notions about their competence; women both perceive and experience a particular form of subordination in greater numbers than men; male elites ensure the maintenance of the status quo, and their own power, by selecting those individuals most like themselves; and finally that sport and leisure companies fail to take women's family responsibilities seriously. Unless companies take seriously the fact that women are always going to produce children, and thus recognise their role as employees as well as parents, then equal opportunity remains an improbability. Thus access to training must be coupled with access to child care for both male and female parents.[4]

If feminism has permeated unevenly the fields of sport and leisure, it has perhaps more comprehensively influenced the sociology of sport and leisure. In the first instance it might be suggested that feminist thought and praxis has influenced this body of knowledge in at least three ways. First, at an empirical level we now know a great deal more about the world of sport and leisure in terms of women's history, women's experiences of sport and leisure, women's participation rates, the representation of women athletes in the media, the body, and the power structure of various sport and leisure institutions.[5] All of these areas have involved challenging existing taken-for-granted assumptions about what counts as proper subject matter for sociological research into sport and leisure. Leisure, previously regarded as an activity carried out away from paid employment, has been redefined to include housewives and others with a dual burden of, for example, domestic and paid labour.[6] In studies of the sport and leisure labour market it has generally been accepted that employment is structured both vertically and horizontally by gender. A shift in emphasis from feminism to gender studies has allowed for a greater interplay between empirical work on both men and women.

Second, the practice of carrying out feminist research has produced a specific question about feminist methodology.[7] A debate
that has mediated both gender studies and sociology but also
highlighted that not all feminists share a common view on
research methodology. In carrying out research into sport and
leisure feminist methodology would raise general questions concerning the social significance of the researcher's gender, the
validity of experience against method, the issue of hierarchy in the
research relationship, the validity of research which does not have
the emancipation of women as a non-negotiable starting point, the
issue of funding and the social composition of the research
councils which make decisions about which research should and
should not be funded, the role of creativity in the research
method, and the extent to which traditional methods, such as
content analysis of newspapers, are appropriate or inappropriate
for recording data on women's experiences of sport and leisure. In
short, it is argued that any methodology that disempowers women
should be resisted.

Alongside the development of empirical studies and the question of a feminist methodology has been a third factor which has
influenced the development of the sociology of sport and leisure,
namely the emergence of a highly significant series of theoretical
debates. Not all feminists have focused upon an overarching
system of patriarchal power, dominance and control, but such
factors have often been starting points for explaining the ways in
which women experience various leisure contexts. No short list of
the various feminist traditions of social thought could be exhaustive but, for example, liberal, Marxist, radical, psychoanalytic,
socialist, existentialist and postmodern varieties of feminist thinking have all attempted to explain, describe and influence women's
oppression. Whatever the explanation, whatever the theory, it has
to be an emancipatory one which acknowledges the impact of
gendered social structures and the nature of gendered social
behaviour upon sport and leisure.

One of the most serious on-going debates amongst those studying gender in the late 1980s and early 1990s is the perceived
inherent racism of many approaches to the subject. Many black
women have argued most vehemently that much of the literature
on gender focuses on white women and the material produced by
both feminists and non-feminists is partial, exclusive and mar-
ginalising.[8] For instance Patricia Hill Collins by placing the ideas

of African-American women at the centre of her work invites both white feminists and African-American men, amongst others, to investigate the similarities and differences among their own standpoints and those of African-American women.[9] At a theoretical level a number of women scholars have attempted to explain the significance of sport and leisure in the lives of Asian and African-American women but at an empirical and historical level concrete studies of black women and the structures that empower or disempower their involvement in the world of sport or leisure have not been forthcoming.

Biology, bodies and femininity

A number of feminists have commented upon the fact that women's involvement in sport and leisure has been historically structured by perceptions, stereotypes, and limitations that have been placed upon women's physical and biological capabilities. One of the barriers which has served to exclude women from certain athletic events or robust leisure activities during pregnancy has been to allege women's biological inferiority – allegations often rooted in malestream notions of science.[10] Feminists rightly point to the huge variation in physical capabilities within either sex and the substantial overlap between the two populations. So how have feminists responded to a form of biological determinism which has served to disempower many women's leisure experiences?

The following are but four responses from feminist writers on this issue. First, many Canadian and American feminist writers on sport and leisure have suggested that the problem with the question of individual differences is that it has been informed by social-psychological, biological, and physiological research. This, it is suggested, has failed to take account of many social and political factors which have determined the discourse about gender sport and leisure.[11] It is argued that the dominant framework for explaining the issue of sex differences, participation and performance has tended to be carried out by a body of knowledge about science and research which itself has not been subjected to feminist analysis and critique. The emphasis on individuals focuses the analysis on such factors as different leisure tastes, styles and consumption and consequently depoliticises the central questions of power and control in explaining the reproduction and maintenance of gender inequality through leisure practices.

Second, the role of the body in such practices has often been viewed as particularly important given the ideological weight that is often invested in the view that the weak female body is directly responsible for women's position in society.[12] Yet others have asserted that rather than being an instrument of disempowerment in terms of physicality women's bodies themselves can be agents of empowerment in terms of sexuality. What is being argued here is that women gain control over their own lives by asserting control through their own bodies. In terms of both physical and social power Sarah Gilroy's research concluded that involvement in physical activity can be empowering and therefore a form of resistance against malestream practices in sport, leisure and physical activity.[13]

A third response has been from feminist biologists who have been critical of some of the feminist interventions on sport and leisure. In counterposing cultural to biological factors it is argued that much of the feminist literature on sport and leisure has unwittingly treated those physical differences as static and somewhat unchangeable. The flaw lies in the habit of viewing biology as essentially fixed. Feminist biologists such as Birke and Vines argue that biology itself can be subject to change and that a truly feminist understanding of women in sport and leisure must take the possible transformation of physiology into account.[14]

Finally some have argued that myths relating to women's physical power have helped to reproduce aspects of hegemonic masculinity by legitimating common sense beliefs about what women can or cannot do. By focusing upon and deconstructing those aspects of social practice concerned with the body and physical activity, biological explanations for the totality of gender differences can be effectively challenged. That is to say that the conflict over biology, the body and ideologies of femininity needs to be exposed to feminist theory which defines a politics of the body and physical power not so much in terms of physical power inequalities between men and women or boys and girls but in terms of social power, social practice and sexuality.[15] The significance of sexual inequality as a social fact varies across a range of sport and leisure practices and is therefore a legitimate terrain for feminist intervention. In the same sense because the sociology of sport and leisure theorises about aspects of gender difference and sexed subjectivity then feminist intervention here must also make a difference.

Different paths to emancipation

Because so much of contemporary feminist theory defines itself in relation to traditional liberal feminism, liberalism provides an obvious place to begin. Liberal feminists assert that female subordination is rooted in a set of customary and legal constraints that blocks women's entrance and success in the so-called public world of sport and leisure. Liberal feminists have argued that because the male dominated public world of sport and leisure has the false belief that women are less intellectually or physically capable, then women are excluded from certain leisure spaces, boardrooms and marketplaces.[16] As a result of this policy of exclusion the true potential of many women goes unfulfilled. Gender justice, insist liberal feminists, requires the rules of the game to be fair for both men and women and that none of the runners in the race for society's goods and services be systematically disadvantaged. Equal opportunities and human rights should mean that opportunities in the world of sport and leisure must be extended to all women, including minority women, fat women, thin women, poor women, handicapped women, lesbian women, and older women. Thus liberal feminist accounts of sport and leisure tend to conceive of women's subordination in terms of social structure and small scale deprivation rather than focus upon the overarching systems of power, patriarchy and control.[17]

Marxist feminist explanations of sport and leisure think that it is impossible for anyone, especially women, to obtain equal opportunity as long as women in sport and leisure continue to service the needs of capital. Marxist feminist ways of seeing sport and leisure have relied heavily upon the notions of ideology, alienation, political economy, division of labour, and power. These have been central to explaining the complex and often contradictory ways in which the structures of class, leisure and patriarchy have articulated with one another at different historical moments.[18] Reflection upon this state of affairs has led to the suggestion that capitalism itself, not just the larger social and political rules under which men are privileged over women, is the cause of women's oppression. As with Marxism more generally, Marxist feminists made a sustained effort to avoid forms of crude economic or class determinism. Both Marxism and feminism are theories of power and its unequal distribution. Both are total theories and both teach that exploitation, domination and subordination produce resistance and a war of movement in a wide variety of spheres, including sport and leisure.[19]

Radical feminists believe that neither their liberal nor Marxist sisters have gone far enough. They argue that it is the patriarchal system that oppresses women, a system characterised by power, dominance, hierarchy and competition. It is not possible to reform such a system. It has, argue radical feminists, to be ripped out at the root, all patriarchal structures and institutions must be demolished. Radical feminists tend to view female biology and sexuality as the key to liberation. What is oppressive is not so much female biology but rather that men have controlled women as child bearers and child rearers. Thus if women are to be liberated, each woman must determine for herself when to use or not to use reproduction controlling and aiding technologies. This is not biological or technological determinism but rather an assertion that if women have certain biological qualities which they themselves have control over, then should such qualities not be used to affirm, celebrate, transform and support women's sporting and leisure roles. This in turn would transform sport and marginalise patriarchal leisure practices.

In many ways it is misleading to suggest that authors or strands of feminism can be neatly boxed off and explained as a taxonomy of different feminisms. Such categories are not homogenous although they do provide different ways of knowing, seeing and explaining women's experiences of life. Postmodern feminists regard the whole enterprise of trying to represent one specific feminist standpoint as neither feasible or desirable. It is not feasible because women's experiences of sport and leisure cut across class, racial and cultural lines. It is not desirable because any search for one form or explanation of the truth is both meaningless and arbitrary. For postmodernists the fact that feminism takes on many forms is to be expected, for women themselves are many and not one. By refusing to centre, cement and congeal the separate ways of seeing and knowing postmodernist feminists argue that they are able not only to resist patriarchal dogma but also distorted forms of rhetoric that claim to be the truth.[20]

Some feminists worry that an over-emphasis on difference may lead to intellectual and political disintegration. While the social divisions between women and the different paths to emancipation may reflect different power struggles over knowledge and methodology all forms of feminist explanation and research are forms of political commitment to the empowerment of women. Pigeon-holing the different characteristics of divergent feminisms side-steps a point of departure which is common to all forms of feminist political practice, namely identifying relationships of oppression and seeking ways of knowing and living which avoid the sub-ordination of women. As the debate over feminist methodology illustrates, any position which disempowers women should be resisted no matter what form of disguise it is presented in.[21]

Gender, bureaucracy and organisational elites

One of the most important points arising out of the feminist literature on sport and leisure is that increasing participation rates in sport and recreation are perhaps not the best indicators upon which to assert a claim of increased opportunity and demo-cratisation.[22] At the heart of this concern is a recognition of the gendered nature of many sport and leisure bureaucracies and organisations. This is not a denial of the fact that an increasing number of women have been employed in managerial or pro-fessional jobs when compared with the first decades of the twentieth century, nor does it mean that many sport or leisure organisations are less patriarchal than they used to be. Rather, it testifies to the fact that the types of areas into which women have moved are often those that tend to be barred from effective organ-isational power.

The starting point for explaining the development of bureau-cratic sport and leisure organisations has often been Weber, who argued that modern bureaucracies showed some or all of the following characteristics: clearly demarcated spheres of com-petence, rules governing the behaviour of staff, recruitment based upon the demonstration of specialised competencies, the occu-pational position of the official is career oriented and involves movement up the hierarchy of authority, and remuneration takes the shape of a fixed regular salary.[23] These have often been seen as imperatives for many forms of modern sport and leisure organ-isations and yet writers such as Clegg have argued that there are many different ways of organising and that the Weberian model of bureaucracy has a specific historical location in the late nineteenth and early to mid twentieth centuries.[24] This is not the place to discuss Clegg's ideas of organisations and what he calls 'circuits of power' but the crucial point that this research establishes is that bureaucracies differ and that any common patterns of organising are due not just to technical necessities but also the embodiment of particular forms and circuits of social and political power.

The work of Hall, Cullen and Slack has suggested that Canadian national sports organisations have tended to re-create themselves and thus reproduce a common pattern of organisational elites which with few exceptions have tended to be male.[25] They argue that research has shown that men's behaviour in work contexts changes in the presence of substantial numbers of women; they become more relationship oriented, more supportive, and less competitive and domineering. Yet from a radical feminist perspective the problem of change for the betterment of women and men is how to create changes so that the values of people in power are not necessarily the values of a fundamentally homogeneous group of specifically white, middle-aged men of privilege. The problems are immense since few sport or leisure bureaucracies readily acknowledge the power of men over women, the public over the private realm, production over reproduction or even heterosexuality over other sexualities.

A further study of Canada's national sports organisations compared 1982 figures with 1985 figures and concluded that although programmes mounted by women in the first half of the 1980s may have assisted women in gaining access to entry-level positions in sport and recreation these have not yet borne fruit at the higher levels of national sport bureaucracies.[26] By 1985 only 7 per cent of Canada's head coaches were women; 17 per cent of the technical directors were women; 24 per cent of the executive directors were women, while women made up an overall 21 per cent of the membership of the boards of directors of Canadian national sports organisations. In a similar study of the power structure of British sports organisations since the 1960s White and Brackenridge concluded that explanations for the male dominance of British sports organisations range from general issues such as the inappropriateness of the male model of sport for women and women's lack of access to political systems, to more specific issues such as the recruitment mechanisms that operate in sports organisations.[27] In contrast Whitson and Macintosh conclude that although small changes in the sports workplace have been achieved (and retarded) these have resulted from both specific struggles around gender and related issues and outside determinations such as economic and technological developments.

A crucial element within feminist critiques of bureaucratic practice is that women have the capacity to go about getting things done not in a better way than men but in a different and equal manner. Feminists often describe the modern women's movement as a distinctive mode of political practice and organisation. In contrast to Weber's formal and substantive rationality, women have suggested that one of the characteristics of the women's movement has been its substantive rationality of collectivist democratic organisation; a claim that is substantiated by considering such practices as the sharing of tasks, skills, information and resources as well as attending to the formal accomplishment of task goals. By contrast the formal rationality of Weberian bureaucracy involves authority residing in individuals, a hierarchical organisation of offices and a maximal division of labour.

Others have viewed the construction of sexuality as the key to understanding gender and bureaucratic organisations. In *Secretaries Talk* Pringle insists that the boss–secretary relation is the classic example of workplace power relations.[28] Pringle clearly wants to establish the fact that forms of power and control in the bureaucratic organisation are based around the construction of sexuality. In other words, the bureaucratic organisation is not de-sexualised and that sexuality is a key discourse in explaining how men and women are positioned as subjects and objects within the modern bureaucratic organisation. Yet despite the enormous potential for examining sport and leisure bureaucracies in terms of organisational sexuality such a starting point all too often removes the focus from the wider field of gender relations. Indeed we would argue that any research agenda on sport and leisure organisations should take as its starting point the relationship between gender and power within different organisational settings. In order to understand how Clegg's circuits of power operate it is necessary to move away from formalist analyses of bureaucracies to a recognition of how they are relatively shaped, not only by specific struggles around particular organisational issues but also by specific types of gender figurations.[29]

One final point concerns the historical specificity of organisational forms. Although organisations such as the Scottish Sports Council (formed in 1972), Sport Canada and Recreation Canada (formed in 1971) and the International Olympic Committee (formed in 1894) were inevitably shaped by a wide variety of social forces – such as patriarchal power relations – sport and leisure organisations and bureaucracies are constantly changing in a fluid way. Earlier we suggested that Weber's classic modern bureaucracy might be best utilised in explaining late nineteenth century and early to mid twentieth century forms of bureaucracy. In the same sense the point that is being made is simply that sport and leisure organisations may gain a certain fixity within a particular historical period but that this cannot be regarded as a permanent state of affairs.

Black feminism and the boundaries of sisterhood

Talking about her reasons for joining the Communist Party and not the Women's Liberation Movement in the late 1960s, Angela Davis comments:

> I felt no connection with what the white women's liberationists were doing. And this was the case with the overwhelming majority of Black women. The feminist movement, even though it was sparked in part by contributions made by Black women, did not attract Black women. This was true for other women of color as well – Chicano women, Puerto Rican women, Asian women, Native American women – who, in some instances, created their own women's organisations. The Black Women's Alliance, later called the Third World Women's Alliance, made it absolutely clear that the target of their efforts was tripartite in nature: racism, sexism and imperialism. Whereas within many of the white women's circles, the focus was personal experience. Their structures were largely designed to allow white women to psychologically overcome the sense of inferiority which they had internalised as a result of the gender-role socialisation they had experienced.[30]

For some time now mainstream white feminism has been criticised for its silences on racism.[31] The complexity of ideas and activism which black feminism represents is not essentially about what black women think of white feminist ideas. Nor is it about defining an exclusive set of voices, for example, for African-American women or Asian women. At the same time the legacy of past struggles against both racism and sexism is a common thread binding many Black women activists. Certainly this legacy of struggle and the forgotten world of black women's history are core themes for many black women writers. But so are other themes such as sexuality, sexual violence, abortion, motherhood,

controlling stereotypical images of Black women, and the separation of biology from much of the ideology that informs many black
feminist ideas. The relevance of feminism for many Black women
activists has often centred around the relevance of feminism as a
vehicle for political mobilisation and social change.[32]

Again Angela Davis talks about her rejection of the women's
movement during the 1960s and early 1970s:

> Well, first of all, if we wish to shed the attitudinal forms of racism
> and class bias inevitable in any racist society, white middle-class
> women cannot continue simply to work among themselves. It
> will not happen as a result of white women attending work-
> shops, learning how to unlearn racism. I'm not trying to com-
> pletely dismiss those workshops, but white women must learn in
> activist contexts how to take leadership from women of color.
> And it may sound like a simple issue but it isn't. Not at all. The
> need for white women to accept leadership from women of
> color flows from the objective relationship between the forms of
> oppression white women suffer – white middle-class women,
> white working-class women – and the forms of oppression
> suffered by women of color. If we actually look at the structure
> of sexism, it has a racist component which affects not only
> women of color but white women as well.[33]

There is no doubt about the dynamic effects that the black
women's movement and black feminism has had not only on the
lives of black women and women of colour but also the Women's
Liberation Movement and feminist thought in general. Yet to
some extent it is fair to say that much of the feminist intervention
into the sociology of sport and leisure has tended to be articulated
in accordance with the structure of white middle-class oppression
and thinking. Very few of the feminist accounts of women in sport
and leisure raise specific questions about the historical specificity
of black women's sport or leisure; or the way in which racism
affects the sport and leisure experiences of many Asian women; or
the specific obstacles which affect the consumption of sport and
leisure for many women of colour.

Placing, for example, African-American or British-Asian women
at the centre of the analysis not only reveals much-needed information about women's experiences and histories of sport and
leisure but also questions taken-for-granted assumptions about
leisure and the body, sport and social mobility, autonomous sports

groups, the exploitation of black women as both athletes and citizens, and the Eurocentric images and models which dominate and inform both the world of sports and the arts.

Black women's experiences and the Afrocentric ideology that informs much of the black feminist tradition also challenges prevailing definitions of sport and leisure in the community. Black women's actions often contribute to a strong sense of community which stands in opposition to the weak market-oriented definition which tends to be at the centre of Sports or Arts Council provision. The definition of community implicit in this market model often sees community as arbitrary and fragile, structured fundamentally by competition and dominations. In contrast Afrocentric, and many working-class, models of community stress connections, caring, and personal accountability.³⁴ Indeed many black sportswomen have had to reject the dominant patterns of sport and leisure provision in order to preserve a stronger sense of sisterhood and sport in the community. Talking about some of her reasons for leaving a predominantly white team for an all-black team one black woman athlete explains:

> I heard about . . . Jah-baddies and they were looking for new players so I says, like, I'd had enough of playing with this white team. . . . I couldn't move up the ladder, I was always in the 'B' team and . . . I knew I was better than some of the white players . . . they didn't want an all-black team like in their top team which it would have been if they'd put the good players in . . . when this opportunity came to join a black team, I says, 'well that's it I'm going'.³⁵

Empowerment in sport and leisure has often meant black women rejecting existing personal, cultural and institutional structures which have historically supported racism. The practice of black feminist thought necessitates an understanding between personal sporting biography and the history of sporting relations in various countries. Many of the personal troubles which black sportswomen in Britain and America experience are in fact related to broader structural dynamics and meanings such as those articulated through racism. Angela Davis is more forceful on this issue when she argues that there is something in the nature of racism's role in society that permits those who have come through the ranks of struggles against racism to have a clearer comprehension of the totality of oppression.³⁶ White women must learn to acknowledge this as a potential starting point for not only understanding black women's experiences of sport and leisure but also oppression in general.

Sojourner Truth's famous question 'Ain't I a woman?' was a question that was asked in the middle of the nineteenth century and yet it remains a pertinent question that might be asked of much of the feminist writings on sport and leisure. There is simply no equivalent text on sport and leisure to that of the contribution made by C. L. R. James in *Beyond a Boundary* (1963) and yet black feminist thought is capable of providing a much-needed radical critique of the sociology of sport and leisure. For example, the existence of athletes such as Anna Quirot, Esther Kiplagat, Lydia Cheromei, Derartu Tulu, Merlynne Ottey, Phyllis Watt, Jennifer Stoute and Hassiba Boulmerka can help open up the history and experiences of black women athletes in Cuba, Kenya, Ethiopia, Jamaica, Great Britain and Algeria. Such case studies are capable of not only opening up a broader understanding of identity politics but also the role of sport in black communities. Yet race, class, national, and gender relations will always be differently combined in different sport and leisure settings, as one sees if one compares the complexities of their combination in South Africa, America or Islamic nations such as Saudi Arabia or Algeria.

The case of Hassiba Boulmerka is illustrative of a much loved Arab-African sporting woman forced to leave Algeria for France in order to escape the backlash from Islamicists and Muslim zealots (*The Independent,* 12 August 1991). Winner of the women's 1,500 metres final at the World athletic championships in 1991, Boulmerka became the first Algerian, the first Arab and the first African woman to win any gold medal at any World athletic championships. On her return to Algeria President Chadli Benjedid greeted her as a national heroine. But Muslim zealots denounced her from the pulpit for baring her most intimate parts (her legs) before millions of television viewers. Furthermore, President Benjeded was denounced for publicly embracing a woman in public. The row underscored the clash between modernity and Islamic traditionalism, the fastest growing social and political force in Algeria; a clash which was all the more surprising given Algeria's position in the Arab world as the torchbearer of modernism, socialism, and successful struggle for independence from colonial rule.

Women were emancipated early in Algeria's national struggle. They were obliged to carry out many tasks their husbands were unable to fulfil because they were dead, imprisoned or fighting against France. Since then, however, the progress made by Algerian women has been under threat. There are only two women ministers in the government and parliament has refused to pass a law to end the traditional practice of men voting by proxy for their womenfolk. Women make up less than a fifth of the paid work-force: 800,000 in a population of twenty-five million. Hassiba Boulmerka has now fled abroad and the Islamicists have lost an opportunity to promote national unity in Algeria. For if ever there was a modern popular figure in Algeria – one who had taken on the world and won – it was Hassiba Boulmerka.

All subjugated knowledges, such as black women's sporting or leisure history and biography, develop in the cultural contexts of oppressed groups. Dominant groups often aim to replace sub-jugated knowledge with their own specialised thought because they realise that gaining control over this dimension of the lives of subordinates simplifies control.[37] While efforts to influence this dimension or an oppressed group's experiences can be partially successful, this level is more difficult to control than dominant groups would have us believe. For example adhering to externally derived standards of beauty leads many African-American women to dislike their skin colour or hair texture. Similarly, internalising Eurocentric gender ideology leads some black men to abuse black women. These may be seen as a successful infusion of a dominant group's specialised thought into the everyday cultural context of African-Americans. But the long-standing existence of a black women's blues tradition, and the voices of contemporary African-American women writers all attest to the difficulty of eliminating the cultural context as a fundamental site of resistance. Certainly an upsurge of black feminist writings on sport and leisure would help to challenge Eurocentric masculinist and feminist thought which pervades the sociology of sport and leisure.

Postmodern feminism

Perhaps more than any other type of feminist thought postmodern feminism has an uneasy relationship with feminism. Often in search of compromise postmodern feminists and other forms of feminism adopt contradictory positions. Feminists applaud post-modernism's criticism of sociology and its denial of a privileged status for male opinion. But postmodernism itself is often denounced for not giving authority to women's voices; they argue that, in the cases of rape, domestic violence and sexual harassment there is a difference between fact and fiction.[38] The victim's account of these experiences, it is suggested, is not just an arbitrary imposition of a purely fictive meaning of an otherwise meaningless reality and as such they warn postmodernists against the total repudiation of either external reality or rational judgement.[39] Postmodern feminists face a possible inconsistency between embracing a relativist form of postmodern philosophy and combining it with a very real commitment to challenge an objective reality.

In short one of the dilemmas for women's studies posed by postmodern feminists is one of theory and truth. It is not surprising that many feminists are willing to embrace postmodern philosophy and yet the postmodern view may ultimately not be any more acceptable than the male-dominated view. Sceptical postmodernists are likely to assume that all versions of the truth are equal while feminists are likely to argue for the superiority of their own point of view. Feminists who are suspicious of the postmodern point of view tend to argue that women need an epistemology where knowledge is possible, where in a search to understand and change the world, their own vision is accepted as valid.

Some women have suggested that one of the strengths of the postmodern feminism is simply one of deconstruction – a voice for the excluded, shunned, disadvantaged, unprivileged, rejected, unwanted, abandoned and marginalised women of the world. The deconstruction approach takes a critical attitude towards everything, including particular ideas or social injustices as well as the structures upon which they are based, the language in which they are thought and the systems in which they are safeguarded. Feminists would support the deconstruction of many of the traditional boundaries which have helped to reproduce male-dominated structures in sport and leisure. Boundaries which women have had to struggle against such as prescription of passive leisure forms during pregnancy; equal prize money for equal effort; perceptions of what is beautiful sport and what is permissible leisure time for women. Yet the problem with the deconstructionist approach is that the critics hardly ever propose an alternative and hence one is left with the impression that deconstructionists and some postmodern feminists find nothing specific about sport and leisure which is worth holding on to – everything goes. The danger here is that a vacuum can be created which neo-liberal theories are all too happy to fill.

Postmodern feminism has had little or nothing to say about sport or leisure. The case against postmodern feminism must be similar to the case against postmodernism, namely, that even if postmodernism was clear about its origins it has tended to remain a mystical term which is high on fashion ability and low in terms of clarity.[40] Feminist critiques of modern sport and leisure tended to be fairly straight-forward; women faced stereotypical notions about their competence; women both perceive and experience discrimination in greater numbers than men; a degree of social self-recruitment by men ensured the maintenance of the status quo within sport and leisure power structures; modernity itself was associated with patriarchal sport and leisure under industrialism and organised capitalism and that traditional class alignment meant that feminist critiques of modern sport and leisure could be easily identified with either the Right or the Left of the political spectrum.

Postmodernism, on the other hand, has tended to suggest that traditional labels such as Right and Left have become increasingly vacuous in analytical terms. Postmodern feminists would therefore support the argument that women's organisations advocating leisure reforms, such as the Women's Sport Foundation in Britain or the Canadian Association for the Advancement of Women and Sport, are best characterised as part of a new social movement which avoids the problem of class-alignment under modernity. If feminism in the age of modernity associated itself with patriarchal sport and leisure then postmodern feminism logically has to talk of post-patriarchal sport and leisure. If not post-patriarchal sport and leisure then surely the discourse of gender and leisure is finally moving away from an exclusive and restrictive focus on women to consider the impact of gendered social behaviour and gendered social structures on both sexes. If modern feminism failed to empower the voice of black women and other women of colour then the resurgence of local, regional and ethnic nationalisms is but a further reminder that perhaps there is no longer a consensus on the direction of progress and that the politics of women's sport and leisure is more diffused and uncertain than it was under modernity.

Concluding thoughts

This chapter has attempted to synthesise and comment upon some of the many themes that have influenced feminist accounts of sport and leisure. It is by no means exhaustive but, by way of summary, it might be suggested that some or all of the following concerns have been central to many feminist accounts of sport and leisure: (i) to consider the structures which have historically exploited, devalued and often oppressed women; (ii) to consider various strategies which are committed to changing the condition of women; (iii) to adopt a critical perspective towards intellectual traditions and methods which have ignored or justified women's oppression; (iv) to explain women's involvement in and alienation from different sport and leisure contexts and practices and (v) to highlight the engendered nature of sport and leisure organisation, bureaucracies and hierarchies. Many of these themes have centred around examples of sport and leisure participation rates; discussions over the legitimate use of the body; media representations of women athletes; concerns over the funding for women's sport and leisure provision; histories and biographies of women's involvement in sport and leisure; economic, cultural, political and religious constraints upon women's consumption of sport and leisure; biological myths concerning sporting performance and the need for female only sport and leisure spaces. While the nature and content of feminist explanations of sport and leisure has changed, the issue of emancipation has always been a non-negotiable starting point.

NOTES AND REFERENCES

1 The Women's Amateur Athletic Association staged its first full-scale championships in 1923. The following year the novelty of a women's international meeting drew 25,000 spectators to London. A year later the 1924 Olympic champion Harold Abrahams argued that women were not built for violent exercise. He could never have dreamed that one day women would run faster and long jump further than himself or that a women would run the 10,000 metres faster than Paavo Nurmi and Ville Ritola when winning their Olympic titles.

2 For a discussion on the gender imbalance in Scottish local government see E. Kelly, 'The Future of Women in Scottish Local Government' in *Scottish Affairs*, no. 1, Autumn, 1992, pp. 66–77.

3 H. Burden, 'Who Cares about Women in Sport?' in *Cosmopolitan*, June, 1992, pp. 12–16.

4 For a useful summary of some of the key issues concerning occupation, change and gender see P. Bagguley, 'The Patriarchal Restructuring of Gender Segregation: A Case Study of the Hotel and Catering Industry' in *Sociology*, vol. 25, no. 4, 1991, pp. 607–25 and S. Roach Anleu, 'Recruitment Practice and Women Lawyers' Employment: An

Examination of In-House Legal Departments in the United States' in *Sociology*, vol. 26, no. 4, 1992, pp. 651–72.

5 A great deal of work still needs to be done to recover the social-history of womens' sport and leisure. The following provide an introduction to aspects of womens' leisure; Fiona Devine, *Affluent Workers Revisited; Privitism and the Working Class*, Edinburgh, Edinburgh University Press, 1992, pp. 145–52; E. Green, S. Hebron and D. Woodward, *Leisure and Gender: A Study of Sheffield Women's Experiences*, ESRC/ Sports Council Joint Panel Report, London, Sports Council, 1987; Jenny Hargreaves, 'Where's the Virtue? Where's the Grace?' in *Theory, Culture and Society*, vol. 3, no. 1, 1986, pp. 109–23; and R. Deem, *All Work and No Play? The Sociology of Women and Leisure*, Milton Keynes, Open University Press, 1986.

6 Workplaces do not convert easily into places of leisure. The two factors that are continually highlighted are (i) that in many women's lives, including their leisure lives, the role of the family is a key influencing factor and (ii) that while the home may provide a peaceful leisure haven for many men it cannot be guaranteed to offer the same haven from work for many women. All members of the household are likely to see the home as a base for some leisure, but in order to make this possible it is often necessary for women to forfeit some of the time that might have been used for leisure.

7 A vast amount of literature has commented upon the notion of a distinct feminist methodology. Feminist theory exposes neutrality as a myth and suggests that the notion of neutrality helps merely to reproduce values that work in the interests of masculinity, elitism and in some cases nationalism. See Liz Stanley, *Feminist Praxis: Research Theory and Epistemology in Feminist Sociology*, London, Routledge, 1990; Caroline Ramazanoglu, 'On Feminist Methodology: Male Reason Versus Female Empowerment' in *Sociology*, vol. 26, no. 2, 1992, pp. 207–12; Martyn Hammersley, 'On Feminist Methodology' in *Sociology*, vol. 26, no. 2, 1992, pp. 187–206 and Loraine Gelsthorpe, 'Response to Martyn Hammersley's Paper on Feminist Methodology' in *Sociology*, vol. 26, no. 2, 1992, pp. 213–18.

8 Various issues of *Feminist Review* have discussed this point. See for example 'The Past Before Us: Twenty years of Feminism', Special Issue of *Feminist Review*, no. 31, Spring, 1989.

9 Patricia Hill Collins *Black Feminist Thought*, London, Unwin Hyman, 1990.

10 The question of the role of biological influences in the development of gender has been a difficult one, and feminists have tended to reject the relevance of such influences altogether. This is the case both for sport and other spheres where malestream thinking and power has lead to a comparative exclusion for many women.

11 An excellent summary of this theme can be found in Sheila Scraton, *Shaping up to Womanhood: Gender and Girls' Physical Education*, Open University Press, Buckingham, 1992, pp. 104–18.

12 See Chris Shilling 'Educating the Body: Physical Capital and the Production of Social Inequalities' in *Sociology*, vol. 25, no. 4, 1991, pp.

653–72. For a general overview of sociological themes on the body see A. Frank, 'Bringing Bodies Back In: A Decade Review' in *Theory, Culture and Society*, vol. 7, no. 1, 1990, pp. 131–62.

13 Sarah Gilroy, 'The embodiment of power: gender and physical activity' in *Leisure Studies*, vol. 8, no. 2, 1989, pp. 163–71.

14 Lynda Birke and Gail Vines, 'A Sporting Chance: The Anatomy of Destiny?' in *Women's Studies International Forum*, vol. 10, no. 4, 1987, pp. 337–47. See also Lynda Birke and Gail Vines 'Beyond Nature Versus Nurture: Process Biology in the Development of Gender' in *Women's Studies International Forum*, vol. 10, no. 6, 1987, pp. 555–70.

15 S. Scraton, op. cit., 1992, pp. 82–7 and pp. 118–19.

16 For an introductory overview to different models of feminist thinking and practice see Rosemary Tong *Feminist Thought: A Comprehensive Introduction*, London, Routledge, 1989. For a similar discussion on sport see A. Hall, 'The Discourse of Gender and Sport From Femininity to Feminism' in *Sociology of Sport*, 1988, vol. 5, pp. 330–40. For a comprehensive review of British feminist theory see T. Lovell *British Feminist Theory*, Oxford, Oxford University Press, 1990.

17 See A. Hall 'How should we theorize sport in a capitalist patriarchy?' in *International Review of Sociology of Sport*, 1985, vol. 20, pp. 109–15.

18 On leisure see Jenny Hargreaves 'The Promise and Problems of Women's Leisure and Sport' in C. Rojek (ed.) *Leisure for Leisure: Critical Essays*, London, Macmillan, 1989, pp. 130–47. See also Jenny Hargreaves 'Sex, Gender and the Body in Sport and Leisure: Has there been a civilising process?' in E. Dunning and C. Rojek (eds) *Sport and Leisure in the Civilizing Process*, London, Macmillan, 1992, pp. 161–82.

19 Many feminists have suggested that any feminism worthy of the name must be post-Marxist and even postmodernist.

20 For a short summary of some of the commonalities and differences between feminism and postmodernism see Pauline Marie Rosenau, *Postmodernism and the Social Sciences, Insights, Inroads and Intrusions*, Princeton, Princeton University Press, 1992, pp. 113–15.

21 Caroline Ramazanoglu, op. cit., 1992.

22 See for example the discussion on sport and gender in A. Hall, T. Slack, G. Smith and D. Whitson (eds) *Sport In Canadian Society*, Toronto, McClelland and Stewart Inc, 1991, pp. 166–74.

23 For an entire range of historical and contemporary debates around the relationship between feminism and organisational theory, see M. Savage and A. Witz (eds) *Gender and Bureaucracy*, Oxford, Basil Blackwell, 1992. The general thrust of this text is to consider the reasons why organisational theory and feminist theory have engaged in a recent dialogue. This has at its starting point the need to move away from general notions of bureaucratic organisation in order to recognise historically and spatially specific ways of organising, which can be shown to rest upon particular gender foundations.

24 Clegg's point is simply that organisations differ and they do so due to the struggles waged by diverse social groups to obtain and resist power. S. Clegg, *Modern Organisations*, London, Sage, 1990.

25 A. Hall, D. Cullen and T. Slack, 'Organisational Elites Recreating Themselves: The Gender Structure of National Sports Organisations' in *Quest*, vol. 41, 1989, pp. 28–45.

26 D. Whitson and D. Macintosh 'Gender and Power: Explanations of Gender Inequalities in Canadian National Sport Organisations' in *International Review for the Sociology of Sport*, vol. 24, no. 2, 1989, pp. 137–50.

27 A. White and C. Brackenridge, 'Who Rules Sport? Gender Divisions in the Power Structure of British Sports Organisations from 1960' in *International Review for the Sociology of Sport*, vol. 20, no. 1, 1985, pp. 95–105. For a similar account of a particular struggle within the American context see J. Hult 'Women's Struggle for Governance in U.S. Athletics' in *International Review for the Sociology of Sport*, vol. 24, no. 3, 1989, pp. 249–60.

28 R. Pringle, *Secretaries Talk: Sexuality, Power and Work*, London, Verso, 1989.

29 S. Clegg, op. cit., 1990.

30 Angela Davis, 'Complexity, Activism, Optimism' in *Feminist Review*, 1989, vol. 37, no. 31, p. 69.

31 G. Tang-Nairn, 'Black women, sexism and racism: Black or anti-racist feminism' in *Feminist Review*, 1991, no. 37, Spring, pp. 1–22.

32 Patricia Hill-Collins, op. cit, 1990.

33 Angela Davis, op. cit, 1989, p. 71.

34 Patricia Hill-Collins, op. cit., 1990.

35 Unpublished research from the graduate programme in Sport, Culture and Society at the University of Warwick. See P. Adudu, Graduate Dissertation, 1991, p. 67. See also Susan Birrell 'Women of Color, Critical Autobiography and Sport' in M. Messner and D. Sabo (ed.) *Sport, Men and Gender Order: Critical Feminist Perspectives*, Illinois, Human Kinetics Books, 1990, pp. 185–98.

36 Angela Davis, op. cit., 1989.

37 Patricia Hill-Collins, op. cit., 1990.

38 For a general summary of the relationship between feminism and postmodern theory, see Rosemarie Tong, op. cit., 1992, pp. 217–33.

39 This point on theory and truth is expanded upon in Pauline Marie Rosenau, op. cit., 1992, pp. 67–77.

40 See Lincoln Allison (ed.) *The Changing Politics of Sport*, Manchester, Manchester University Press, 1993, pp. 10–11.

Chapter 8

Fields of power, habitus and distinction

In mapping out the intellectual project of the French sociologist Pierre Bourdieu, at least two main points should be noted. First, he seeks to tackle issues which are key concerns within modern social theory. Second, research on sport, leisure and the body occupies a central place within this project. Such a coupling is very rare. This interweaving of his concerns with sport, leisure and the body, on the one hand, and broader sociological issues on the other, are well summed up in the opening section of his work *Distinction*:

> To understand the class distribution of the various sports, one would have to take account of the representation which, in terms of their specific schemes of perception and appreciation, the different classes have of the costs (economic, cultural and 'physical') and benefits attached to the different sports – immediate or deferred 'physical' benefits (health, beauty, strength, whether visible, through 'body-building' or invisible through 'keep-fit' exercises), economic and social benefits linked to the distributional or positional value of each of the sports considered (i.e. all that each of them receives from its greater or lesser rarity, and its more or less clear association with a class, with boxing, football, rugby or body-building evoking the working classes, tennis and skiing, the bourgeoisie and golf, the upper bourgeoisie), gains in distinction accruing from the effects on the body itself (e.g. slimness, sun-tan, muscles obviously or discreetly visible, etc.) or from the access to highly selective groups which some of these sports give (golf, polo, etc.).[1]

As with his analysis more generally, Bourdieu's study of sport and leisure attempts to construct a model of these social practices by examining what people actually do in these practices without

losing sight of the wider patterns of social life. His essential proposition appears to be that the appeal of sport and leisure practices to social groups lies in distinctive uses of the body. These
practices act as taste signifiers in a constant struggle to gain or
maintain distinction. For Bourdieu, the task is to relate specific
sports to the tastes and preferences of social groups and to assess
the 'rewards' accruing relative to the type of 'investment' made.
This concern with the particular without losing sight of the general
is one of the distinguishing features of Bourdieu's work. There is
however, another reason why Bourdieu is worthy of consideration:
his work is 'good to think with'.[2] That is, by thinking in con-
junction with and in opposition to his work, the sociological enterprise is enhanced. Bourdieu himself addressed this issue when
commenting on a sociology of sociology. This is what he had to say:

> If, for example, you take the relations between Weber and Marx
> . . . you can view them in another way and ask how and why one
> thinker enables you to see the truth of the other and vice versa.
> The opposition between Marx, Weber and Durkheim, as is
> ritually invoked in lectures and papers, conceals the fact that
> the unity of sociology is perhaps to be found in that space of
> possible positions whose antagonism, apprehended as such,
> suggests the possibility of its own transcendence. It is evident,
> for instance, that Weber saw something that Marx did not, but
> also that Weber could see what Marx hadn't because Marx has
> seen what he had . . . every sociologist would do well to listen to
> his/her adversaries as it is in their interest to see what he/she
> cannot see, to observe the limits of his vision, which by defini-
> tion are invisible to him.[3]

So what is it that Bourdieu enables us to see? Let us spell out how
he allows us to begin to see through a thicket of sociological
conundrums. Underpinning his research are a number of key
aims. Bourdieu's central task is to transcend the 'epistemological
couples' which have arguably bedevilled sociological research.
These 'couples' include agency-structure debates, micro-macro
linkages and the freedom and determinism dichotomy. Bourdieu
seeks to outflank these dichotomies by focusing on the 'dialectical'
relationship between objective structures and subjective phenomenon. He describes his own work as 'constructivist structuralism'
or 'generative structuralism'. In this regard Bourdieu's aim is to
'make possible a science of the dialectical relations between the

objective structures . . . and the structured dispositions within which these structures are actualised and which tend to reproduce them'.[4] That is, at one and the same time, Bourdieu wants to examine both the objective structures which unconsciously act to orient and constrain social practice and the subjective dimension which focuses upon the social genesis of mental structure.

In order to accomplish this task, Bourdieu argues that the development of a new way of thinking and mode of asking questions about social life is required. Here again Bourdieu is challenging another dualism, in this case that between theory and empirical work. He wishes to eschew the choice between grand theory and narrow empiricism. His research craft centres around a spiral between theory, empirical work and back to reformulating theory again. A two-way uninterrupted traffic between theory and evidence is advocated as the best way to comprehend the genesis of both the person and of social structures.

In utilising a range of quantitative as well as qualitative research methods, Bourdieu also challenges the crude formulations found in objectivity and subjectivity research debates. By adopting a variety of methods, Bourdieu is guided by the notion that the subject matter of sociology is the interweaving of conscious and unconscious processes in social life. For Bourdieu, in describing his position as 'participant objectivation', social practice is a product of processes that are neither wholly conscious nor wholly unconscious. While seeking to avoid the excesses of voluntarism and of structuralism, however, Bourdieu has still been referred to as a 'poststructuralist'. The jury is still out on whether this label is correct or indeed whether in adopting the strategy proposed he does in fact, dissolve the 'epistemological couples' referred to.[5]

To assist in this radical reorientation of the sociological enterprise, Bourdieu has also developed several key concepts which act as 'thinking tools'. Three of the most important are practice, habitus and field. These will be considered in a discussion of the sporting body. Attention will then focus on two related issues, sport, social fields and class relations and leisure, lifestyles and distinction.

Sport practices, habitus and the body

For Bourdieu, the study of the sporting body highlights issues which are central to the sociological enterprise. Addressing its importance, he argued: 'I think that sport is, with dance, one of the terrains in which is posed with maximum acuteness the problem of the relations between theory and practice and also between language and the body.'[6] In tracing the importance of sporting practices, it is necessary to map it out as part of Bourdieu's theoretical terrain. The concepts of practice, habitus and field are sensitising concepts and are used by Bourdieu to construct a framework for examining, at one and the same time, society and human conduct. The concept of social practice is designed to perform two functions. Bourdieu uses it in order to overcome or circumvent a range of dualisms including individual-society, agency–structure, freewill–determinism and mind–body. It is also a concept that highlights the way that the body enacts marks or habits that have been absorbed and reproduced through practices occurring in a structural context. Bourdieu thus feels able to deal with how day-to-day practices interweave as part of a wider tapestry of social life. Several key points regarding the concept can be identified.

For Bourdieu, culture is incorporated bodily within structural social contexts. Hence, social practice is the outcome of a dialectical relationship between agency and structure. In this way, the body is viewed as a site of social memory. This involves the individual culturally learning, refining, recognising, recalling and evoking dispositions to act. Echoing his point about dialectical relationships, Bourdieu argues that social practices are neither objectively determined, nor exclusively the product of freewill.[7] What is being raised here is not just the dualism of individual and society but also the relationship between consciousness and unconsciousness as aspects of a person's social make-up. For Bourdieu, however, it is not solely a question of nature versus nurture but rather, the dialectical aspects of nurture. It is a question of the 'society written into the body, into the biological individual', yet by so doing, the individual is empowered to act back on the social world.[8] In this way, we return to his more general questioning of the processes by which culture is incorporated bodily.

Given Bourdieu's concern to trace how day-to-day affairs are part of wider schemes of living, it is of little surprise that social practices are viewed as occurring across time and space. Social practices are processes through which we live out our daily lives. But they are not random. There is a pattern, a sequence and a structure to such social practices. Despite this patterning, social practices are not wholly consciously organised and/or orchestrated.

For Bourdieu, the production of social practices involves a blend or balance between the conscious and the unconscious, between the intended and the unintended. Again, Bourdieu is trying to reconcile recognising the strategies of social actors but acknowledging that the 'practical accomplishment' of daily life involves reliance on the utilisation of what is conventionally termed 'second nature'.

Bourdieu uses a variety of examples to illustrate how the practical accomplishment of daily life involves 'second nature'. For present purposes one of the more relevant examples is his reference to the dynamics of games to illustrate the nature of the processes involved. In steering away from seeing the 'things of logic' as the 'logic of things', Bourdieu observes:

> To avoid this, you have to include in the theory the real principle behind strategies, namely the practical sense, or, if you prefer, what sports players call a feel for the game, as the practical mastery of the logic or of the imminent necessity of a game – a mastery acquired by experience of the game, and one which works outside conscious control and discourse (in the way that, for instance, techniques of the body do).[9]

Though Bourdieu was not the first to recognise how the study of games can shed light on more general sociological issues, his comments allude to how the study of games can reveal processes of social practice in action. The practical sense or logic of social actors involves then the expression of dispositions that lie at the intersection of the conscious and unconsciousness. Recognising this also enables the researcher to grasp that the sports performers' seeming inability to cognitively describe their actions is less to do with inarticulateness, and much more to do with the fact that such activities, and indeed day-to-day practices more generally, result not from a process of reasoning from preset rules, but stem from 'systems of action'. More specifically, individuals participate in systems of action without 'formal' understanding. That is, the practical action is learned but is also formally forgotten as an object of consciousness. This practical notion, though originally developed as part of a conscious learning process, is remembered as a habitual response. These habits are so successfully learned that they become sedimented in the body. They become the body. As with sports and leisure performers, so too with social actors, it is the doing that counts. Bourdieu is here attempting to weave together issues of freedom and constraint and the conscious and unconscious processes of social life. Addressing this issue and the role that sport plays in this regard, Bourdieu argues:

> Thinking about this understanding of the body, one could perhaps contribute to a theory of belief. . . . I think there is a link between the body and what in French we call 'esprit de corps' ('corporate loyalty' or 'team spirit'). If most organisations – the Church, the army, political parties, industrial concerns, etc. – give such a big place to bodily disciplines, this is to a great extent because obedience is belief and belief is what the body grants even when the mind says no. . . . It is perhaps by thinking about what is most specific about sport, that is, the regulated manipulation of the body, about the fact that sport, like all disciplines in all total or totalitarian institutions, convents, prisons, asylums, political parties, etc., is a way of obtaining from the body an adhesion that the mind might refuse, that one could reach a better understanding of the usage made by most authoritarian regimes of sport. Bodily discipline is the instrument par excellence of every kind of 'domestication'.[10]

This 'domestication' process begins as the child enters the world. From the very early stages of child development, the person is having to weave together conscious and unconsciousness dimensions of social practices. If we follow the pattern of general motor skill development, such as the process of crawling, balancing, walking, running and jumping, it can be observed that the individual leans towards conscious control over their body parts. This control tends to be formal, rigid, awkward and less fluid. They have to 'think' about their movement. Gradually, through repetition, the degree of syncronicity increases. Self-conscious control of actions decreases. Simultaneously, movements become more flowing, continuous and fluid. Movements become 'second nature'. This is what Bourdieu had in mind when he argued:

> What is 'learned by body' is not something that one has, like knowledge that can be brandished, but something that one is . . . [such knowledge is] . . . never detached from the body that bears it and can be reconstituted only by means of a kind of gymnastics designed to evoke it, a mimesis which . . . implies total investment and deep emotional identification.[11]

These comments raise fundamental questions about the early social-isation of children into play, games, sports and leisure activities. Not only does this have pedagogical implications for those involved in physical education, the sports sciences, and leisure studies, but it reveals in vivid form the importance of the area for social science as a whole. Based on this approach, sport and physical education can be seen to be ideologically laden and instrumental in establishing and expressing class, gender and national identities. But, for Bourdieu, sport and physical education are not ideologically fixed or pre-determined. These practices can act as a potential site of resistance. The making of bodies is contested terrain. Indeed, it is in the context of body matters that 'the fundamental principles of the arbitrary content of the culture' are forged.[12] The task facing social scientists is to trace and analyse the processes involved. But this is not an easy matter. As Bourdieu notes:

> The principles embodied in this way are placed beyond the grasp of consciousness, and hence cannot be touched by volun-tary, deliberate transformation, cannot even be made explicit; nothing seems more ineffable, more incommunicable, more inimitable, and, therefore, are more precious, than the values given body, *made* body by the transubstantiation achieved by the hidden persuasion of an implicit pedagogy.[13]

These social practices tell us something about day-to-day life more generally, and we ignore them at a cost. These practices both enable and constrain individuals from childhood to grave and involve an interpretation of what it is to be a human being. These embodied actions structure how an individual thinks, feels and acts. The production and reproduction of these practices within the individual reflects both the membership of humanity as a whole but also of specific communities.

For Bourdieu, the ability to absorb appropriate embodied actions is the key to developing specific feelings which enable the individuals to be at ease with their self and with others of the same community. This applies equally to sport and leisure subcultures. The knowledge of what it is to be a boxer, for example, involves the development of a body habitus. Here lessons are absorbed about manners, customs, style and deportment that become so ingrained in the boxer that they are forgotten in any conscious sense. The 'accumulative practice of the same' ensures that the boxer's motor schema is drawn on intuitively.[14] Being a competent social actor and having mastery over social practices involves then a feel for the game. This is developed and maintained by a deeply embodied habitus. Addressing this link between habitus, the feel for the game and the social game, Bourdieu observed:

> The habitus as the feel for the game is the social game embodied and turned into a second nature. Nothing is simultaneously freer and more constrained than the action of a good player. He (*sic*) quite naturally materialises at just the place the ball is about to fall, as if the ball were in command of him – but by that very fact, he is in command of the ball. The habitus, as society written into the body, into the biological individual, enables the infinite number of acts of the game – written into the game as possibilities and objective demands – to be produced; the constraints and demands of the game, although they are not restricted to a code of rules, impose themselves on those people – and those people alone – who, because they have a feel for the game, a feel, that is, for the immanent necessity of the game, are prepared to perceive them and carry them out.[15]

Conceived of in this way, habitus is a concept that allows the researcher to outflank the conceptual knots of individual and society, agency and structure and nature versus nurture. For Bourdieu, habitus refers to a set of dispositions that are created and reformulated in the unification of objective structures and personal history. Habitus is then 'an acquired system of generative schemes objectively adjusted to the particular conditions in which it is constituted'.[16] Habitus is the product of the internalisation by an individual of social structures. This internalisation occurs concomitant with the occupancy of specific social positions within what Bourdieu terms a 'social field'. This does not mean that everyone has the same habitus, but that people who occupy the same position within the social world tend to have a similar habitus. We will return to the concept of field when we examine sport and social class. At this stage, it is important to grasp that it is a person's habitus that 'engenders all the thoughts, all the perceptions, and all the actions consistent with these conditions and no other'.[17]

The process of internalisation involves the embodiment of certain dispositions within human beings. This operates at two levels: a conscious level, in which the individual deploys strategies to achieve certain tasks; and an unconscious level in which certain acts are conducted that are below the level of consciousness and language. Several crucial questions arise with regard to how habituses work in practice. Does the conscious or the unconscious have primacy? Does a person's habitus work in a fixed, deterministic manner or in a flexible, elastic pattern? Does a person's habitus reside inside a person's head, in the actual practice of interaction with others or in 'generative schemes' sedimented deep within a person's body?

At first sight there are no clear-cut answers in Bourdieu's work. In some instances Bourdieu uses the term with reference to an individual's embodiment. On other occasions, habitus is used to capture the idea of social practices involving a collective homogenous phenomenon. If his work is read from the vantage point of one or other of the dualities he rejects, then the reader is left feeling that no formal conclusion has been reached: that habitus means all things in different situations. Bourdieu appears aware of this. Practice is seen to mediate between an individual's habitus and the social world. While it is through practice that habitus is created, this process of practice also creates the social world. For Bourdieu:

> This paradoxical product is difficult to conceive, even inconceivable, only so long as one remains locked in the dilemma of determinism and freedom, conditioning and creativity. . . . Because the habitus is an endless capacity to engender products – thoughts, perceptions, expressions, actions – whose limits are set by the historically and socially situated conditions of its production, the conditioned and conditional freedom it secures is as remote from a creation of unpredictable novelty as it is from a simple mechanical reproduction of the initial conditionings.[18]

Habitus then is an embodied internalised schema that structures but does not determine actions, thoughts and feelings. Though it functions beyond the reach of introspective scrutiny and control by the will, it is utilised in practical action. In this the body occupies a central position. For those studying sport and leisure practices, the significance of this should not be underestimated. Why should this be the case? Within the framework being mapped out social identity is considered to be a process of learning and relearning classifications, codes and procedures which structure social exchanges. According to Bourdieu, these habituses:

> ... embed what some would mistakenly call values in the most automatic gestures or the apparently most insignificant techniques of the body – ways of walking or blowing one's nose, ways of eating or talking – and engage the most fundamental principles of construction and evaluation of the social world, those which most directly express the division of labour . . . or the division of the work of domination.[19]

We have already noted that habitus refers to an acquired system of generative schemes. These schemes are firmly implanted within the body. This would not surprise psychologists working with the area of motor skills. However, given their disciplinary term of reference, they are unable to conceive of the linkage between the occupancy of a social position and the development of a specific motor schema. Utilising the term 'bodily hexis' as a bridging concept between the individual's interior and exterior world, Bourdieu highlights how a socio-cultural perspective provides a more adequate conceptualisation when he writes that 'bodily hexis is political mythology realised, embodied, turned into a permanent disposition, a durable manner of standing, speaking and thereby of feeling and thinking'.[20]

As habitus operates at an unconscious level, people's manners, deportment and demeanour signify a great deal about their personal history and present occupancy of a specific social position. Conceived of in this way, the body acts as a social memory. The very basics of culture are imprinted and encoded in both a formal and informal manner. That is, through taken for granted socialisation processes, the child assimilates and memorises social properties common to those in a similar social situation. In some instances, formal teaching plays a part and the child learns and internalises certain attributes. Both processes go on in play, games, sport and physical education.[21]

A range of writers have deployed aspects of Bourdieu's ideas: some have examined body styles, eating habits and fitness regimes, while others combine elements of Bourdieu with feminist scholarship to assist in explaining the gendered construction of people's bodies, sporting practices and social relations. In addition, researchers in Britain and North America have quarried Bourdieu's work to provide a conceptual framework to make sense of the 'schooling of the body', the rationalisation and scientisation of the body in the sports sciences, and the disciplining of the body within sport more generally.[22] Bourdieu is unusual as a major social theorist in that he himself has applied the main corpus of his work in the study of sport and leisure practices. It is to this we now turn.

Sport, social fields and class relations

Bourdieu, in drawing together several themes from his work – power, culture and body habitus – highlights in the following passage the connections between sport, social fields and class relations:

> Sport, like any other practice, is an object of struggles between the fractions of the dominant class and also between the social classes . . . the social definition of sport is an object of struggles . . . the field of sporting practices is the site of struggles in which what is at stake, inter alia, is the monopolistic capacity to impose the legitimate definition of sporting practice . . . this field is itself part of the larger field of struggles over the definition of the legitimate body and the legitimate use of the body.[23]

On what basis then do social actors choose between the different sport and leisure practices which, at any given time and place, are offered to them as possible? Rejecting both 'naturalistic' and 'voluntaristic' explanations, Bourdieu constructs a sophisticated analysis for the development of sport and for the existing pattern of consumption. Reference to the concepts of field, supply and demand, capital, habitus and social class provide the key to understanding his approach.

In seeking to map out the practice of everyday life, Bourdieu developed a heuristic device which would sensitise the reader to several key elements. Known as his 'generative formula', Bourdieu expressed it in the following way: (habitus) or (capital) + field = practice.[24] A person's competency in and mastery of practice within a specific field – or in the overall social space – is dependent on their habitus and possession of capital. We have already outlined the main features of Bourdieu's use of the concept habitus. Here we will direct attention to the related concepts of field and capital before spelling out how class habitus and sport practices are intertwined.

In Bourdieu's work a field is defined as a social arena – sport is one such field. Within a field, struggles take place. This struggle can be over specific resources and stakes and access to them. A field is defined by the stakes which people play for. These can include cultural goods, intellectual distinction or political/economic power. Each field has its own logic and taken for granted structure. That is, each field is partially autonomous. Nevertheless, broader social and economic conditions are embedded within each specific field. Fields are characterised by struggles for dominant positions. These struggles help to conserve and transform a field. Positions within a field are determined by the allocation of specific capital to actors who are thus structurally located in the field. But these positions are not static. Once attained, a person's position interacts with a person's habitus to produce different postures and actions. These then have an interdependent effect on the economy of position – taken within a field. Bourdieu captured several elements of fields in the following passage:

> The existence of a specialised and relatively autonomous field is correlative with the existence of specific stakes and interests: via the inseparably economic and psychological investments that they arouse in the agents endowed with a certain habitus, the field and its stakes (themselves produced as such by relations of power and struggle in order to transform the power relations that are constitutive of the field) produce investments of time, money and work, etc. . . . In other words, interest is at once a condition of the functioning of a field . . . in so far as it is what 'gets people moving', what makes them get together, compete and struggle with each other, and a product of the way the field functions.[25]

A field then is a structured system of social positions. The nature of the system defines the experience of the field for the occupants. This system is characterised by a series of unequal power relations. The positions occupied by participants within the field can be viewed as more or less dominant, more or less subordinant. The occupancy of a position of domination or subordination is both reinforced by and also reflects the access to the goods or resources which are at stake in the field. This 'capital' can take the form of economic, social, cultural and symbolic goods or resources. The structure of the field is defined – at any given moment – by the balance between the occupancy of specific positions and the distributed capital. Struggle is a dominant feature of fields as agents use 'strategies' to preserve or improve their occupancy of positions relative to the defining capital of the field.

Although each field is relatively autonomous, Bourdieu views them as part of the overall 'social space'. Viewing social reality as a 'space', he argues that this is comprised of 'multiple fields'. These fields have relationships to each other, and, have specific points of contact and/or overlap. The social space or reality of an individual is connected through time (his/her 'life trajectory') by occupancy of a series of fields within which they struggle more or less success-fully – for the various forms of capital available. Given Bourdieu's methodological structures, the structure of a specific field or indeed, the overall social space, cannot be determined a priori. Rather the character of struggle for ascendency must be estab-lished through empirical research. So what has been found out with regard to sport and leisure?

Two broad areas can be identified that illustrate work on sport and leisure. These are firstly, the link between tastes and preferences with class habitus and secondly, the emergence and contemporary pattern of the supply and demand within the sport and leisure fields. We will examine the issue of taste more closely when we focus on lifestyles, leisure and distinction. Here, we will concentrate on the elements of supply and demand in the sports field. Several questions therefore arise. Is there an area of sport production that has its own logic and its own history? If there is, how is the demand for sports products produced and how do people acquire the 'taste' for sport – either as participant, spectator or consumer? Clearly Bourdieu argues that there is distinct field in which sport is produced. The pattern of sporting practices within the field of sport is seen to reflect the dispositional attitude to the body. This disposition is class specific. Class attitudes to the use of the body influence the kinds of sports taken up, the kinds of style associated with a sport and the cultural status of the specific sport.

Answers to these questions and issues require consideration of the emergence of the contemporary pattern of supply and demand in the sports field. Rejecting a simple continuity thesis connecting modern sport with ancient festivals, games and pas-times, Bourdieu argues that it is more adequate to talk of a 'break' with the past. During the course of the nineteenth century a field of competition within which sport was defined as a specific practice came into being. It is from this moment on that it becomes possible to speak of sport in the modern sense. This field included public and private associations, producers and vendors of equipment, the service side and the marketing area. Though this production field relates directly to broader economic and social conditions of society, it nevertheless has a relatively autonomous history with its own current of events.

Examining how this terrain was constituted, Bourdieu identifies two main phases: the initial genesis, and the popularisation of sport products. In the initial phase there occurred a major shift from popular pastimes and games to 'sports'. Echoing his general analysis on fields, Bourdieu notes that it was members of the aristocracy and bourgeoisie who 'took over' popular games and pastimes and simultaneously changed their meaning and function. These groups were to be come the dominant group in the sports field. These groups set in train several interconnected processes. A rationalisation process, ensuring predictability and calculability over performance unfolded. Standardisation of rules occurred and organisations devoted to the administration and promotion of the sports field emerged. These processes were combined with the forging of a political philosophy of sport emphasising fitness, fair play and amateurism.

Enjoying a monopolistic capacity in the sports field enabled members of the aristocracy and gentry to define what was the legitimate definition of sport practice and the legitimate function of sport activity. The moral ideals of the English public schools – which the sons of these dominant groups attended – promoted the amateur code and an emphasis upon chivalrous manliness. For Bourdieu, this initial phase was a decisive one in the subsequent emergence of the contemporary pattern of the field of sport. Through to today, he argues:

> Sport still bears the mark of its origins. Not only does the aristo-cratic ideology of sports as disinterested, gratuitous activity, which lives on in the ritual themes of celebratory discourse, help to mask the true nature of an increasing proportion of sporting practices, but the practice of sport such as tennis, riding, sailing or golf doubtless owes part of its 'interest', just as much nowadays as at the beginning, to its distinguishing function and, more precisely, the gains in distinction which it brings.[26]

These gains to which Bourdieu refers are seen as at their greatest when the distinction between noble and vulgar practices are com-bined with opposition between participation in sport and the mere consumption of sporting entertainments. The popularisation of sports involved not popular sports produced by the people, but rather, spectacles produced for the people by the very groups who compose the sports field. Bourdieu observes that the public are 'very imperfectly equipped with the specific competence needed to decipher it [media sport] adequately'.[27] Expressed in this way, it is perhaps less surprising that a cultural dupe thesis can be seen lurking within the Bourdieu account of popular culture.

Under the impetus of spectacularisation, sport products become a mass commodity consumed as part of the field of sporting entertainments, which is itself part of the broader field of 'corporate business'. This popularisation process – from elite schools and clubs to mass sporting associations – does result in some sports being played across a range of social classes. But Bourdieu is quick to point out that this popularisation 'is necessarily accompanied by a change in the functions which the sportsmen (*sic*) and their organisers assign to this practice'.[28] This change in function relates not only to the spread of sport to different classes but also to gender and ethnic groups. In the following passage Bourdieu addresses several of these issues:

> A sport such as rugby presents an initial ambiguity. In England, at least, it is still played in the elite 'public schools', whereas in France it has become the characteristic sport of the working and middle classes of the regions south of the Loire (while preserving some 'academic' bastions such as the Racing Club or the Paris Université Club). This ambiguity can only be understood if one bears in mind the history of the process which, as in the 'elite schools' of nineteenth-century England, leads to the transmutation of popular games into elite sports, associated with an aristocratic ethic and world view ('fair play', 'will to win' etc.) . . . entailing a radical change in meaning and function . . . which, in a second phase, transforms elite sport into mass sport, a spectacle as much as a practice.[29]

Different classes, gender and ethnic groups do not 'agree' on the profits (physical, cultural and symbolic) expected from sport. Different classes derive different types of profit from sport in terms of health, slimness, relaxation and social relationships. Though some sports are practised by all classes, e.g. golf, both the setting and actual practice itself involves different bodily dispositions and different expectations of returns on type and volume of cultural, symbolic and economic capital invested. Just as there is a 'universe of class bodies and bodily practices' so too is there a 'universe of sporting bodies'. The task is to map out these on to the social space.

In accounting for the logic of sport practices, two broad issues need to be addressed. The supply dimension of sporting practices involves the particular definition of sporting and entertainment practices that is put forward by dominant groups at a given place and moment in time. This supply meets a demand. This entails the expectations, interests and values that people bring to the sports field. Actual sport practices develop as a result of the ongoing struggle and realignment between these two dimensions. While Bourdieu acknowledges that the field of production helps to produce the need for its own products, he concludes:

> The logic whereby agents incline towards this or that sporting practice cannot be understood unless their dispositions towards sport, which are themselves one dimension of a particular relation to the body, are reinserted into the unity of the system of dispositions, the habitus, which is the basis from which lifestyles are generated.[30]

It is essential then, in examining the specificity of the field of sport, to relocate it back into the wider network of practices. The common origin of all such fields is the system of tastes and preferences that is embodied as a class habitus. In constructing his model of sporting practices, Bourdieu is therefore keen to point to the fact that consideration must be given to positive and negative determining factors such as spare time and economic and cultural capital. But this alone is not enough. It must be recognised that the variations in the meaning and function given to sport practices by various classes and class fractions must be the core of the investigation. It must be understood that:

> Class habitus defines the meaning conferred on sporting activity, the profits expected from it; and not the least of these profits is the social value accruing from the pursuit of certain sports by virtue of the distinctive rarity they derive from their class distribution.[31]

Observations of this kind relate not only to sport practices but also to wider leisure pursuits. It is to these we now turn.

Leisure, lifestyle and distinction

Taking as his departure point the notion of taste, Bourdieu notes that the occupancy of a specific position within the field and the wider social space is reciprocally connected with the expression of a specific habitus and that, in turn, this habitus produces a specific lifestyle. Tracing this interconnection reveals that lifestyles cannot be studied in isolation. Lifestyles – and leisure practices – must be woven to broader relationships within the social space. For Bourdieu, this expression of taste is:

> The generative formula of lifestyle, a unitary set of distinctive preferences which express the same expressive intention in the specific logic of each of the symbolic sub-spaces, furniture, clothing, language or body hexis . . . taste is the basis of the mutual adjustment of all the features associated with a person.[32]

It is through the expression – or should it be deployment – of taste that people maintain similarities or differences between themselves and others. Through this process people establish a sense of identity. These taste choices function as a 'sort of orientation', they give the person a sense of *heimat* in which the occupants of a given place in social space are 'guided' towards both the social positions, practices and goods 'which befit the occupants of that position'.[33]

Taste choices then classify but also classify the classifier. In classifying, classifiers distinguish themselves by their choices, but by so doing ensnare themselves. This is not a process that occurs by chance. Identifying what he terms a 'hierarchy of legitimacies', Bourdieu notes that cultural goods and tastes are ranked within and between spheres of legitimacy. How in practice a leisure activity is assigned to a specific sphere stems from the exercise of cultural power. This approach was developed by Bourdieu over a considerable period of time – from his early work in Algeria through to his detailed analysis of contemporary France. The approach is best expressed in his work *Distinction*.[34] In this he provides us both with a framework and a broad substantive base on which to consider lifestyles and leisure practices.

Implicit within the discussion of taste, outlined in bare bones form above, is the idea that such choices are inherently social. Bourdieu is here critiquing the idea that taste choices stem either from the essence of the object being examined or from some innate quality within an individual. Neither are adequate. Nor, indeed, is the idea that taste choices are the prerogative of an individual unfettered by social influences. In the following passage Bourdieu addresses these issues when arguing for a scientific study of culture:

The science of taste and of cultural consumption begins with a transgression that is in no way aesthetic: it has to abolish the sacred frontier which makes legitimate culture a separate universe, in order to discover the intelligible relations which unite apparently incommensurable 'choices', such as preferences in music and food, painting and sport, literature and hairstyle. This barbarous reintegration of aesthetic consumption into the world of ordinary consumption abolishes the opposition, which has been the basis of high aesthetics since Kant, between the 'taste of sense' and the 'taste of reflection', and between facile pleasure, pleasure reduced to a pleasure of the senses, and pure pleasure, pleasure purified of pleasure, which is predisposed to become a symbol of moral excellence.[35]

Far from being innate, people learn lifestyle and leisure preferences, and the process of learning is contoured along class lines. In the opening section to *Distinction*, Bourdieu is also mapping out another key feature of his work on lifestyles and leisure. He rejects the dichotomy between high and low culture. He dissolves classical culture notions into a study of culture as a whole. In doing so, he is probing the social function of lifestyle and leisure choices. In this he traces how the cultural preferences of various groups serve to unify some and demarcate others. These cultural preferences reflect the occupancy of a position within a specific field and the wider social space. Struggles between these groups permeate all their social interaction and taste choices. In fact, these taste choices arise out of, and are mobilised in, these struggles for status. In these struggles, and by the expression of taste choices, an individual establishes both their own identity and self position. The dynamics of the consumption of lifestyle and leisure choices positions the individual within the field and thereby creates their view of themselves and of others.

Leisure choices – types of holiday (Malaga or Oslo); education 'days-out' (the Robin Hood Centre or avante garde art gallery with creche); sporting practices (American football or golf); musical taste (Showaddywaddy or classical jazz); food and drink preferences (wine, lager or real ale); types of reading (Jackie Collins or Ibsen) – all reflect lifestyle schemes. These schemes are contoured along social class lines. In mapping out French tastes Bourdieu identifies three broad groupings – the legitimate, middle brow and popular. As we have already noted, their preferences reflect this classification scheme and by making choices on this basis, the classifier is classified.

The processes identified in the field of sport are also at work in the leisure field. That is, leisure practices are characterised by market competition, principles of supply and demand, and tendencies towards monopolisation are evident. Access to culturally valued leisure goods and services are restricted and the power chances of particular classes of individuals are contoured by the volume of 'capital' they thus possess. This capital is not just economic, but is also cultural (e.g. education, knowledge of high culture and art) and symbolic (presentation of self-demeanour).

In order to understand how access to and maintenance of a position of power is achieved reference has to be made to cultural capital with its own structure of value and rates of convertibility into social power. Different classes and class fractions are involved in a constant struggle to turn the social practice of 'field' to their advantage. They do so in two ways. Firstly, they attempt to monopolise access to the production of leisure goods (hi-fi equipment) or leisure services (high status fitness centres). Secondly, they attempt to rename, legitimise or marginalise leisure practices (fox-hunting and the hippy convoy).[36] Those classes which possess a high volume of both economic and cultural capital are clearly in a stronger position to define what leisure activities are legitimate, deemed pleasurable and possible to practice and consume. What is at stake here is the power to define what counts as taste and thereby either to accumulate or loose status and distinction.

Given that Bourdieu acknowledges that there is a constant struggle over lifestyles and leisure activities, this suggests that he does not conceive of the exercise of power in a deterministic and unidimensional manner. In *Distinction*, we see that lifestyles and leisure practices are struggled over and a degree of resistance to dominant definitions is evident. Such an analysis connects to the fact that different social classes and class fractions actively pursue different tastes that are a reflection of their position within the field and wider social space. But this divergence of tastes also reflects the ability of different groups to cling to marginal or residual forms of leisure pursuits.[37]

To express the divergence of taste differences in this manner is perhaps to emphasize to too great an extent a theme in Bourdieu's work which highlights the conscious strategies of different classes. Rather, if we return to one of Bourdieu's other building blocks, namely habitus, it can be noted that greater emphasis is given to the unconscious assimiliation of tastes contoured along class lines. Insider tastes are naturalised and accepted as 'common sense', while tastes pursued by outsiders are treated with suspicion and distain. In this connection Bourdieu observes:

> The habitus is necessity internalised and converted into a disposition that generates meaningful practices and meaning-giving perceptions. . . . That is why an agent's whole set of practices (or those of a whole set of agents produced by similar conditions) are both systematic, in as much as they are the product of the application of identical (or interchangable) schemes, and systematically distinct from the practices constituting another lifestyle.[38]

Let us try to illustrate these processes at work with reference to the interrelated issues of food, fitness, lifestyle, social class and consumer culture. A class's body habitus is made up of all the dispositions towards one's body, themselves determined and conditioned by the material conditions of existence. This is evident throughout the course of a single day and the life of the person, e.g. birth, body size, volume, walking, ways of eating/drinking, hygiene, everyday demeanour, speaking, learning, sitting, running, resting, sleeping, dying. Bourdieu explained these issues at some length:

> It is the relation to one's own body, a fundamental aspect of habitus, which distinguishes the working classes from the privileged classes, just as, within the latter, it distinguishes fractions that are separated by the whole university of a lifestyle. On the one side, there is the instrumental relation to the body which the working classes express in all the practices centred on the body, whether in dieting or beauty care, relation to illness or medication, and which is also manifested in the choice of sports requiring a considerable investment of effort, sometimes pain and suffering (e.g. boxing) and sometimes a gambling with the body itself (as in motor-cycling, parachute jumping, all forms of acrobatics, and to some extent, all sports involving fighting, among which we may include rugby). On the other side, there is a tendency of the privileged classes to treat the body as an end in itself, with variants according to whether the emphasis is placed on the intrinsic functioning of the body as an organism, which leads to the macrobiotic cult of health, or on the

appearance of the body as a perceptible configuration, the 'physique', i.e. the body-for-others.[39]

From these observations it is clear that Bourdieu is probing how the tastes pursued by different classes become 'naturalised'. These tastes act as a set of classificatory practices unconsciously assimilated. While their own tastes are naturalised, those tastes of others are regarded with suspicion and hostility. The differential formation of habitus for different groups and classes results in a 'natural' disposition to produce certain practices and to classify and judge the practices of others. In effect, habitus is the generative principle of taste differences. Choices regarding the appropriateness and validity of leisure goods and practices are grounded in these sets of distinctive preferences which in turn form the basis of different lifestyles.

For Bourdieu, taste and lifestyle preferences are a product of a specific habitus which in turn can be related to the volume of economic and cultural capital possessed. Bourdieu conceives of a grid of different habituses which can in turn be related to the grid of capital volume and the grid of lifestyle choices.[40] Body practices are analysed in terms of more general lifestyle tastes and how these are structured by their relationship to the habitus of particular class fractions and groups. For example, in the following passage Bourdieu links the issue of food, body maintenance activities and body styles:

> Whereas the working classes are more attentive to the strength of the (male) body than its shape, and tend to go for products that are both cheap and nutritious, the professions prefer products that are tasty, health-giving, light and not fattening.[41]

The reference to gender is important to note. Women of the various social classes and class fractions have their own specific body habitus structured by the balance of power between the sexes within and between such groups. Movement through the life course is also managed differently by different classes. Such differences become visibly inscribed on to the body and are accompanied by different dispositions towards the body and different investments of leisure time into bodily practice. Workers who use their bodies all day in their manually-based economic practice have little time for pretensions such as jogging and health-related fitness centres. They react to the bodily practices of the health-related fitness movement not only with a sense of 'strangeness' but also hostility. For male working-class manual workers the emphasis is on activities such as weightlifting and activities associated with strength.

In contrast, the middle classes are not concerned to produce a large, strong body, but rather a slim, athletic and fit body. Here the concern is with style, restraint and individualised practices (jogging, yoga, golf, squash, tennis, riding). Some leisure activities, according to Bourdieu, are:

> . . . predisposed for bourgeois use when the use of the body it requires in no way offends the sense of the high dignity of the person, which rules out, for example, flinging the body into the rough and tumble. . . . Ever concerned to impose the indisputable image of his own authority, his dignity or his distinction, the bourgeois treats his body as an end, makes his body a sign of its own ease.[42]

Located in a different occupational grouping, (the media, advertising, marketing, public relations, fashion, the helping professions) it is Bourdieu's contention that the middle-class habitus provides a sense of unease, alienation and embarrassment towards the body. The new middle class are 'pretenders' who aspire to be better than they are and who thus betray the insecurity of their investment orientation to life in the way that they watch, check and correct the body, self-consciously aware of the gaze of others. Activities such as jogging, aerobics and health clinics are related to this middle-class occupational concern with self-presentation. In this way the body becomes a sign for others which is frequently glamourised and presented as expressive leisure. Given the occupations which are monopolised by such a grouping, these body techniques and practices are promoted, transmitted, purveyed and stylised as part of the legitimate lifestyle, i.e. their lifestyle. This keenness to generalise their own bodily dispositions meshes with the promotion and creation of 'consumer culture'.[43]

Different classes and class fractions derive different types of profit (economic, cultural and symbolic) from leisure in consumer culture. This finds expression in terms of health needs, body shaping, quest for emotional fulfilment and social relationships. Though some leisure activities are practised by sections of all classes – listening to Pavarotti – both the setting and the actual 'practice' itself involves different bodily dispositions and expectations on the return on the 'investment' made. Such an analysis also holds true whether consideration is given to tourism within or between countries, or across continents. The 'secret' of high status tourism is not simply the accumulation of a 'sun tan' (if at all, given recent skin cancer scares), but rather to gain an educative/ enlightening cultural experience and a prized authentic native artefact – at not too high a price! The aim is to go where no plebians from one's own national culture have gone before.

Concluding thoughts

We argued at the beginning of this chapter that Bourdieu is 'good to think with'. Let us try to indicate how this is so in relation to the study of sport and leisure. The learning of a sport is an embodied process. The process of becoming a player of a specific sport involves a subtle blending of the conscious and the unconscious. As the 'novice' becomes more expert, the repertoire of skills becomes deeply embedded in a person's habitus. But this process is not culturally neutral. The learning of an appropriate habitus reflects the occupancy of a specific position within the field. In turn, this is embedded in wider political and cultural struggles that structure the learning experience. The study of sport provides a vivid demonstration of the construction of the body habitus in motion. Within Bourdieu's project, the sport setting is a rich context for the analysis of the relation between body habitus and the moment of individual choice.

We also discover from thinking with Bourdieu that the choice of 'learning' a sport or leisure activity is not a question of free choice and individual taste. This choice is socially structured, reflecting the possession and deployment of varying degrees and combinations of economic, cultural and symbolic capital. Taste reflects and embodies class disposition, a body habitus. The body is the most indisputable materialisation of class taste. Supply and demand issues that regulate sport and leisure consumption are also marked by power struggles. In these struggles, dominant groups are able to regulate access to culturally valued goods and services. They also utilise leisure pursuits to achieve and/or maintain gains in distinction and define what counts as legitimate or illegitimate practices.

Insights of this kind rest, of course, on certain methodological assumptions. Bourdieu attempts to both outflank empty empiricism and a priori theorising and to avoid falling into the trap of dualistic thinking that is characteristic of individual– society, agency–structure, freedom–determinism and nature–

nurture debates. More specifically, Bourdieu is also careful to avoid drawing a too direct and unidimensional relationship between a sport and a social position. In spelling out his alternative, Bourdieu also maps out the starting points for a programme for the sociology of sport. He writes:

> In fact, the correspondence, which is a real homology, is established between the space of sporting practices, or, more precisely, the space of the different finely analysed modalities of the practice of different sports, and the space of social positions. It is in the relation between these two spaces that the pertinent properties of every sporting practice are defined. And the very changes in practices can be understood only on the basis of this logic, in so far as one of the factors which determine them is the desire to maintain in practice the gaps which exist between different positions. The history of sporting practices must be a structural history, taking into account the systematic transformations entailed for instance by the appearance of a new sport (Californian sports) or the spread of an existing sport.[44]

From this it is clear that Bourdieu is arguing that the researcher must begin with an overall view of the structure of the space of sporting and indeed leisure activities. Further, he argues that the dynamics of change involved in leisure practices can only be understood if the researcher grasps the transformation involved in the overall social structure. In order to do this, it is necessary to relate the particular field to the social universe of class fractions that define and appropriate sport and leisure practice. Bourdieu goes on to argue that 'the priority of priorities is the construction of the structure of the space of sporting practices whose effects will be recorded by monographs devoted to particular sports'.[45] Recommending this development of culturally 'thick' monographs devoted to particular sports still involves a crisp description of the overall social space and the distribution of people within it.[46] Here, as elsewhere, Bourdieu's analysis of sport and leisure is concerned to uncover the structure within individual practice. In his analysis of games, the main task lies in discovering the moment(s) when structure is transcended and reconstituted through dispositional schemes. The study of games therefore allows for the probing of freedom and constraint in a controlled setting. Here, then, we have a programme for the sociological study of sport that provides significant promise for the discipline as a whole.

Bourdieu, however, is not without his critics.[47] It would be remiss in this critical appreciation if we did not identify some of the more salient criticisms. Does Bourdieu overcome the dualisms he purports to outflank? Is it sufficient to sidestep these dualisms rather than to seek to resolve or synthesise them? Given the manner in which Bourdieu employs the concept of habitus, is there sufficient account given to agency? Several critics see his approach as a sophisticated variant of structuralism or of post-structuralism in which objective structures unconsciously act to orient and constrain social practice. As such, or so the criticism goes, little is seen of the strategies employed by individual actors or of the enabling features of social life. Indeed, another tension can be identified in his work. What is the relationship between the conscious and the unconscious? To what extent does second nature predominate over practical, cognitively oriented social interventions?

Little account is seen to be given to the production of the sport and leisure fields. That is, questions of political economy are avoided and the creativity of the performer is also overlooked.[48] On a related note, other critics point to the question of individual choice, taste, body habitus and class position and wonder whether the relationship is conceived of in a too deterministic and mechanistic manner? Likewise, the relationship between field, multiple fields and social space is viewed as too deterministic and insufficient attention is given to identifying the mechanisms or processes involved in change in the overall social system of dispositions. One further omission is also identified. While class and class fractions figure prominently in his work, the gendered nature of social life is downplayed. To each of these criticisms Bourdieu has responded.[49] It will be for the reader both to judge the adequacy of these critiques and counter-critiques, and to assess the fruitfulness of Bourdieu's programme for the sociology of sport and leisure.

NOTES AND REFERENCES

1 P. Bourdieu, *Distinction. A Social Critique of the Judgement of Taste*, London, Routledge, 1986, p. 20.
2 Richard Jenkins makes this point in his splendid review of Bourdieu's work. Unfortunately, in his otherwise excellent, wide ranging and searching evaluation, he deliberately chose to exclude discussion of Bourdieu's analysis of sport and its position within the writer's

empirical/theoretical field. R. Jenkins, *Pierre Bourdieu*, London, Routledge, 1992, p. 12. No justification for this omission is offered. We hope what follows in some small way offsets this oversight.

3 P. Bourdieu, *In Other Words: Essays Towards a Reflexive Sociology*, Cambridge, Polity Press, 1990, pp.35–6. This argument underpins our rationale for the book as a whole. Each of the chapters should be read in this way. Reading theorists in this way assists in the development of the sociological imagination and avoids the 'violence of abstraction'.

4 P. Bourdieu, *Outline of a Theory of Practice*, Cambridge, Cambridge University Press, 1977, p. 3.

5 For reviews of P. Bourdieu, see R. Brubaker, 'Rethinking classical theory. The sociological vision of Pierre Bourdieu', *Theory and Society*, no. 14, 1985, pp. 745–75; R. Hawker, C. Mahar and C. Wilkes (eds) *An Introduction to the Work of Pierre Bourdieu*, London, Macmillan, 1990; R. Jenkins, *Pierre Bourdieu*, London, Routledge, 1992; D. Robbins, *The Work of Pierre Bourdieu*, Milton Keynes, Open University Press, 1991.

6 P. Bourdieu, op. cit., 1990, p. 166.

7 ibid, 1990.

8 ibid, p. 63.

9 ibid, p. 61.

10 ibid, p. 167.

11 ibid, p. 168.

12 P. Bourdieu, op. cit., 1977, p. 96.

13 ibid, p. 94.

14 L. Wacquant, 'The social logic of boxing in black Chicago: towards a sociology of pugilism', *Sociology of Sport Journal*, no. 9, 1992, pp. 221–54.

15 P. Bourdieu, op. cit., 1990, p. 63.

16 P. Bourdieu, op. cit., 1977, p. 95

17 ibid, p. 95.

18 ibid, p. 95.

19 P. Bourdieu, op. cit., 1986, p. 466.

20 P. Bourdieu, op. cit., 1977, pp. 93–4. This observation also applies to sport psychologists working within the sport sciences.

21 P. Bourdieu, op. cit., 1990, pp. 156–67.

22 A number of writers have drawn on the work of Bourdieu to examine different aspects of the sports phenomenon. See S. Laberge and D. Sankoff, 'Physical activities, body habitus and lifestyles' in J. Harvey and H. Cantelon (eds) *Not Just a Game: Essays in Canadian Sport Sociology*, Ottawa, University of Ottawa Press, 1988, pp. 267–86; C. Shilling, 'Educating the body: physical capital and the production of social inequalities' in *Sociology*, no. 25, 1991, pp. 653–72; R. Gruneau, 'The critique of sport in modernity: theorising power, culture and the politics of the body' in E. Dunning, J. Maguire and R. Pearton (eds) *The Sports Process*, Champaign, Ill: Human Kinetics, 1993, pp. 85-110; John Hargreaves, 'The body, sport and power relations' in J. Horne, D. Jary and A. Tomlinson (eds) *Sport, Leisure and Social Relations*, London, Routledge, 1986, pp. 139–59; J. Harvey and R. Sparkes, 'The politics of the body in the context of modernity' in *Quest*, no. 43, 1991, pp. 164–89.

23 P. Bourdieu, 'Sport and social class' in *Social Science Information*, no. 17, 1978, pp. 819–40.
24 P. Bourdieu, op. cit., 1986, p. 101.
25 P. Bourdieu, op. cit., 1990, pp. 87–8.
26 P. Bourdieu, op. cit., 1978, pp. 819–40 and 825–7.
27 ibid, p. 829.
28 ibid, p. 832.
29 P. Bourdieu, op. cit., 1986, p. 209.
30 P. Bourdieu, op. cit., 1978, p. 209.
31 ibid, p. 835.
32 P. Bourdieu, op. cit., 1986, pp. 173–4.
33 ibid, p. 466.
34 ibid.
35 ibid, p. 6.
36 For a discussion of the significance of the hippy convoy, see C. Rojek, 'The Convoy of Pollution', *Leisure Studies*, no. 7, 1988, pp. 21–32.
37 These concepts have been fruitfully utilised by Peter Donnelly in 'Sub-cultures in sport: resilience and transformation' in A. Ingham and J. Loy (eds) *Sport in Social Development*, Champaign, Il: Human Kinetics, 1993, pp. 119–46. Though drawing on the work of Raymond Williams, there is an overlap here with the concerns raised by Bourdieu.
38 P. Bourdieu, op. cit., 1986, p. 170.
39 P. Bourdieu, op. cit., 1978, pp. 819–40 and 838.
40 These issues are fruitfully explored by several Canadian writers. See S. Laberge and D. Sankoff, op. cit., 1988, and J. Harvey 'The politics of the body in the context of modernity', *Quest*, no. 43, pp. 164–89.
41 P. Bourdieu, op. cit., 1986, p. 190.
42 P. Bourdieu, op. cit., 1986, p. 218.
43 For a penetrating analysis of these issues, see M. Featherstone 'Leisure, symbolic power and the life course', in J. Horne, D. Jary and A. Tomlinson (eds) *Sport, Leisure and Social Relations*, London, Routledge, 1986, pp. 113–38.
44 P. Bourdieu, op. cit., 1990. p. 158.
45 ibid, p. 158.
46 The project begun by Bourdieu examining the field of sports in France has continued, with recent work by two French writers being the most prominent. See L. LaFrance and C. Pociello, 'Structure and evolution of the field of sports in France (1960–1990)' *International Review for the Sociology of Sport*, no. 28, 1993, pp. 1–23.
47 In addition to the work of Richard Jenkins, reference should be made to the following: R. Laermans, 'The relative rightness of Pierre Bourdieu: some sociological comments on the legitimacy of post-modern art, literature and culture' *Cultural Studies*, 1992, pp. 248–60; D. Gartman 'Culture as class symbolisation or mass reification? A critique of Bourdieu's *Distinction American Journal of Sociology*, no. 97, 1991, pp. 421–47. It should be pointed out that these writers' critique Bourdieu on radically different – and competing – criteria!
48 For some critics there is insufficient attention given to issues of political economy. That is, how the supply of goods is contoured and

shaped by the culture industries which create demand via slick advertising and marketing strategies is overlooked. See D. Gartman, op.
cit., 1991, pp. 421–47. The agency dimension of the production
process is also arguably over looked. That is, the capacity of performers (sports and leisure performers) to transcend the here and
now, and give meaning to the products they produce, is ignored.
Though Marcuse, for example, would want to explore the role the
cultural industries played in this regard, he too was interested in the
transformative qualities of art, see H. Marcuse *The Aesthetic Dimension,*
London, Macmillan Press, 1978, Bourdieu appears to serve us up,
however well done, a sociology of consumption.

49 His interviews provide a sound base on which to examine the ade-
quacy of his responses. See P. Bourdieu, op. cit., 1990; L. Wacquant,
'Towards a reflexive sociology: a workshop with Pierre Bourdieu' in
Sociological Theory, no. 7, 1989, pp. 26–63.

Chapter 9

Beyond modernity and the problems of postmodernism

Late twentieth-century theories of postmodernism have embraced a variety of movements, a diversity of disciplines and a complex number of concepts. There remains an intense controversy over the merits of the postmodernist contribution to the analysis of culture and society. Postmodernism first gained currency in the fields of architecture and art history but gradually permeated a vast number of disciplines as a general cultural and political critique of modernity. As an umbrella term for a number of concepts postmodernism was based upon a negation of modernity and the deconstruction of everything associated with it. In a simple sense postmodernists have attempted to deconstruct any tight definitions or academic theories which might be associated or even popular within modernity. More precisely if modernity can loosely be taken to refer to a number of Western social, economic and political forms which were brought into being from at least the eighteenth century, then postmodernism refers to a reaction and dissolution of those very same forms such as Marxism, Christianity, capitalism, Fascism, liberal democracy and feminism.[1]

According to one writer postmodernism refers to a general social condition characteristic of the economically advanced societies, a condition which came into being during the twentieth century but accelerated dramatically during the 1970s and 1980s.[2] Yet it would be a mistake to think of postmodernism as simply a time period or a phase of development beyond modernity since one cannot make sense of any postmodernist intervention in this way. Many have suggested that postmodernity is a case of modernity coming to terms with itself, a realisation of the grand hopes and failures born out of 1960s politics, a postmodern condition emancipated from false consciousness, a condition which for postmodernists is based on a realism and frustration which has been born out of the political struggles of the past thirty or forty years. Above all else postmodernism, in this sense of the term, has developed out of a reaction to the 1960s.[3]

For many postmodernism is not just a historical period or phase of development but also a critique or a comment about contemporary scholarship. In many ways postmodernist style is just a matter of choosing your own definitions or concepts and disputing that which had gone before. These challenges are endless and include: a rejection of grand theory; a rejection of any methodological conventions; a dismissal of policy recommendations; a rejection of any knowledge claims which obscured postmodernist versions of the truth and a rejection of any rigid disciplinary boundaries. For postmodernists any conventions, tight definitions or a taxonomy of academic disciplines were dismissed as being remnants of a failed modernity. Beneath all this sound and fury lay a genuine anxiety. An anxiety which was rooted within a fear for the future and despair from the past. For such people not only was faith in the future in short supply but also the state of the present was so grim that they called into question the intrinsic social, cultural, political and economic value systems of Europe, the United States of America and the former Union of Soviet Socialist Republics. Indeed the whole question of progress or modernism was subjected to an intense interrogation.[4]

The issues are complex and amongst both the critics and supporters of postmodernism there is a considerable degree of conceptual confusion. On the one side there are self-confessed non-sociologists like Foucault and Baudrillard whose respective positions suggest that the conditions of existence of the social and human sciences is precarious. On the other side sociologists such as Touraine and Giddens acknowledge the presence of fundamental problems confronting both modernity and the discipline of sociology. For sociologists such as Giddens and Touraine the question of postmodernity remains peripheral while for others such as Bauman postmodernity has to be placed firmly on the sociological agenda.

Any initial overview might view postmodernism as being attached to at least three different movements: (i) a style or mood born out of a reaction and dissatisfaction with modernism in art and literature; (ii) a trend in French philosophy or more specifically within post-structuralist theory; and (iii) the latest cultural and political age which is seen to be a product of some sort of shift in world history and the collapse of grand systems which are designed to explain and resolve everything. Yet the idea of the postmodern is by no means a new development within sociological discourse. In the late 1950s C. Wright-Mills commented upon the modern age being succeeded by a post-modern period; Daniel Bell made several critical references to the developments in the 1960s of a post-modern temper while Peter Berger briefly used the term in connection with the idea of modernity having 'run its course'.[5]

In the first instance contemporary critical discussion has tended to be dominated by such figures as Francois Lyotard, Jean Baudrillard, Michel Foucault and Jacques Derrida. For instance, Jean Francois Lyotard is perhaps best known for a memorable feat of succinctness, his three-word definition of postmodernism 'incredulity towards meta-narratives'.[6] In addition there has been an ever present concern over the need to reconsider the focus or object of sociological inquiry in the light of the impact of a range of parallel changes in society and/or the social. The question is do these manifestations point to the existence of a postmodern condition in which the grand narratives or foundations of modern knowledge have been eroded, if not displaced, and the objects of investigation transformed by a new social and economic moment? More recently Lyotard has expanded upon a subtle relationship between the right to speak and the duty to announce. It is suggested that if our speech announces nothing then it is doomed to repetition and consequently the conservation of existing meanings. In his own words Lyotard's project is to find ways of saying the unsayable, resisting the urge to totalise and unify and 'not to supply reality but to invent allusions to the conceivable which cannot be represented'.[7] If Lyotard was confusing then Baudrillard hardly faired any better. When asked to define the new wisdom the reply was: 'I cannot explain and will not explain. Post-Modernism for me is nothing. I don't worry about this term. I am very exhausted with this Post-Modernism. All that I will say is that Post-Modern maybe is Post-Modern.'[8]

At first postmodernism had a distinctly European presence. A presence which may at one level have seemed insignificant and yet at another level it marked a distinct shift from the artistic style and critical discourse of the 1960s. A period which had been overtly influenced by American thinking. By the 1980s it was European artists and theorists who were at the forefront of the postmodern condition. While some of the seminal critics of both modernity and postmodernism were non-Europeans, in the last instance the postmodernist intervention and the response to it, was essentially led by non-Americans.[9]

In the philosophy of Alasdair MacIntyre one finds a hostile critique of not just an atomised and privatised way of life, but also modernity itself.[10] At first sight it would be easy to associate much of this writer's thinking with the left, but MacIntyre distances himself from both the left and Marxism, a philosophy which he refers to as 'one of the games played by children of the bourgeiosie'. This dismissal of the Marxist critique of modernity stems from a fundamental contradiction identified by MacIntyre. He sees Marxists both condemning capitalism as morally bankrupt yet at the same time considering advanced bourgeois social formations as containing many of the prerequisites of a truly human socialist society. If modernity or late twentieth-century capitalism is composed of individuals who are acquisitive, self-seeking and morally deficient then where are the human resources for the creation of a good postmodern order?

This critique of modernity is also critical of utilitarian philosophy which is equally guilty of failing to provide either a rational foundation or an acceptable morality from which any potential postmodern order might emerge. For MacIntyre, the modern self is an individual who has been totally desocialised and dehistoricised. The apparent answer to this malaise is to return to premodernity for a classical view of ethics and the self. Within the classical tradition the self is a socially and historically rooted being with given obligations. It is only through an understanding of the total human nexus in which one moves that the virtues of identity can be confronted. Progress from modernity, argues the writer, can only be achieved if the emotive, fragmented individual undertakes a unifying quest which is rooted in an adequate sense of the traditions to which one belongs. Here I am, what I am and self can only be realised as a virtue of a particular human nexus as the child of these parents, as a member of this village, community or nation.[11]

It is not difficult to see why postmodernist thinkers might be attracted to this particular philosophy. Like MacIntyre, postmodernists have questioned the superiority of the present over the past and the modern over the premodern. Some postmodernists look with nostalgia on the past and particularly upon the self-managing, self-reproducing popular culture of premodern times.

The emotional, the sacred, the particular, the traditional, the religious sentiment and the personal experience are all elements which would attract postmodernist thinkers to the work of Alasdair MacIntyre. Furthermore several postmodern social scientists have supported a re-focusing on what has often been taken for granted, or what has been forgotten, indeed on anything that the modern age has failed to understand in any particular detail. A basis for this has often meant a return to the ancient and premodern.

Ancient sport symbols, nostalgia, and postmodernism

When compared with other traditions of social thought which have informed research agendas on sport and leisure, the post-modern influence has been relatively limited. However, in Slowi-kowski's insightful examination of the Olympic flame ceremony, and other ancient sport symbols, several postmodern concerns are clearly evident.[12] A classical concern with ancient and premodern Greece, the contemporary images of ancient Greek sport symbols and the collective nostalgia and emotion evoked by the Olympic flame ceremony at the opening of the modern Olympic Games are all genuine terrain for the postmodernist. Since postmodern memory asserts that there is no special value in the new, and that all modern representation is fraudulent, then it is not surprising to find a nostalgia and romanticism over the classical past as a particular critical theme in Slowikowski's research.[13]

Rooted in antiquity, the ancient Olympic flame ceremony was closely connected with ancient beliefs and practices concerning sun-worship, purification and the search for the truth. As a tradition within the modern Olympic Games, Slowikowski suggests, the antiquity of the ancient torch symbol confers a degree of import-ance and classicism upon the modern Olympic Games which sur-passes the original significance of the object itself.[14] For that which is associated with the ancient and premodern is deemed to be far more authentic than any modern form of popular culture. The primitive and the ancient are seen to be closer to the truth and yet many of the symbols of the golden age are brought alive in the present from the moment one catches sight of the Olympic flame or the Olympic torch runner.

A further link with the premodern is communicated through the Olympic vegetation crop, or laurel leaves, which often adorns the necks of victorious Olympic athletes as they stand on the medal rostrum. Here Slowikowski argues that the postmodern athletic vegetation crop is a bridge to a displaced meaning and, as such, the vegetation-crowning ceremonies tell us not who we are but who we wish we were.[15] They serve as a contemporary expression of a postmodern concern over the role of tradition and whether a return to romantic nationalism, neo-classicism, or whatever else, serves as either a philosophically viable critique of modernity or simply as a means through which we commune with the mythical links of our ancient Greek past.

Despite the general rejection of grand theory and history, the pursuit of postmodernism has often involved a search for authenticity by looking for roots and connections in the past. In modern popular culture Greek athletic symbols are often popularised and institutionalised thus defining in *our* terms not only who the ancients were but who we would like to be. Postmodernists would have us believe that such motifs as the Olympic torch, the vegetation crop and sporting versions of Greek vases embellished with black Greek athletic running figures give millions access to an era which in many other ways remains inaccessible.

It is not as if such romantic associations with the past are viewed within the social and political context of the premodern era. The search for authenticity is undertaken not just because post-modernists want to say certain things about classicism and roman-ticism, but more importantly, the search for authenticity serves as a critique of modern assumptions about *the truth*. Almost all post-modernists reject the quest for truth because such a goal or ideal is viewed as the epitome of modernity. Truth is viewed as an Enlightenment value and subject to dismissal on these grounds alone. Truth makes claims to order, rules, values, logic, rationality and reason, all of which are questioned in the postmodern critique of modernity.[16]

One of the fundamental feelings associated with a multitude of sporting ceremonies is nostalgia. Collective nostalgia has often been described as a condition in which symbolic objects or tradi-tions become highly public and widely shared. The Olympic flame ceremony is but one symbolic object which triggers collective nostalgia, romantic feelings and emotions about a premodern era. Yet it would be wrong to argue that what it signifies is a form of postmodern representation. While the romantic and emotional is valued, the notion of any type of representation is alien to most postmodern thinkers. They argue that representations are but distortions. More specifically, modern representation is perverse, artificial, mechanical, incomplete, fraudulent and wholly inadequate for a postmodern age.

While it might be inappropriate to place a specific postmodern label upon the work of Slowikowski, her research on ancient sport symbols, ancient Greek culture and the modern Olympic Games has served as a basis for highlighting a number of postmodern themes. Five particular postmodern concerns are to be found in her work: (i) a suggestion that we have moved beyond modernity and that the boundaries between old and new images have been effaced; (ii) that postmodernity can be identified as a product of some sort of shift in world history – a shift which, in part, involves a rejection of grand systems which claim to explain everything; (iii) the search for the authentic and the process by which ancient symbols are transformed into postmodern images; (iv) a concern with feelings, emotions and nostalgia for a premodern era which can be used as critique of the supposedly harsh, uncaring, unromantic modernity; and (v) a close affinity for American versions of Cultural Studies.

Scarcity, seriousness and the elevation of play

Not only is modernity viewed as being uncaring, harsh and unromantic but it is also deemed to be 'serious' and lacking a play element in its culture. Consequently a particularly strong theme within the post-1970s aesthetics of production has been the elevation of play, pleasure and a regime of desire.[17] A further theme which is worthy of mention is the idea that a postmodern condition or a postmodern social order would produce the possibility of a post-scarcity system in which the quest for excitement, pleasure and leisure would be a distinct possibility. For those familiar with the sociology of leisure debates from the 1970s, both of these themes must seem like old wine in new bottles.

During the early 1970s Daniel Bell heralded the emergence of a post-industrial society which would be radically different from what he saw as nineteenth-century capitalist society and twentieth-century industrial society.[18] The traditional capitalist from business and commerce was to be replaced by a new technical professional class. The concept of post-industrial society was not a picture of a complete new social order but an attempt to explain significant transformations in the social structure of the existing advanced industrial nations. The scientist, mathematician, computer technologist and economic theorist were to form the basis of what Bell called a 'distinct knowledge' class.

As with other theses proclaiming the demise of capitalism, the concept of a post-industrial society assumed the decline of manual labour, the rapid growth of white collar posts and a greater expenditure on higher education, research and development. The production of technology and theoretical knowledge was to give rise to a new social structure. It would also transform a capitalist formation which was seen to be dominated by the large scale production of goods. For Bell and others the promise of the post-industrial order was that it contained the possibility of moving beyond a concern for crude material goods and returning to a genuine debate over the nature of good society.[19]

While Marxists warned of the constraints, totalitarianism and one-dimensional nature of any society dominated by technology, post-industrial theorists promised the end of scarcity and an increase in leisure time for all. The end of scarcity theme postulated that a major change would occur in the relationship between work and reward. Thus, argued Bell, for the first time people would be faced with the real permanent problem of an increase in leisure time secured by the advancement of science and compound interest.[20] In other words, technological efficiency would result in what Jenkins and Sherman, amongst others, referred to in the 1980s as the leisure shock.[21]

The post-scarcity theme has more recently been discussed within the context of a move beyond modernity, a move beyond capitalism and a move towards postmodernism. The continual pursuit of capital accumulation is an activity which postmodernists associate with modernity. A pursuit which it is argued cannot continue forever since capitalist accumulation is not self-sustaining in terms of finite resources. A post-scarcity system, contends Giddens, would necessitate a global redistribution of wealth, significant alterations in modes of social life and a realism towards the rates of potential economic growth.[22] Various concerts involving artists, musicians and sports people are often cited as an indicator of mass popular support for a move towards helping developing nations and modern global crises such as famine and AIDS. Several leisure forms have been implicated in various moves to raise a general awareness and consciousness about First World greed and the consequences for global welfare. Some postmodernists tend to argue that not only is there a potential for a post-scarcity system but also that socialised economic organisation on a world scale is a possibility within a caring postmodern order.

The end of scarcity, and the pleasure from leisure, are both compatible with a further theme to be found in postmodern aesthetics. The postmodern construction of pleasure and the elevation of the importance of play serves as a further critique of modernity which is seen to be serious and lacking any impulse for play.[23] Beneath these endless postmodern assaults on modernist traditions lies the belief that a reassertion of the play element in human culture can be used to dethrone the seriousness of modernity. For example, postmodern thought would argue that some people's desire to collect travel experiences is but a comment on the seriousness of modernity. A reaction to a lost play element. There is much in Huizinga's conception of play that postmodern aesthetics would warm to.[24] Most importantly, Huizinga identified disinterestedness and freedom as two distinctive aspects of the play element in human culture. Huizinga saw the play element in Western civilisation as involving a variety of utilitarian functions. For postmodernists, play tends to become an end in itself. Play in itself suffices on the grounds that it is intrinsically satisfying.

Several criticisms could be levelled against these aspects of a postmodern order characterised in part by a post-scarcity system, a decline in seriousness, pleasurable leisure and the elevation of the play element in human culture. Yet rather than repeat the critiques of the 1970s we should like to limit ourselves to two fairly crucial observations. While the principles behind the redistribution of wealth, a concern for global welfare, pleasure from leisure and the elevation of play are all worthy concerns, the reality of the present is that such goals, at least in the early 1990s, remain utopian. In the United States of America, race riots in Los Angeles during May 1992 highlighted the poverty and frustration that remain nearly twenty-five years after Martin Luther King spoke of his dream. In the divided United Kingdom a British electorate arguably voted through their pockets and returned a Conservative majority at the general election of April 1992. Such events and an escalating gap between rich and poor both within and between many nations are not the healthiest of indicators upon which to proclaim the promise of change; a change centring upon a post-scarcity system, a decline in seriousness, an elevation of the importance of play and leisure or the economically advanced societies of the Western world saying enough is enough in terms of capital accumulation.

What needs emphasizing again and again is that the politics of postmodernism and the demand side of postmodernism are both closely associated with particular politics and particular lifestyles of the post-1960s era. The demand side of postmodernism is deeply rooted amongst people born in the late 1950s, 1960s and beyond, people who take for granted not only coloured television and yuppie suburban lifestyles, but also abundant recreational facilities. If one bought into it, the consumption of postmodern culture was/is essentially a game in which the one with the most toys won. The politics of postmodern art is often closely associated with the Thatcher years in Britain and the Reagan years in America. Indeed MacIntyre's assertion that Marxism was the game played by children of the bourgeoisie might be more appropriately targeted at many postmodernists.[25] Only recently have some postmodern artists worked out a distinct approach to the themes of unemployment, poverty, inequality and other blind spots of Conservative Britain and a Republican America.

Disneyland, hyper-reality and deconstruction

In Hollywood, Disneyland and the culture of the yuppies, Baudrillard's vision of America expresses a much broader discontent with Republican America under Reagan. Seeking a source of hope in postmodern America the high-priest of postmodernism finds none. It is condemned as a country without hope.[26] In stark contrast to the political intelligence of President J. F. Kennedy, former President Ronald Reagan is viewed as the sorcerer of a triumphal illusion, the magician of a tranquil, uneasy, unreal life in which postmodern America is but a hyper-reality of the real thing. Civilisation within this polity is seen to be non-existent, a cultural desert in which nothing is authentic or worth salvaging. Despite this emptiness, Baudrillard's message is simply that European aesthetics and culture cannot survive in the face of American domination.

It is not surprising that the leisure citadels of Hollywood and Disneyland bear the brunt of this writer's cryptic pen. For Baudrillard, Disneyland is authentic because it does not attempt to be real while everything outside of this leisure palace, which is reputed to be real, is in fact imagery or simulacrum.[27] Disneyland is presented as imaginary in order to suggest that the world outside is real whereas what the writer is actually saying is that all of Los Angeles and indeed the surrounding United States of America is no longer real but simulated and hyper-real. While many Marxists have deconstructed the Disneyland myth and tried to expose its ideological functions, Baudrillard's riposte to this approach is to argue that there is nothing to choose from between the self-deceiving attitude of the cultural critics on the left and those who champion the voluntarist, pleasurable dimensions of the Disneyland experience. Both are condemned as theorists attempting to reinforce yet another mythical message which claims to be the truth.

By transforming the whole of the United States of America into an empty desert of hyper-reality Baudrillard chose to focus his attention purely on the stereotypes, images and symbols which both insiders and outsiders have of America and Americans. The term hyper-reality is coined to refer to the collapsed reality of modernity and the model of illusion and simulation that has replaced it. Baudrillard's America excludes racial tension, crime, poverty, baseball, religious fundamentalism and SuperBowl mania. It includes the hyper-reality of images, icons, signs, faces, simulations, and illusions which are regularly presented through television, cinema, electronic billboards and even motel graffiti. Leisure spaces and recreation environments are reduced to being sites of consumption and simulation.[28] Reality has been replaced by words and images with the signifiers becoming both the bedrock of postmodern America and the symbols of a romantic protest against the complexities of the modern world.

Deconstruction and hyper-reality are but two of the keys to understanding Baudrillard's texts. The deconstruction of hyper-reality is, in the first instance, rooted in the deconstruction of reality. The notion of deconstruction is as close as one gets to outlining any sort of postmodern method of investigation. The goal of deconstruction is simply to undo all constructions of reality, tear texts apart and consequently reveal all the assumptions and contradictions inherent within the modern world.[29] Deconstruction is avowedly, intentionally and intensely subjectivist and anti-objectivist. It is extremely difficult to criticise a deconstructive argument or method simply because no clear viewpoint is expressed other than openness. As a general method it would appear to entail finding an exception to any generalisation and pushing this exception to the limit so that the generalisation and ultimately reality seem to be absurd. The exception eventually undermines the reality and in turn becomes hyper-reality itself.[30] The distinctions between reality and unreality become blurred and consequently hyper-reality emerges as a copy for which there is no original. Thus the leisure citadels of Disneyland and Hollywood symbolise, for Baudrillard, the desert of American culture which is neither real nor unreal but hyper-real.

As for questions of power and social transformations, they no longer matter within the postmodern scheme of social order. Power is no longer the result of cause and effect – nor is it tied to the material relations of production – but rather it is tied ambiguously to the cybernetic systems of mass communication. Real power is seen to be replaced by dead power which inhabits and dominates postmodern society.[31] The simulated dead power of postmodernity is, for postmodernists, seen to be everywhere and yet having no centralised locus or position. As for the social distribution of power Baudrillard sees no difference between those who enforce power and those who submit to it.[32] Given the ubiquitous ambiguity of power within a postmodern social order the same writer sees the search for either the maintenance or the overthrow of any existing power relations as completely futile.[33] Hence by sketching a transition from a capitalist productivist society to a cybernetic order the vision of the future is reduced to a vision of a postmodern populace engulfed by an all consuming nihilism and meaningless.

Concluding thoughts

Even if one accepts that modernism no longer holds the promise of aesthetic, cultural or political transformation, it is far too easy to be fooled by the promise of postmodernism. Because it operates outside the parameters of conventional wisdom in the social sciences, it is viewed by some as being progressive and yet for others it is a diametrically opposed phenomenon. Neither Marxists, feminists or socialists who turn to postmodernism are likely to be completely satisfied. The modern world remains fragmented, chaotic and uncertain but to speak of a postmodern era is perhaps a bit premature.

Those on the right who favour postmodern influences tend to do so not because of its political relevance but because of certain strands within some aspects of postmodern thinking such as deregulation, increasing individual freedom of choice, the dismantling of the welfare state and its anti-state and anti-bureaucratic stance. Those on the right who tend to criticise postmodernism tend to view it as being decadent, amoral, opportunistic, hedonistic, disruptive and even a refuge for disillusioned Marxists.[34]

Those on the left who favour postmodern thinking tend to emphasize those aspects which are closest to Marxist or Neo-Marxist traditions of social and political thought. Neo-Marxists have been drawn to the anti-state, anti-hierarchy, and anti-centralisation aspects of postmodern thinking. Some have suggested that postmodernism is constructive because it alerts the left to some of the weaknesses in its own assumptions. For example, deconstruction for some classical Marxists is viewed as having a left political content which is capable of destabilising assumptions about the status quo in several areas. Those who are critical of postmodernism tend to reject it on a number of grounds such as idealism, lack of objectivism, relativism and as a modern form of utopian thinking. Marxists would clearly have problems with postmodernism's anti-theoretical, anti-historical stance.

While a number of general criticisms might be levelled at different aspects of postmodern thought a number of specific fundamental problems seem to exist with postmodernism in general.[35] Although the history of the concept might be traced back to at least the 1960s there is still no general agreed meaning of the term postmodern. The list of characteristics inherent within postmodern culture is constantly shifting and although the term has increased its currency value since the 1980s the debates that cut across literature, architecture, art, pop music, film, television and sport, are far from coherent or even uniform. There is a problem of theory or anti-theory as the case may be. While accepting the view that the sociology of knowledge is but an accumulative product of time and place, it is difficult to accept the epistemological relevance of postmodernism when no epistemological relevance of postmodernism exists other than, deconstruction, anti-theory and a frustration with the failing promise of the 1960s. Postmodernism tends to collapse important questions of periodisation and history and as such any account which fails seriously to take account of social and cultural history must ultimately be prone to the charge of presenting a detached representation of reality.[36] It would appear that the idea of a new postmodern era in either sociology or history must for the time being be rejected and yet none of this means that postmodernism is likely to disappear.

Certainly the emergence of a global order is no longer as utopian as it was during the pre-1960s era, however global alliances are continually under threat. Nationalist tensions and conflicts are but one source of unrest which currently undermine any notion of global order, global harmony or even a global co-ordinated polity. Such tensions may be crudely divided into two categories. Firstly, those tensions which directly relate to problems of nationality.[37] These may be about nations seeking to establish and strengthen lost sovereignty – Lithuania, Georgia, Scotland, Estonia; or looking to achieve independence for the first time in modern history – Wales, or attempts to extend existing degrees of autonomy – Catalonia, the Ukraine; or concerns over civil rights of minority groups such as the Germans in the South Tyrol, the Slovenes in Austria, the Hungarians in Transylvania and Slovakia.

Secondly, those tensions which directly relate to existing frontiers or demarcation lines and generally include disputes between governments. While the Helsinki agreements (Helsinki Final Act of 1975) bind all European states not to attempt to change existing borders, except by mutual agreement, the potential for conflict is forever present. In the West, such conflicts might include those over Northern Ireland. In Eastern and Southern Europe there is the reluctance of the United Germany to recognise Poland's Western frontier the Oder-Neisse Line. The Macedonia question forms a deeply buried Doomsday machine under Bulgaria and Greece, while in the Caucasus the tensions between Armenia, and Azerbaijan are about frontiers, minorities, nationality and religion all at once.

Postmodernism has hardly touched the Islamic countries, Asia or Latin America while modernism is always vulnerable to its enemies and in a perennial need for radical renewal. Europe, and indeed large sections of the world, during the early 1990s is a very different place from that which existed at the start of the 1980s or the postmodern decade. It is perhaps more meaningful to talk of postmodernism as a phase in the development of a more radicalised modernity. Such a position is capable of exposing some of the basic tensions and contradictions within modern institutions while at the same time rejecting the anti-theoretical, anti-historical stance implicit within postmodernism. It is precisely this approach which Giddens adopts in his comparison of some of the key differences between Post-Modernity and Radicalised Modernity and which is presented in Table 1 merely as a summary of some of the key issues which have been central to much of the thinking around postmodernism in the social sciences.[38]

Table 1 A Comparison of Conceptions of 'Postmodernity' and 'Radicalised modernity'

Postmodernity	Radicalised modernity
1 Understands current transitions in epistemological terms or as dissolving epistemology altogether.	Identifies the institutional developments which create a sense of fragmentation and dispersal.
2 Focuses upon the centrifugal tendencies of current social transformations and their dislocating character.	Sees high modernity as a set of circumstances in which dispersal is dialectically connected to profound tendencies towards global integration.
3 Sees the self as dissolved or dismembered by the fragmenting of experience.	Sees the self as more than just a site of intersecting forces; active processes of reflexive self-identity are made possible by modernity.
4 Argues for the contextuality of truth claims or sees them as 'historical'.	Argues that the universal features of truth claims force themselves upon us in an irresistible way given the primacy of problems of a global kind. Systematic knowledge about these developments is not precluded by the reflexivity of modernity.
5 Theorises powerlessness which individuals feel in the face of globalising tendencies.	Analyses a dialectic of powerlessness and empowerment, in terms of both experience and action.
6 Sees the 'emptying' of day-to-day life as a result of the instrusion of abstract systems.	Sees day-to-day life as an active complex of reactions to abstract systems, involving appropriation as well as loss.
7 Regards co-ordinated political engagement as precluded by the primacy of contextuality and dispersal.	Regards co-ordinated political engagement as both possible and necessary, on a global level as well as locally.
8 Defines postmodernity as the end of epistemology/the individual/ ethics.	Defines postmodernity as possible transformations moving 'beyond' the institutions of modernity.

Source: A. Giddens, *The Consequences of Modernity*, Cambridge, Polity Press, 1990, p. 150.

While the postmodern intervention is likely to be present for a while it is difficult to see any consensus or even a political agenda emerging from postmodern politics. Certainly as far as the sociology of sport or leisure is concerned the question of postmodernism must remain a question and not an answer. While Guilianotti's work on Scottish football fans in Italy in 1990 clearly illustrates that aspects of postmodern thinking have some explanatory significance, many would suggest that postmodernism as epistemology has lost its way.[39] Undoubtedly the issue of a transformation of modernity has crystallised a number of fundamental problems for the sociology of sport and leisure but whether postmodernity is the most appropriate term to capture and explain such problems remains questionable.

A brief glance at the sociology of knowledge would also indicate that, like many other emerging epistemologies of the past, postmodernism in the 1980s sought to replace that which had gone before. The new generation of gurus lead by Baudrillard, Derrida, Lacan, Lyotard and others spoke in strange oaths. The new ways sought to replace the existing gatekeepers of knowledge with their new speak. The unspeakable new language and thinking of postmodernism was spoken. New professors of elitism could now go to dinner parties, talk only about *Telly Addicts*, *Batman*, and *Film X*, and not be put down by bossy show-offs who professed to an intimate knowledge of what they defined as high culture. But then, all the upsurge of postmodern activity stopped as if it had lost its way. It had made itself unintelligible, it had no common core values and therefore was prone to universal abandonment. So postmodernism remains at one and the same time both a critique of modernity while being in a mess itself. In short postmodernism seems to have suffered from a collapse of consensus over what constitutes postmodernism while at the same time signalling that modernity itself has shifted and disintegrated.

NOTES AND REFERENCES

1 Postmodernism tends to challenge all global, totalistic, all encompassing views be they political, religious or social. A wide variety of introductory articles and texts is available. See in particular R. Boyne and A. Rattansi (eds) *Postmodernism and Society*, London, Macmillan, 1990; M. Featherstone, 'In Pursuit of the Postmodern: An Introduction', *Theory, Culture and Society*, 1988, Vol. 5, pp. 195–215; A. Giddens, *The Consequences of Modernity*, Cambridge, Polity Press, 1990;

P. M. Rosenau, *Postmodernism and the Social Sciences: Insights, Inroads and Institutions*, Princeton, Princeton University Press, 1992; and B. Smart, *Postmodernity*, London, Routledge, 1992.

2 The argument put forward by Bauman is that postmodernity in essence is modernity coming to terms with itself. While many of the characteristic features of modern social life and thought have more or less been there from the beginning, the implications of modernity have only recently become more apparent. Postmodernism then is merely a current phase of a modernist tradition. See A. Bauman, *Intimations of Post Modernity*, London, Routledge, 1991.

3 This point is developed fully in T. Gitlin, 'Postmodernism defined at last', *Utne Reader*, 1988, July/August, pp. 52–9.

4 This rather dismal contribution to the postmodern debate took place in nearly every discipline. Politicians on both the right and the left grew in arrogance, the cold war warriors flexed their muscles, fundamentalist preachers gathered their flocks while many writers, intellectuals and artists lost confidence in the past, foresaw gloom in the future and prophesised the doom of civilisation.

5 See R. Billington, S. Strawbridge, L. Greensides and A. Fitzsimons (eds) *Culture and Society*, London, Macmillan, 1991, pp. 172–94. This division has relied upon the discussion by B. Smart 'On the order of Disorder of Things: Sociology, Postmodernity and the End of the Social' in *Sociology*, 1990, no. 24 (3), pp. 397–416.

6 See P. Aspden 'Saying the unsayable in silence', *The Times Higher Education Supplement*, 1993, 26 February, p. 2.

7 ibid, p. 2.

8 See Helen Fielding 'Teach yourself post-modernism', *The Independent on Sunday*, 1992, 15 November, pp. 21–2.

9 The seminal postmodern critics of the 1980s with the rather questionable exception of Charles Jencks and Frederick Jameson, were not Americans. This was in stark contrast to the 1960s and 1970s during which time a US hegemony had a distinct influence upon artistic debate and fashion both in Europe and the United States of America.

10 This discussion of MacIntyre has tended to limit itself to a consideration of A. MacIntyre, *After Virtue*, Duckworth, London, 1981.

11 For a concise but critical discussion of MacIntyre's postmodern philosophy, see R. Turnbull and C. Beveridge, 'Towards Postmodernism: An Introduction to MacIntyre', *Cencrastus*, 1988, Autumn, no. 31, pp. 1–10.

12 Slowikowski's critique of the way in which ancient Greek symbols are identified, mythologised and represented in the present is a reminder to those advocates of postmodern approaches which either reject social-totality or trans-historical explanation. See S. Slowikowski 'Ancient Sport Symbols and Postmodern Tradition' in R. Renson, M. Lammer, J. Riordan and D. Chassiotis (eds) *The Olympic Games Through the Ages: Greek Antiquity and it's Impact on Modern Sport*, Athens, Hellenic Sports Research Institute, 1991a, pp. 400–11.

13 See in particular S. Slowikowski 'Burning Desire: Nostalgia, Ritual and the Sport – Festival Flame Ceremony' in *Sociology of Sport Journal*,

1991b, vol. 8, no. 3, pp. 239–57; and S. Slowikowski 'Festivals and Culture in Ptolemaic Egypt', unpublished paper presented at the eighteenth annual North American Society for Sport History Conference, 1990, Banff, Alberta, Canada.

14 This remark specifically refers to the antiquity of the ancient torch symbol as it is used in contemporary modern Olympic Games. Drawing on the work of Hobsbawm and Ranger the writer is careful to recognise that in so far as there is reference to an historic past by invented traditions the peculiarity of invented traditions lies in the fact that their connection with the historic past or authentic culture is largely fictitious. See E. Hobsbawm and T. Ranger (eds) *The Invention of Tradition*, Cambridge, Cambridge University Press, 1983, pp. 1–14.

15 S. Slowikowski, 1991a, op. cit., p. 403.

16 This negation of truth is associated with the dark side of postmodern thought. The sceptics who speak of the immediacy of death, the demise of the subject and the impossible search for truth. A position which is rooted in a frustration with modernity and a belief that no social or political project is worthy of commitment.

17 R. Dunn 'Postmodernism, Populism, Mass Culture and Avant-Garde' in *Theory, Culture and Society*, 1991, vol. 8, no. 1, pp. 111–35.

18 D. Bell, *The Coming of Post-Industrial Society*, London, Penguin Books, 1976.

19 For a useful summary and critique of Daniel Bell, see A. Swingewood, *A Short History of Sociological Thought*, London, Macmillan, 1984, pp. 312–25; and A. Giddens, *Sociology*, Cambridge, Polity Press, 1989, pp. 648–56.

20 D. Bell, 1976, op. cit., p. 119.

21 C. Jenkins and B. Sherman, *The Leisure Shock*, London, Methuen, 1981.

22 The question of whether the notion of a post-scarcity system is a meaningful concept for contemporary modernity is considered in A. Giddens, *The Consequences of Modernity*, Cambridge, Polity Press, 1990, pp. 165–6.

23 This play impulse in postmodernism, argues Dunn, needs to be seen in relationship to the ascendency of entertainment values associated with mass culture. Postmodernists suggest that the goals of relaxation and fun associated with mass leisure often threaten to undermine or contaminate serious modern art. Whether this is the case or not, for postmodernists, the sense of purposelessness and enjoyment associated with play and leisure serves to undermine the high seriousness and deliberateness of modern art. See R. Dunn, op. cit., p. 120.

24 J. Huizinga, *Homo Ludens: A Study of the Play Element in Culture*, Boston, Beacon Press, 1955.

25 A. MacIntyre, 1981, op. cit.

26 J. Baudrillard, *America*, London, Verso, 1989, p. 117. This discussion of Baudrillard's America has drawn heavily upon two relatively recent reviews of this text. See A. J. Vidich, 'Baudrillard's America: Lost in the Ultimate Simulacrum', *Theory, Culture and Society*, 1991, vol. 8, no.

2, pp. 135–44 and N. K. Denzin, 'Paris, Texas and Baudrillard on America', *Theory, Culture and Society*, 1991, vol. 8, no. 2, pp. 121–33.

27 The term simulacrum simply refers to a copy of a copy from which no distinction can be made between the original and the model or the real and the unreal.

28 For one of the few pieces of work to evaluate the significance of the work of Baudrillard for the analysis of leisure, see C. Rojek, 'Baudrillard and Leisure', *Leisure Studies*, 1990, vol. 9, no. 1, pp. 7–20.

29 See P. M. Rosenau, 1992, op. cit., pp. 118–23.

30 Most postmodernists contend that there are no methods or rules of procedure to which they must conform. By rejecting the formal rules of social science methods postmodernists are essentially declaring that anything goes. As substitutes for scientific methods or ethnographies postmodernists tend to look for feelings, personal experience, empathy, emotion, intuition, subjective judgement and imagination. But the actual content of these terms and the methods involved remain vague and open to interpretation.

31 This discussion on power has drawn on the work of David Andrews 'Sport, Cultural Studies and Postmodernism: Some Observations on Baudrillard', *Working Papers in Sport and Society*, University of Warwick, 1992/93, no. 1, pp. 12–28.

32 This discussion of Baudrillard is to be found in D. Kellner, 'Postmodernism as Social Theory: Some Challenges and Problems', *Theory, Culture and Society*, 1988, vols 2–3, no. 5, pp. 246–52.

33 ibid, p. 249.

34 Such critics also view postmodernism as undermining customary, established family structure and traditional religious values. In the social sciences right-wing critics also see postmodernism as overthrowing traditional methods and research orientations without replacing them with anything else.

35 During the late 1980s the whole question of the dark side of the postmodern political orientation was brought to the public's attention by the Heidegger affair in Germany and the de Man affair in the United States of America. Both actively supported the Nazis while at the same time disguising or denying the extent of their involvement.

36 J. Wolff, 'Postmodern Theory and Feminist Art Practice' in R. Boyne and A. Rattansi (eds) op. cit., 1990, pp. 187–208.

37 N. Ascherson, 'Old Conflicts in the New Europe' in *The Independent*, 18 February 1990, pp. 6–10.

38 A. Giddens, *The Consequences of Modernity*, Cambridge, Polity Press, 1990. p. 150.

39 R. Giuliannotti, 'Scotland's tartan army in Italy: the case for the carnivalesque' in *Sociological Review*, 1990, vol. 39, pp. 503–27.

Chapter 10

Dependency and globalisation:
Sport, leisure and global processes

How is it possible to make sense of the global patterning of sport and leisure practices? The sheer variety of local practices seems to defy an attempt to record and catalogue them in their entirety. That is not our aim. Here, we have taken a different tack. Drawing on 'traditions' associated with dependency theory and 'globalisation' research, we intend to map and make sense of the place of culture within the context of global processes. We then locate sport and leisure practices with this broader global framework. We suggest that dominant, emergent and residual patterns of sport and leisure practices are closely intertwined with globalisation processes. Initially, we describe the form and dynamics of the global condition. Preliminary discussion of the global sport and leisure pattern is also undertaken. Specific attention is then given to the contribution of dependency theory and globalisation research.

Globalisation processes are not of recent origin. Nor have they occurred evenly across all areas of the globe. These processes – involving an increasing intensification of global inter-connectedness – are very long-term in nature.[1] Nevertheless, the more recent history of these processes would suggest that the rate of change is gathering momentum. Despite the 'unevenness' of these processes, it is more difficult to understand local or national experiences without reference to these global flows. The flow of leisure styles, customs and practices from one part of the world to another, 'long-haul' tourism and global events, such as music festivals and the Olympic Games, are examples of these processes at work.

Every aspect of social reality – people's living conditions, beliefs, knowledge and actions – is intertwined with unfolding globalisation processes. These processes include the emergence of a global economy, a transnational cosmopolitan culture and a range of inter-national social movements. A multitude of transnational or global economic and technological exchanges, communication networks and migratory patterns characterises this interconnected world pattern. Not only are people, and nation states, seen to be woven together in a tighter and deeper interdependency network. These globalisation processes are believed to be leading to a form of time- space compression. That is, people are experiencing spatial and temporal dimensions differently. Time and space are 'collapsed'. There is a speeding up of time and a 'shrinking' of space. Modern technologies enable people, images, ideas and money to criss-cross the globe with great rapidity. This leads, as noted, to a greater degree of interdependence, but also to an increased awareness of a sense of the world as a whole. People become more attuned to the notion that their lives and place of living are part of a single social space – the globe.

These themes can be illustrated, in preliminary form, with reference to the consumption of sports events and of leisure cloth-ing. Consider the example of ice-hockey. Citizens of countries spread across the globe regularly tune in by satellite broadcasts to National Hockey League (NHL) matches. In these games perform the best players drawn from North America, Europe and Asia. The players use equipment – sticks, skates, uniform, etc. – that is designed in Sweden, financed in Canada, assembled in Ohio, (USA) and Denmark. This is then sold on to a mass market in North America and Europe. This equipment – skates for example – is made out of alloys whose molecular structure was researched and patented in Delaware (USA) and fabricated in Japan. Several transnational corporations are involved in the production and consumption phases of this global cultural product.[2] The product screened to the consumer is itself provided by a global media-sport production complex and is viewed on a television that itself was manufactured as part of a global telecommunications network.[3]

The leisure wear industry can also be used to highlight how people's consumption of cultural goods is bound up with global processes. As a fashion item, the wearing of sports footwear has become an integral feature of consumer culture. One premier brand is Nike. The purchase and display of this footwear are but the final stages in a 'dynamic network' involving designers, producers, suppliers, distributors and the parent or broker company, in this case, Nike. Though its headquarters is located in Oregon, the range of sub-contractors involved straddles the globe. Its suppliers and production companies are located in different South-East Asian countries, Thailand, Singapore, Korea and Taiwan. Its designers attempt to provide shoes with a world-wide demand that will also appeal to local tastes. Local franchise operations ensure appropriate distribution backed by global marketing strategies. Here again, Nike uses the media-sport production complex by endorsing sports stars and/or sports leisure festivals. In addition, Nike use advertising within the television schedules that carry these sports and other programmes deemed appropriate. Similar processes are at work in other areas of fashion and the music industry.[4]

Several writers have identified key features of this global process. Anthony Giddens, for example, points to four interconnected features of the world-system. These are, the world capitalist economy; the nation-state system; the world-wide diffusion of modern technologies and the associated division of labour; and the emergence of a world military order.[5] To this list should be added the cultural dimension of globalisation processes. In a manner that shares some common ground with Giddens, Robertson also seeks to map what he terms the 'global field'. Concerned with the way the world is ordered, he highlights four main aspects of the global field. These are national societies; individuals or selves; relations between nation societies or the world system of societies and humankind. Each of these aspects is interconnected. According to Robertson, a probing of these interconnections helps map the 'global human-condition'.[6]

There are two important points that also need to be grasped. First, while the various aspects identified do interweave, they also retain a degree of relative autonomy from each other. There is no global strait-jacket. Second, the interweaving of these themes of societies, individuals, international relations and humankind do not follow any single inexorable path. Many different variants to the existing global pattern were possible in the past and the making of future global patterns is also open-ended and subject to different permutations.[7] Discussion of the stages or phases that are associated with this global process – and the position of leisure and sport developments within this broad process – is undertaken in the section dealing specifically with globalisation research.

Given this perceived growth in the multiplicity of linkages and networks that transcend nation-states, it is not surprising that some writers identify a concomitant development of 'transnational cultures' or indeed, a 'unitary global culture'.[8] This process is seen to entail a shift from ethnic or national cultures to 'supranational' forms based upon a 'cosmopolitan' communication and migrant network.[9] Whatever the merits of this conclusion – and it is subject to considerable debate – clearly cultures communicate, compete, contrast and conflict with each other in a more inderdependent manner than was previously the case.[10]

This intermingling and status competition between cultures occurs on a global scale and is patterned along five main dimensions or 'scapes'.[11] These are: 'ethnoscapes' that are produced by the international movement of people such as tourists, migrants, exiles and guest workers; the 'technoscapes' that are created by the flow between countries of the machinery and plant flows produced by corporations (transnational as well as national) and government agencies; the 'financescapes' that centre on the rapid flow of money and its equivalents around the world; the 'mediascapes' in which the flow of images and information between countries is produced and distributed by newspapers, magazines, radio, film, television and video; and finally, the 'ideoscapes' that are linked to the flow of ideas centrally associated with state or counter-state ideologies and movements.[12]

All five dimensions can be detected in late twentieth-century leisure and sports development. Thus, at the level of 'ethnoscapes' the global migration of professional sports personnel and artistic performers has been a pronounced feature of recent decades. It appears likely that this will continue to be so in the future. The flow across the globe of goods, equipment and 'landscape' and 'heritage' items (e.g. sports complexes, golf courses, works of art) has grown to the position of a multi-billion dollar business in recent years. As such, it represents a transnational development in the leisure and sports spheres at the level of 'technoscapes'. Regarding 'financescapes', clearly the flow of finance in the global leisure and sports arena has come to centre not only on the international trade in personnel, prize money and endorsements, but on the marketing of leisure and sport along specific lines, e.g. the Disneyfication of theme parks. The transformation of American sports such as basketball, baseball and American football into global sports is also part of this process.[13] Closely connected to these dimensions has been a development at the level of 'mediascapes'. This 'media-sport/leisure production complex' projects images of individual sports and arts labour migrants, leisure forms and specific cultural messages to large global audiences. The marketing of the opera singer Pavarotti or the pop singer Michael Jackson are examples of these processes at work. The pervasiveness of the media-leisure/sport-capital nexus, has forced a range of leisure practices, in 'local' places, to align themselves to this global model. Failure to do so would place in question their ability to survive in the global media-marketplace. At the level of ideoscapes, global sports festivals such as soccer's World Cup and the Olympics and music festivals such as Live Aid, have come to serve as vehicles for the expression of ideologies that are trans-national in character.

It was noted earlier that the main aspects of globalisation that Robertson identifies do retain a degree of relative autonomy. This is also seen to apply to these dimensions or 'scapes'. One additional point needs to be grasped however. In the interweaving of these 'scapes' there develop 'disjunctures'. That is, according to Appadurai, disjunctures causing a series of diverse, fluid and unpredictable global conditions and flows. Competing and distinctive cultures are thus involved in an infinitely varied, mutual contest of sameness and difference.[14] Global flows such as Europeanisation, Americanisation, Hispanicisation, Orientalisation and Africanisation intertwine in complex, unpredictable ways. Cultural diversity is emphasized in which 'Western' modernity is increasingly questioned, challenged and undermined. Not all observers of the global human condition agree with this assessment.[15] Though they concur that cultural interchange is a crucial area of investigation, a different portrayal of global culture is emphasized. Let us examine this issue with reference to consumer culture and leisure practices.

Consumer culture is associated with the rise of mass consumption in the late nineteenth and early twentieth century. This was accompanied by what Featherstone describes as a general reorganisation of symbolic production, everyday experiences and practices.[16] The central features of consumer culture as it developed entailed the availability of an extensive range of commodities, goods and experiences. These could be consumed, maintained, planned and dreamed about.[17] A crucial feature of this culture was (and is) the creation of an overproduction of signs and associated feelings. The production of this consumer culture is said to be formed through the economic and political domination of the United States. That is, the global consumer culture that now exists is said to involve an Americanisation process. The global media are seen to communicate signs, symbols, practices and cultural icons across the globe that are American in origin, content and ideology.

In analyses of the alleged Americanisation of 'British' culture, especially popular culture, attention has focused on the Americanisation evident in areas such as films, records, TV programmes, clothes, advertising and consumer products more generally. Several competing explanations have been offered but they tend to centre around the degree of individual 'choice' and the impact which Americanisation has on the indigenous culture as a whole. Concern over Americanisation is not new. As early as the 1890s, conservative social critics were making disparaging remarks regarding the visits of American tourists to Europe.[18] Significantly, such observations were occurring in a more general climate of concern regarding what conservative social critics, such as Spengler and Eliot, saw as a threat to 'high culture', namely the emergence of mass society. Writers such as Spengler equated 'mass society' with mediocrity and the atomisation of the 'masses', and argued that it rendered individuals susceptible to manipulation by those who controlled the mass media. It is perhaps not surprising that, following the First World War when American cultural products began to appear on the British scene, this development was seen by mass society theorists as symptomatic of a 'levelling down' of standards. Americanisation was the symbol of mediocrity.[19] As Chambers put it: 'America . . . clearly dominated images of leisure from the 1920s onwards'.[20] American influence was evident in several areas of popular culture, notably film, music and dance. During the late 1940s and 1950s, this 'foreign contamination' of popular culture in general was enhanced by the adoption of its more public manifestations by Britain's emerging youth subcultures. American rock-'n'-roll, in particular, was perceived to be a source of corruption, embodying all that was 'trash' in American culture.[21]

Significantly, criticism of Americanisation in the 1950s and 1960s was not confined to conservative cultural critics who saw such trends as a threat to the texture of authentic working-class culture as well. Here, American television programmes and consumer products were the source of concern.[22] During the 1960s, the concerns of the left began to be reinforced by the work of the Frankfurt school. Writers such as Adorno, Marcuse and Horkheimer launched powerful critiques against popular culture, equating it with consumerism and holding that it engendered 'false aspirations' and satisfied 'false needs'. These critiques share with mass-society theories the notion that the users of popular culture are 'cultural dupes'. Analyses of the culture industries employing critical theory have not overlooked the global impact of Americanisation on the mass media and popular cultural forms. Subsequent work has argued that the media are American and that this Americanisation constitutes a form of cultural imperialism.[23] By the late 1980s, what Collins describes as a 'moral panic' appears to have developed regarding the dominance of American programmes on European television schedules.[24] The icon of this dominance, to which the European Commission drew attention when criticising the impact of non-European television, was *Dallas*.

The alleged effects of Americanisation have, however, been challenged by several writers working within cultural studies. Kaplan, for example, argues that the Americanisation thesis contains within it an undifferentiated and over-simplified view of popular culture.[25] The receptivity of popular culture to American culture wares, she maintains, is both active and heterogeneous. Indeed, since these cultural wares contain no 'fixed ideological message', they can be reacted to differently by different national audiences.[26] Similarly, Hebdige rejects the idea of the 'homogenising influence of American culture'. In contrast, he argues that 'American popular culture offers a rich iconography, a set of symbols, objects and artefacts that can be assembled and re-assembled by different groups in a literally limitless number of combinations'.[27]

The work of Bigsby reinforces this position. He argues that, during cross-cultural diffusion, American culture 'suffers a sea-change', it 'assumes a new identity', and becomes, in effect, a 'superculture, a reservoir of shifting values'.[28] In arguing for the possibility of the emergence of a 'new identity', Bigsby is allowing for the capacity of individuals to reinterpret the American cultural product into something distinct. He further argues that Americanisation is an 'emblematic' not a causal source of change. Further, with regard to Americanisation, insufficient attention has been paid in the literature to the pleasure experienced in consuming American popular culture. That is, when distinctions are made between 'personalised consumption' and 'mass consumerism', the pleasure gained in the latter is seen as inauthentic and as in some way serving to endorse the system that produced it. In contrast,

Webster notes that the 'pleasure of the consumer is not exhausted in his or her contribution to record company profits'.[29] According to Ang, the images of American films and television programmes have become 'signs which no longer indicate something like Americanness but visual pleasure as well'.[30] Webster similarly remarks that American images do not just give pleasure: they signify pleasure. At their core, such issues reflect the debate regarding the portrayal of people and the balance of power between them and the global 'culture industries'.

There are several contentious issues here. These debates centre around questions of homogeneity and heterogeneity; unity and diversity; integration and fragmentation and universalism and particularism. Is the global condition understandable in terms of a single causal explanation, i.e. capitalism, Westernisation, or, more specifically, Americanisation – or is a multi-causal, interconnected set of processes involved? As will now be shown, dependency theory and globalisation research tend to reach different conclusions regarding the nature of the explanation offered and the conclusions reached concerning these issues.

Dependency and sport: Domination and resistance

In dependency research global cultural flows are seen to reflect the activities of representatives of nation states and/or 'multinational' corporations. These activities entail a form of domination of one culture over another. Issues of power, control and the ability of 'indigenous' people to interpret, understand and/or resist cultural manipulation and domination are central concerns. Significantly, the media, as we have just highlighted, are the most common focus for discussion. The idea of the 'invasion' of an indigenous culture by a foreign one is the commonest way of articulating the process involved.[31] Two main emphases can be identified in cultural imperialism accounts. In one, the focus is placed on a 'world' made up of a collection of nation states in competition with each other. One manifestation of this is 'Yankee imperialism', in which the task is to win the 'hearts and minds' of foreign people. This sentiment is evident in Klein's insightful study into baseball in the Dominican Republic.[32] Another approach views the 'world' as an integrated political-economic system of global capitalism. Here the focus is on the activities of multi- or transnational corporations. McKay and Miller fruitfully employ elements of this approach to examine Australian sport.[33] In this section we intend to review critically accounts of development and dependency literature and then see how this research has been applied to the study of sport and leisure practices.

The notion of dependency refers to a paradigm or set of paradigms in the sense that there is no one theory of dependency but several competing theories and explanations. Dependency research first gained impetus as a result of extensive Latin American debates on the problems of under-development.[34] The debate emerged as a direct reaction to the conventional ways in which economists, sociologists and political scientists had tended to treat the problems of developing societies. The dependency paradigm that subsequently emerged in the 1940s was a penetrating yet flawed critique of developmental theory, particularly of its implications for the Third World. Many people have attempted to define and chart the history of dependency theory.[35] Here we have selected several prominent schools of thought with a view to contrasting earlier and more recent approaches. More specifically, we shall refer to three broad schools of thought that influenced the debate until the initial disintegration of the dependency debate during the late 1970s. They are: (i) the early structuralist tradition of the United Nations Economic Commission for Latin America (ECLA); (ii) the Marxist-imperialist tradition that emerged in the 1960s; and (iii) the world system theorists who emerged in the later 1960s and 1970s.

A central catalyst in the foundation of many early dependency arguments was a group of economists who worked for ECLA between the late 1940s and 1960. The early structuralist position, as epitomised by the work of Raul Prebisch, who emphasized the part played by external factors in the underdevelopment of Latin America.[36] His early work suggested that Latin American underdevelopment was entirely due to its heavy reliance on the export of primary products in an international free trade market. Here, an unequal exchange value for raw materials worked against the interests of the Latin American economy. Every quantum of Latin American raw materials bought in return a small quantum of imports from the developed economic core of the industrial centre. Although the theory of unequal exchange value was not clearly expressed in Prebisch's early writings, he did view external issues as a key factor in explaining Latin American underdevelopment as early as 1950.

Early structuralism therefore attempted to present a theory of development that particularly emphasized the structural imbalances between the centre and the periphery. Dualism in this instance referred to the systematic, observable differences between the economic structure of the rich world in contrast to the economic structure of the poor world. The same analysis could equally be done at a regional, national or international level depending on the unit of analysis in each case. Prebisch concluded that underdevelopment was not the same as undevelopment or lack of development. Underdevelopment resulted from a specific process in which one part of the world developed at the expense of the other. The early work of ECLA under the guidance of Prebisch should not be underestimated. This initial, albeit economic, argument proved to be a useful catalyst or starting point for many subsequent dependency formulations. Yet, like many other dependency models, the early structuralist model never really managed to formulate an adequate theory of development. Unfortunately, the approach to development was invariably reduced to a one or two dimensional explanation. It was an approach that specifically stressed external factors and primarily viewed development and underdevelopment in terms of capital accumulation. Even within ECLA itself, there was a reaction against the view that dependency could be explained easily in terms of external factors.[37]

Unlike the early ECLA economists, Sunkel and Paz chose a broader inter-disciplinary approach.[38] For instance, they found a Marxist approach to imperialism a perfectly acceptable framework for explaining development while also arguing that such an approach tended to neglect what happens within countries subject to imperialism. Certainly they developed a wider socio-political and economic framework as opposed to a purely economic framework of analysis. For instance, commenting upon some of the external and internal class contradictions, Sunkel argued that foreign factors should be seen not as external.[39]

The 1960s and early 1970s writings of Sunkel certainly provide a more complex framework for understanding dependency and underdevelopment than that promoted by Prebisch and the early structuralists. Sunkel's work on transnational corporations, for instance, cuts through national boundaries and attempts to understand historical processes. Several criticisms can be offered of this approach from the vantage point of globalisation research. First, despite the development of a wider framework, Sunkel's analysis is still essentially economistic. Economic factors also are the major driving force behind Sunkel's approach to development. Secondly, like many other dependency theorists, Sunkel's analysis rests upon several dichotomies such as external and internal, development and underdevelopment, centre and periphery and integration and disintegration. These provide potential obstacles to understanding societies or even global systems as a complex web of dependent and interdependent people. This problem is immediately removed if one considers such terms as development and underdevelopment as referring to activities that are primarily carried out by people and because of domination and dependency that result from one group having greater power chances than the others. Finally, Sunkel reduces the activities of individual human beings to a matter of insignificance. It is essential to realise that social development occurs via the various meaningful but structurally located actions in which people engage.[40]

A more sociological contribution to the dependency paradigm came out of the Latin American Institute for Social Economic Planning (ILPES). Cardoso's work is often regarded as a classic example of dependency theory.[41] Both Cardoso and Faletto have argued that the notion of development used by many dependency theorists tended to be a reflection of the *Gemeinschaft/Gesellschaft* dichotomy developed by Ferdinand Tonnies.[42] They raised two points of concern: (i) that neither concept was broad enough to explain existing social situations, nor specific enough to distinguish between those structures that determine lifestyles, tastes and culture; and (ii) that both concepts failed to explain the various stages of economic development and the corresponding social structures that characterised traditional and modern social formations.

Cardoso explicitly refrained from formulating a new theory of dependency. He repeatedly rejected the idea that dependency theory should be thought of as a theory independent of Lenin's theory of imperialism.[43] In this sense, the work of both Cardoso and Faletto is similar to that of other Marxists such as Santos and Ray Mauro Marini. In order to explain the process of exploitation within the periphery, Marini introduced the concept of super-exploitation.[44] He also used the term 'superimperialism' in an attempt to translate Lenin's definition of imperialism to dependent capitalism. Dos Santos also argued that the concept of dependency capitalism should not be formulated outside an imperialist framework.[45] Dependency and imperialism were viewed as complementary terms by Dos Santos.

With regard to Latin America, Cardoso (1972) made the case for capitalist development taking place within a dependent situation.[46] This analysis began with the assumption that modern capitalism and imperialism differed from the explanation given by Lenin. Capital accumulation was seen to be more a consequence of corporate control as opposed to simply financial control. Monopoly capitalism and development, for Cardoso, were not necessarily contradictory terms in that dependent capitalist development had become a new form of monopolistic expansion into the Third World. However, this development was oriented towards a limited upper class type of market and society.

In moving towards a class model of dependency, Cardoso offered several criticisms of the existing dependency paradigm. These were: (i) that any analysis based on the naive assumption that imperialism unifies the reactions and interests of dominated nations is a clear oversimplification of what is really going on; (ii) that there was a need for historically grounded empirical studies of dependency; and (iii) that many static dependency theories were often misleading.[47] On the one hand, new trends in international capitalism resulted in an increased interdependence based upon production activities while, on the other hand, international capitalism also gained a disproportional influence within industry. This type of criticism led Cardoso to argue that dependency should be viewed, not as a separate external variable but as a variable within a system of relations among different social classes. Thus, like Gunder Frank and Dos Santos, Cardoso argued that dependency should be traced through the historical process as a form of class relations.[48]

There is much to commend in the work of Cardoso and Faletto. The emphasis upon social and political patterns of domination is a major advance, we believe, over the structuralist models formulated by Prebisch and the other ECLA economists. By emphasizing historically shifting patterns of development they promoted a more dynamic elucidation of dependency theory. In this way they highlighted the distinction to be made between dependency as a static, historical condition and dependency as a dynamic historical process. The concept of process promoted an analysis of the historically relevant factors through which a region or nation had become dependent. Like many Marxist accounts of dependency, the work of Cardoso could be said to be guilty of a form of economic determinism. That is, for Cardoso, the key driving force behind the analysis is to be found in a materialist explanation of development. One difficulty with such an approach is that it rests upon the adoption of the false conceptual dichotomy of base and superstructure. There are innumerable 'superstructural' relations that can be explained without necessarily adopting a Marxist-imperialist approach to dependency. As early as 1968, Dos Santos defined dependency as:

> a situation in which the economy of certain countries is condi-
> tioned by the development and expansion of another economy
> to which the former is subjected. The relation of inter-
> dependence between two or more economies, and between
> these and world trade, assumes the form of dependence when
> some countries expand and can be self-sustaining, while other
> countries can do this only as a reflection of that expansion.[49]

The above statement is often regarded as a classic definition of dependency. Yet, while Dos Santos did not alter his general position during the early 1970s, he did provide a somewhat broader approach to the problem of dependency and underdevelopment. Dos Santos' approach to dependency emerging during the early 1970s is often viewed as a new dependency theory. Dos Santos identified three different forms of dependence that affected Latin American development: (i) colonial dependence; (ii) financial-industrial dependence; and (iii) technological-industrial dependence.[50] Each of these forms of dependence was dominent during a particular historical epoch. The first form of dependency was characteristic of many of the dependency relations formed by colonial monopolies of land, mines and labour in conquered colonies. Financial-industrial dependence emerged during the latter part of the nineteenth century when heavy financial invest-ments were made by the advanced countries in the production of raw materials and agricultural products in the periphery. Finally, the third form of dependence appeared after the Second World War and developed as a result of technological dependence. It is this third form of dependence that is specifically referred to as the new dependence. The important point made by Dos Santos is that, while dependency should be thought of primarily as a form of imperial relations, these relations shifted and historically took on different forms.[51]

It is possible to include the earlier work of Frank within this broad group of Marxist dependency theorists who influenced the debate in the late 1960s and early 1970s.[52] While Cardoso, Faletto, Marini and Dos Santos all represented an approach that emphasized particular, concrete, empirical studies of dependency, Frank might be classified more appropriately as a world systems theorist in the sense that both his earlier and later works emphasize the need for a global analysis. The developmentalist perspective was replaced by a world perspective. Its fundamental unit of analysis is not a particular nation-state but the world as the only social system, a totality of geoeconomic, geopolitical and geocultural processes. Whether we are dealing with the history of the system as in Immanual Wallerstein's analysis, or whether our attention is primarily directed towards the economic predicament of a continent as in Frank's research, this basic global perspective is maintained throughout.[53]

The development of underdevelopment thesis that was expressed in Frank's earlier writing emphasized that commercial monopoly rather than feudalism and pre-capitalist economic forms was the essential factor by which national and regional metropolises exploited and appropriated economic satellites. This capitalism on a world-wide scale produced a developed metropolis and therefore an underdeveloped periphery. The same process, argued Frank, could also be identified as occurring within nations or between regions depending on the unit of analysis used. His central thesis focused on the contradictions that had emerged as a result of capitalism. Capitalism, it was argued, generated under-development in the peripheral satellites whose economic surplus was expropriated, while generating economic surplus and develop-ment in the metropolitan centres. While his earlier work revolved entirely around the metropolis-satellite model of expropriation of resources, his later work was concerned more with class links and structures.[54] The prime linkage between the dominant class of the metropole and the subordinate classes of the hinterland was the *lumpenbourgeoisie* or *comprador* class. This referred to the bour-geoisie of the underdeveloped societies who blocked or hindered regular capitalist social formation in the dependent countries. According to this view any class in a dependent country that collaborated with the capitalist metropole consequently became a tool of manipulation.

The crucial theoretical innovation proved to be the relational idea of core and periphery or metropolis and satellite. The division of labour that was integral to the emergence of capitalism in the sixteenth century, Frank argued, did not only create a class divide as Marx saw it. A division in the world economy between core areas or strong states and peripheral areas or weak states/stateless nations also occurred. This divergence of economic and political power was not simply a matter of relativity but was also relational. Capitalism, the argument goes, could only come into being by a parallel emer- gence of an interstate political system. The point is similar to the one made by Wallerstein when he argues that:

> Political empires are a primitive means of economic domina- tion. It is the social achievement of this modern world, if you will, to have invented the technology that makes it possible to increase the flow of the surplus from the lower strata to the upper strata, from the periphery to the centre, from the majority to the minority, by eliminating the 'waste' of too cumbersome a political superstructure.[55]

Consequently all states or areas cannot develop simultaneously. Development, it is argued, can only take place at someone else's expense. Frank maintains that capitalism functions through the mechanism of unequal exchange that maintains inequalities between the metropolis and satellite. While Cardoso, Faletto, Dos Santos and Marini all argue for concrete historical analysis of the periphery, world system theorists such as Frank and Wallerstein emphasize the need for a more holistic approach.

The main theme of world system centres on the dynamics of historical capitalism. The logic of capitalism permeates global pro- cesses. Several key elements of this approach can be identified. Dating from the sixteenth century onwards a 'world system' of com- merce and communication has developed. This world system has produced a series of economic and political connections based on the expansion of a capitalist world economy. For Wallerstein, the world capitalist economy is oriented around four sectors. The core states dominate and control the exploitation of resources and production.[56] Their wealth derives from their control over manufacturing and agri- culture, and are characterised by centralised forms of government. Those states that are linked by various kinds of dependent trading are referred to by Wallerstein as being semi-periphery to the core. Peri- pheral states are those that depend on selling cash crops directly to the core states and are seen as at the outer edge of the world economy. For Wallerstein, however, there were states that were, until colonial expansion, relatively untouched by commercial development. Their dependency and indeed that of those states at the periphery of the world economy has been established and maintained by the legacy of colonialism. These nations are enmeshed in a set of economic relations that enrich the industrial areas and impoverish the periphery. The driving force of globalisation is seen to be located in the logic of the capitalist world economy. As yet, this latter approach has not been taken up extensively by scholars studying global sports and leisure development. This is not so with other strands of dependency work. Let us see what has been established.

In accounts of the emergence and development of sport several strands of development and dependency research is evident. The modernisation approach, closely linked to functionalism, was the dominant paradigm in sociology until the early 1970s. Essentially concerned with how traditional societies reach modernity, modernisation theory has focused on the political, cultural, economic and social aspects of this process. Consideration is given to the development of political institutions that support participatory decision-making. The growth and development of secular and nationalist ideologies is examined. The emergence of a division of labour, the use of management techniques, technological innovations and commerical activities are also the subject of attention. These changes are accompanied by urbanisation and a decline of traditional authorities. In his review of the emergence of modern sport, Gruneau points to a range of literature that has used this approach.[57] Its application has not been confined to the 'origins' of sport. Several writers have been said to use ideas drawn from this approach to account for aspects of global sports development.[58] Wagner, for example, maintains that the 'long-term trend is toward greater homogenisation in world sports culture'.[59] Rejecting a cultural imperialist or, more specifically, an Americanisation thesis, he argues 'there is an internationalisation, a joining of interests, with sport culture flowing in all directions'.[60] Wagner goes on to discuss a range of sports, basketball, soccer and the martial arts. In doing so, he rejects a 'cultural dependency' position and concludes that the emulation of American sport is not so much indicative of Americanisation 'so much as it is international modernisation'. While Wagner believes that 'we make too much of cultural dependency in sports' others disagree.[61]

Studies of imperialism or neo-imperialism are more usually associated with Marxist writings that try to explain the colonialism of specific nation states, especially Western nation states, in terms of its necessity for capitalist expansion. At least three dimensions of these colonial ventures have been noted. These include the search for new markets to sell products, the search for new sources of raw materials and the search for new sources of 'cheap' or 'skilled' labour power. This process is seen to help Western economic development and, at the same time, impoverish the rest of the world. Large business corporations, as well as state organisations have played and continue to play a leading role in these developments. While the formal possession of empires has largely disappeared, with the concomitant rise in self-governing countries, a form of economic neo-imperialism has developed in which Western countries are able to maintain their position of ascendancy by ensuring control over the terms upon which world trade is conducted. Though one of the first approaches within the field, it still has its devotees. Ideas of this kind have surfaced in the literature on sport. Consider Baker and Mangan's collection of papers on sport in Africa, Mangan's own work on the games ethic and imperialism, Cashman's exploration of the phenomenon of Indian cricket, Eichberg's earlier work critically examining the neo-colonial aspects of the Olympic movement and Arbena's evaluation of literature relating to Latin America.[62]

Eichberg's study probes several of the issues identified. He suggests that Olympism is a 'social pattern' that reflects the 'everyday culture of the Western (and East European) industrial society'.[63] He highlights several negative consequences of Olympism, including drugs, violence and the scientification of sport. Eichberg maintains that these excesses are not accidental or marginal but logically related to the configuration of Western Olympic sport with its emphasis on 'quicker, higher, stronger'. Olympism is seen to reflect the colonial dominance of the West and its spread across the globe has been remarkably successful. Yet, Eichberg argues, it is increasingly subject to resistance. Alternatives to Olympism are emerging. These alternatives include a resurgence of national cultural games, open air movements, expressive activities and meditative exercises. He concludes that 'the age of Western colonial dominance is coming to an end – and with it the predominance of Olympic sports' and that 'new physical cultures will arise . . . from the different cultural traditions of the world'.[64] These bold statements are open to debate but can only be resolved empirically. As yet, the jury is still out.

In several respects dependency theory links with neo-imperialist accounts. Both are concerned with the uneven manner and form of global development. Further, the origins and nature of the dependency of specific nations varies according to how far a country was colonised and by whom. There are, as noted, several strands evident in this metatheory. These include dependent underdevelopment, dependent development and dependency reversal. In the first strand it is argued that the global capitalist system operates actively to underdevelop the Third World. This is done largely but not exclusively through multinational corporate activity. Third World countries' impoverishment is the direct result of their subordinate position in relation to the industrialised countries. The wealth of the industrial countries is at the expense of Third World countries, the latter being economically dependent on the former. Exponents of this strand argue that no genuine development is possible while this system is in place.

This dependent underdevelopment strand appears unable to account for growth of some Third World countries. Hence, advocates of this general approach coined the idea of dependent development. That is, the growth of some Third World countries is acknowledged, but this is viewed as limited in nature. But while dependent development is conceived of as possible, such an approach still does not appear to grasp that certain countries can break out of the 'double bind' of dependent development. In this context, a further revision of the basic approach is evident in which reference is made to dependency reversal. In this approach it is conceived possible that certain Third World countries and/or institutional sectors of Third World countries can escape and reverse the previous disadvantageous relations with developed countries. At present, as will be clear from this review, no one approach dominates within dependency theory. Despite this, variants of dependency theory have been used extensively in the study of sport.

Several studies have, not surprisingly, examined Latin and South America.[65] This approach has also been taken up by Jarvie in his study of the Highland Games.[66] In this substantively grounded research Jarvie avoids a crude application of dependency theory, and blends aspects of Gramsci, dependency theory and figurational sociology. He concludes that

dependency can only be adequately explained if it turns to the examination of the historical relations and conflict between

Scotland and the British state and, in particular, the ways in which a distinct civil society and a distinct cultural identity has been developed alongside political control through Westminster.

Adopting this strategy allows dis- cussion of Scottish sport to be located within broader debates about 'dominant cultural power'.[67]

Bruce Kidd's study of sport in Canada is also located within a broader analysis of the development of Canadian national culture.[68] Noting the potential importance of sport in the strengthening and enunciation of national identity, Kidd observes that the commodification/Americanisation of Canadian sport has served to undermine this potential. Focusing on the National Hockey League as a 'critical case' in this regard, he highlights how both the ideological marketing strategy of the NHL and the general process of commodification between the two world wars served to 'accelerate the disintegration of beliefs and practices that had once supported and nurtured autonomous Canadian institutions'.[69] For him, an explanation of these processes lies not in Americanisation *per se* but in a critique of capitalism. He writes in this regard:

> Explanation lies neither in US expansion nor national betrayal, but in the dynamics of capital. Once sport became a sphere of commodity production . . . then it was almost inevitable that the best Canadian hockey would be controlled by the richest and most powerful aggregates of capital and sold in the richer and more populous markets of the US. The disappearance of community control over Canadian hockey strengthened a much larger process – the centralisation of all popular forms of culture.[70]

Alan Klein's study of Dominican baseball is also an example of dependency research at its best.[71] Grounded in a careful and sophisticated anthropological approach, he probes the contradictory status and role of baseball in relations between the Dominican Republic and the United States of America. Klein insightfully observes:

> Because baseball is the only area in which Dominicans come up against Americans and demonstrate superiority, it fosters national pride and keeps foreign influence at bay. But the resistance is incomplete. At an organisational level American baseball interests have gained power and are now unwittingly dismantling Dominican baseball. Therefore, just when the Dominicans are in a posi-

tion to resist the influence of foreigners, the core of their resistance is slipping away into the hands of the foreigners themselves.[72]

Despite the fruitfulness of this approach, within social science more generally, attention has increasingly been given to what has been termed 'world systems theory'. As noted, however, there has not been much work done using this approach. It is possible however, to view the trade of sports or arts talent from 'peripheral' countries to 'core' countries from this perspective. This approach alerts us to the extent to which hegemonic powers exploit other nations in their search for new markets to sell sport forms, leisure products, equipment and cultural merchandise. Further, in the context of sports and arts labour migration, the activities of hegemonic states centres on the search for new sources of 'skilled' labour whose early development was resourced by these former colonial countries. The global sports and leisure system can thus be seen to operate largely but not exclusively through multinationals or organisations dominated by First World nations. This system operates actively to underdevelop the Third World by excluding them from the centre of political decision-making process and from the economic rewards derived from the world sports/leisure economy. Indeed, it could be argued that the core states dominate and control the exploitation of resources and production. A de-skilling of semi-periphery and peripheral states occurs on the terms and conditions set by core states. The most talented workers, in whom peripheral or semi-peripheral states have invested time and resources, are lured away to the core states whose wealth derives from their control over athletic and artistic labour and the media-sport/leisure production complex. Non-core states are thus in a position of dependent trading: their athletic or artistic labour being the equivalent of the cash crops that they sell in other sectors of the world economy.[73]

Whether the attention of dependency researchers focuses on the imperatives of multinational capitalism or the spread of the cult of consumerism, a homogenising trend is allegedly identified. While the scale and pace of the process is disputed, the general drift towards the convergence of cultures is accepted. Several problems arrive with this picture. One way that these problems can be expressed is as a series of 'sensitising' questions that need to be asked about accounts drawing on cultural imperialism. What constitutes Westernisation and/or Americanisation? Is it simply a question of the presence of a cultural product from a 'foreign' culture or does it involve a 'seachange' in the conscious and subconscious makeup of people? How 'intended' is the process described? How complete does the process have to be for domination to be said to have occurred? What ability do people have to understand, embrace and/or resist these processes? What constitutes the 'indigenous/authentic' culture that the foreign culture is said to threaten?[74] Some writers have abandoned the attempt to answer these questions and have sought to reconceptualise the debate.

Globalisation and the global sports/leisure process

Several writers suggest that reference to the concept of global- isation helps reorientate the analysis.[75] Globalisation is viewed as a far less coherent or culturally directed process. That is, the inter- dependency and interconnectedness of all global areas unfolds in a far less purposeful way than dependency theory suggests. Global- isation occurs as a result of the complex dynamics of political, economic and cultural practices. These do not, of themselves, aim at global integration, but nonetheless produce it. The effect then of globalisation is to weaken the cultural coherence of nation states. This includes those nations who are more powerful within the interdependent world order. How does this contrast with dependency theory?

Several objections to variants of dependency theory are raised by exponents of globalisation research. Whereas dependency theories use mono-causal explanations to explain the global condition, e.g. Americanisation, globalisation research emphasizes the need for multi-causal analysis. Globalisation research also disputes whether there is a trend towards homogenisation. In contrast, Robertson and Featherstone maintain that the unity of nation states is being dissolved, identity pluralised and a partial mixing of global cultures occurring. In globalisation accounts, emphasis is placed on the emergence of global diversity. Citizens of different nations in various parts of the world are becoming aware of 'otherness' and recognising difference. Polyculturalism is said to be one of the main features of global processes.[76]

Yet, a related feature of these processes is the re-assertiveness of 'local' identities. Global cultural flows are not embraced unwittingly. Rather, people interpret and actively use those cultural products they consume in the global marketplace. From this, some observers have concluded that the dynamics of globalisation is powered by an 'infinitely varied mutual contest of sameness and difference'.[77] The tendency towards dichotomous thinking regarding global culture is also inappropriate. Instead of endlessly arguing about whether homogeneity or heterogeneity, integration or disintegration, unity or diversity are evident, it is more adequate to see these processes as interwoven. Nor is it a question of either/or but of balances and blends.[78]

Several writers have taken up these themes and issues. Here we will concentrate on the work of Featherstone, Giddens and Robertson. In his critique of 'post modernism', Giddens argues that 'post modernity' is an extension of the project of modernity.[79] His concern is with what he terms 'high' modernity. While he dismisses the claims of postmodernists, he himself wishes to emphasize certain discontinuities between recent history, (the past three or four hundred years) and the very long term past. These discontinuities include: the great rapidity and global scope of change; the uniqueness of modern institutions; the commodification of products and labour and the reliance on inanimate sources of power.[80]

Globalisation is viewed as one of the more visible consequences of this process of modernity: it entails the enlargement of modernity. For Giddens, 'modernity is inherently globalising' and that 'one of the fundamental consequences of modernity . . . is globalisation'.[81] We have already noted that Giddens identifies four main features of the world-system. These form part of his 'institutional analysis of modernity'. In this analysis, he emphasizes that globalisation involves a profound re-ordering of time and space in social life. Global networks of communication and complex systems of production and exchange combine to produce a diminishing grip of local circumstances over people's lives. For example, decisions on the global money markets affect national interest rates that, in turn, have a direct impact on the home mortgage loans. The rate of home repossessions is thereby related less to domestic considerations and more to decisions made by financiers in the Bundesbank, and elsewhere. This process therefore entails a 'disembedding' of social relations. Social relations are lifted out of their local context of interaction and are recombined across time and space. For Giddens:

Globalisation can thus be defined as the intensification of worldwide social relations which link distant localities in such a way that local happenings are shaped by events occurring many miles away and vice versa. . . . Local transformation is as much a part of globalisation as the lateral extension of social connections across time and space.[82]

Let us leave aside, for the moment, the issue of local transformations and the dialectical aspects of the processes involved. The question that we want to address now is how this framework might help us make sense of the global sports and leisure system. Unfortunately, no systematic or substantive work completed by Giddens refers to this issue. Neither have his devotees in the sociology of sport or leisure completed such work. Clearly, however, the media-sport/leisure complex can be viewed from a vantage point of a global institutional analysis of modernity. This complex entails the movement of people, an interdependent network of production and exchange of goods, styles and bodily practices that are framed and reframed by a global web of communication companies. Through this complex, the individual is 'transported' to venues across the globe. Sport or leisure interaction and social relations are no longer dependent upon simultaneous physical 'presence' within specific locations. No longer does the sports fan or music buff have to declare, 'But I was there!'. In discussing the broader process, Giddens observes that 'larger and larger numbers of people live in circumstances in which disembedded institutions, linking local practices with globalised social relations, organise major aspects of day to day life'.[83]

For Giddens, the local and global have become interlocked. Global processes therefore express fundamental aspects of what he terms 'time-space distantiation'. These processes involve, as noted above, the conflation of presence and absence. Though he does not write about sport or leisure occasions, it is not difficult to see how their global manifestations exhibit the same characteristics as broader examples of local global interchange. That is, sport and leisure festivals such as Wimbledon or the New Year's Day concert from Vienna also involve 'an interlacing of social events and social relations "at a distance" with local contextualities'.[84]

By arguing that globalisation does not simply refer to the diffusion of Western institutions and the crushing of 'other' cultures, Giddens avoids one of the alleged pitfalls of dependency theory. Neither is the globalising of social life complete. The process is, in fact, contradictory. The very decline of the dominance of the West is, he maintains, the result of the global spread of the institutions he identifies as the main features of the world system.[85] Nevertheless, several problems have been identified with this approach.[86] First, Giddens neglects to incorporate within his framework the study of culture. Second, his account provides no examination of cultural variation or of the contestation of global culture. Third, though other cultures are referred to, no elaboration of their development, or potential development, is provided in Giddens' view of the future.

For Robertson, globalisation refers, 'in its most general sense, to the process whereby the world becomes a single place'.[87] He is keen to avoid the suggestion that this notion of a 'single place' entails a crystallisation of a cohesive system. Yet, he maintains, globalisation does involve the development of a global culture. This culture, he argues, is not a homogeneous, binding whole, but refers to a 'general mode of discourse about the world as a whole and its variety'.[88] Concerned to trace the way in which the world is ordered, Robertson maps out, as noted earlier, what he refers to as the 'global field'.

In tracing the pattern of this global field that results from an interweaving of societies, individuals, international relations and humankind as a whole, Robertson maintains that a reference to a single causal process must be avoided. Globalisation is not the direct outcome of inter-state processes. Rather, these processes need to be understood as operating relatively independently of conventionally designated societal and socio-cultural processes. He stresses the relative autonomy and 'logic', and long-term nature of the processes involved. While he refers to the development of a global culture, Robertson also stresses, as noted, that globalisation processes do not lead to homogeneity. For Robertson, global processes involve both the particularisation of universalism and the universalisation of particularism.[89] That is, these processes are marked by heterogenious tendencies and characteristics. In sum, 'globalisation is . . . best understood as indicating the problem of the form in terms of which the world becomes "united" but by no means integrated'.[90]

The process by which people have come to understand the world-system as a whole has a long history. In mapping out the global condition, Robertson identifies five main phases in this long process.[91] The details need not concern us here. We wish to concentrate on what Robertson refers to as Phase III, the 'take off' phase. Lasting from around the 1870s until the mid-1920s, this phase involved the process through which the 'increasingly manifest globalising tendencies of previous periods and places gave way to a single, inexorable form'.[92] This form centred on four reference points: national societies, generic individuals, a single 'international society' and a singular notion of humanity as a whole. These globalisation processes are evident in several areas: the growth of agencies that straddle the globe (the League of Nations); the establishment of global awards and prizes (the Nobel prizes); the emergence of a global communications system (telegraph, telephone, radio, etc.); and the emergence of a standardised notion of human rights. As part of this general framework, Robertson is also keen to explore how standardised notions of 'civilisation' emerged during this period. Whereas some observers view ethnic reassertiveness as running counter to globalisation processes, Robertson does not see these processes as mutually exclusive. Indeed, he suggests that 'the contemporary concern with civilisational and societal (as well as ethnic) uniqueness – as expressed via such motifs as identity, tradition and indigenisation – largely rests on globally diffused ideas'.[93]

Significantly, it was in this 'take off' period that contemporary notions of national/ethnic identity and culture were formed. This has received considerable attention in work on globalisation by Hall and other writers.[94] It is also important to note that standardised notions of sport, and the global diffusion of sport forms by international agencies and associations, also occurred in this period. The links between sport, identity and ethnicity have similarly become an area of investigation.[95] Unfortunately, while Robertson refers to the Olympics as an example of the establishment of global competitions in this period, he does not elaborate on this connection. The links between leisure, identity and global culture are more fully developed by Featherstone, and it is to his work that we now turn.

During the period of intense globalisation, roughly 1880 to 1920, Featherstone suggests that more nations were drawn together in a tighter global interdependency and set of power balances. This period also produced intense forms of nationalism, and what Robertson himself termed, 'wilful nostalgia'.[96] National cultures thus sought to reinvent traditions of the nation and to marginalise local ethnic and regional differences. For Featherstone, this entailed the invoking of a collective memory. This was done through the performance of ritual, bodily practices and commemorative ceremonies. Royal jubilees, the Olympic Games, international competitions and national days all performed this function. These practices became 'echoes of the sacred' where the fundamental elements of national culture and identity were revealed. Leisure events came to express myths, invoke memories, emphasize heroes and embody traditions. These tied popular consciousness together.[97]

In this earlier phase of globalisation, leisure practices functioned to bind nations together around specific invented traditions. In contrast, the more recent phase of globalisation dating from the 1960s is forcing nation states to reconstitute their collective identities along more pluralistic and multi-cultural lines. Significantly, leisure practices also take on new meanings. Featherstone notes in this connection:

> Such festive moments [such as Woodstock] in which the everyday routine world becomes transformed into an extraordinary sacred world enabled people to temporarily live in unison, near to the ideal. Subsequent gatherings often incorporate rituals which re-invoke the aura of the sacred. . . . Televised rock festivals such as the Band Aid, Food Aid, the Nelson Mandela concert and other transnational link-ups may also invoke a more direct sense of emotional solidarity which may reawaken and reinforce moral concerns such as the sense of common humanity, the sacredness of the person, human rights, and more recently the sacredness of nature and non-human species.[98]

Although global consumer culture can be perceived to be destroying local culture, Featherstone argues that it can also be used for reconstituting a sense of locality. In Europe, for example, Celts, Basques and Bretons are reasserting their identity and use leisure events to promote this. Given the moral concerns about humanity, human rights and environmentalism identified by Featherstone as permeating some leisure events, it is not surprising that he believes that global consumer culture is leading to polyculturalism and a sense of otherness. Global leisure practices do not therefore involve a homogenisation process (Americanisation). In contrast, for Featherstone, 'the tendency . . . within consumer culture to reproduce an overload of information and signs would also work against any coherent integrated universal global belief on the level of content'.[99] The very prevalence of images of the 'other' contained in global sport and leisure practices may both decentre the West and put other cultures more centre stage. The challenge to Western Olympism is a case in point. It would appear safe to say that sport and leisure practices will also be part of this global cultural contest.

Concluding thoughts

The confusion, uncertainty and a sense of powerlessness experienced by people caught up in globalisation processes can be overcome. Globalisation processes involve a blend between intended and unintended practices. While people have to cope with the problems of interdependency that globalisation engenders, the fact that these processes are relatively autonomous ensures that people can intervene. Global practices still lie within the province of human actions. What people require to empower themselves in this regard is more reality-congruent knowledge.

How then to make sense of the global sports/leisure process? If one or other of the theoretical perspectives reviewed became the guiding light in the study of this area, or of the sociology of sport and leisure more generally, then certain consequences would flow from this decision. Some existing areas of research would receive less priority. Other research areas now considered crucial would be refocused. Further, research areas that are now neglected by sociologists would receive greater prominence. The process of making sense of the global sports/leisure process is itself contested terrain. Yet the object of this critical review and synthesis of literature has not been an attempt to privilege any one perspective. It has sought to assess, in a relatively detached manner, the merits of different traditions and how they have manifested themselves in sociological work on sport and leisure over the past three decades and more. This has held true with regard to this analysis of research conducted from a dependency or globalisation perspective.

In conducting this review some common hallmarks of good sociology have emerged. Such hallmarks might include the necessity to ask questions about structured processes understood to be concretely situated in time and space; an attempt to make sense of the unintended as well as the intended outcomes of various social transformations; an attention to the meaningful interplay between individuals' lives and structural contexts and the development of a more reality-congruent body of knowledge. In the long term, we would be happy for these hallmarks to permeate all sociological work on sport and leisure. Based on the review of the traditions examined we would suggest that historically grounded questions must be the compelling driving force and not an optional extra within either the sociology of sport or the sociology of leisure. The result would be a historically grounded sociology of sport or sociology of leisure of far greater intellectual and practical power than its current incarnation.

Clearly, multi-paradigmatic rivalry and abstract generalities have tended to obscure the fact that much common ground exists between many so-called competing intellectual traditions of thought on sport and leisure. For example, much common ground exists between Bourdieu, Elias, Simmel, Weber and cultural studies work on sport and leisure. These traditions have a common respect for history, an analysis of power relations at the core of their general frameworks, and a common emphasis on the cultural diversity and richness of social reality. In the same way, much common ground also exists between various traditions of feminism and Marxism. Furthermore, as the social meanings attached to bodies of work change over time, new forms of reconciliations between bodies of knowledge might be possible. The work of Gregor McLennan, for example, provides one of the most coherent, logical and historically grounded attempts to reconstruct, engage and move forward the debate concerning the relationship between Marxism and pluralism.[100] While differences do exist, for example, between the figurational and cultural traditions of work on sport and leisure, they need no longer view each other as anathema.

As we suggested earlier, the observation that Bourdieu charges at contemporary sociology also relates to the sociology of sport and sociology of leisure literature of the 1980s: namely, that there is a high correlation between the type of cultural capital that different researchers have at their disposal and the form of sociology that they defend as the 'only' legitimate one.[101] A consequence of this power struggle over knowledge has been that much intellectual curiosity and energy has been spent ensuring that one favoured tradition counts for more than others, rather than examining whether the basis for much of this fragmentation of knowledge and multi-paradigmatic rivalry is itself based upon false premises. False oppositions or dichotomies, such as theorist and empiricist, subjectivist and objectivist, and structure and agency, are not only fictitious but also dangerous because they lead to a violence of abstraction. These oppositions are real enough in the sociological field but they have no scientific or historical foundation. We cannot, whatever paradigms we think in or challenge, seriously claim permanent authority even for our facts, let alone our judgements. Nevertheless the project of the honest sociologist, or even historian, must surely be to reveal what really happened. If there is anything to be learned from this, it is that attention to the specific and the particular, will take us much further forward than violent abstractions or sterile pre-emptive generalities. We would be happy for historically grounded questions to be the compelling driving force within the sociology of sport and leisure rather than an optional extra. The sociology of sport and leisure in the 1990s needs not only persuasive examples of historical analysis combined with fruitful theorising, but also a tighter fit between theory and evidence. Our job remit for *Sport and Leisure in Social Thought* was to provide an introductory text to introduce students not only to a range of sociological theory, but also to the sociology of sport and leisure. We hope that the end product is of some assistance in these maturing fields of the sociology of sport and the sociology of leisure. We also hope that this text provides a useful introduction to sociological thought *per se.*

NOTES AND REFERENCES

1 See R. Robertson, *Globalisation: Social Theory and Global Culture*, London, Sage, 1992; S. Mennell, 'The Globalisation of Human Society as a very long-term social process: Elias's theory', *Theory, Culture and Society*, no. 7, 1990, pp. 359–73. In Chapter 6 we referred to the contribution that process sociology makes to the study of globalisation processes and to the specific study of sport and globalisation. While we do not intend to repeat those arguments in this chapter, clearly this tradition makes a major contribution to the area. This has also been recognised by Robertson, 1992, op. cit., see Chapter 7, though we do not concur with his evaluation.

2 See R. B Reich, *The Work of Nations: Preparing Ourselves for Twenty-First Century Capitalism*, New York, 1991, Knopf, cited in D. Sabo, 'Sociology of Sport and New World Disorder', *Sports Science Review*, no. 2, vol. 1, pp. 1–9.

3 For more extensive discussion of this see J. Maguire, 'Globalisation, sport development and the media-sport production complex', *Sports Science Review*, no. 2, vol. 1, 1993, pp. 29–47.

4 M. T. Donaghu and R. Barff, 'Nike just did it: international sub-

contracting and flexibility in athletic footwear production', *Regional Studies*, no. 24, 1990, pp. 537–52.

5 A. Giddens, *The Consequences of Modernity*, Cambridge, Polity Press, 1990.

6 R. Robertson, op. cit., 1992.

7 For discussion of this see B. Smart, *Postmodernity*, London, Routledge, 1993.

8 This position is reviewed in A. D. Smith, 'Towards a global culture?' *Theory, Culture and Society*, no. 7, 1990, pp. 171–92; F. H. Tenbruck, 'The dream of a secular ecumene: the meaning and limits of policies of development', *Theory, Culture and Society*, no. 7, 1990, pp. 193–206.

9 R. Robertson, op. cit., 1992.

10 B. Smart, op. cit., 1993.

11 A. Appadurai, 'Disjuncture and difference in the global cultural economy', *Theory, Culture and Society*, no. 7, 1990, pp. 295–311.

12 ibid., 1990.

13 See J. Maguire, 'More than a sporting touchdown: the making of American football in England 1982–1990', *Sociology of Sport Journal*, 1990, pp. 213–37; J. McKay and T. Miller, 'From old boys to men and women of the corporation: the Americanisation and commodification of Australian sport', *Sociology of Sport Journal*, no. 8, 1991, pp. 86–94; J. McKay, G. Lawrence, T. Miller and D. Rowe, 'Globalisation and Australian Sport', *Sport Science Review*, no. 2, 1993, pp. 10–28.

14 See A. Appadurai, op. cit., 1990.

15 We are thinking here of the following writers: R. Gilpin, *The Political Economy of International Relations*, Princton, Princton University Press, 1987, J. Rosenau, *The Study of Global Interdependence*, London, Francis Pinter, 1980, I. Wallerstein, *The Modern World System*, New York, Academic Press, 1974.

16 See M. Featherstone, Global culture, *Theory, Culture and Society*, no. 7, 1990, pp. 1–14. M. Featherstone, *Consumer Culture and Postmodernism*, London, Sage, 1991.

17 ibid., 1991, see Chapter 8.

18 C. Bigsby, (ed.), *Superculture: American Popular Culture and Europe*, Ezek Books, London, 1975. For a definition of Americanisation see R. A. White, 'Backwater Awash: The Australian Experience of Americanisation', *Theory, Culture and Society*, no. 1, 1983, pp. 108–22.

19 D. Hebdige, 'Towards a Cartography of Taste 1935–1962' in B. Waites, et. al., *Popular Culture: Past and Presnet*, Croom Helm, London, 1982. See also D. Hebdige, *Subculture: The Meaning of Style*, Methuen, London, 1979.

20 I. Chambers, *Popular Culture, The Metropolitan Experience*, Methuen, London, 1986, p. 151.

21 ibid., 1986, pp. 152–8.

22 Hebdige, 1982, op. cit., pp. 198–9.

23 Examples include H. Schiller, *Mass Communication and American Empire*, Boston, Beacon Press, 1969; J. Tunstall, *The Media are American*, London, Constable, 1977 and A. Mattelart, *Multi-national Corporations and the Control of Culture: The Ideological Apparatuses of Imperialism*, Hassocks, Harvester, 1977.

24 R. Collins, 'Wall-to-Wall *Dallas?* The US-UK Trade in Television', *Screen*, no. 27, vols. 3-4, 1986, pp. 66–77, p. 67. See also S. Emanuel, 'Culture in space: the European cultural channel', *Media, Culture and Society*, no. 14, 1992, pp. 281–99.

25 C. Kaplan, 'The Culture Crossover', *New Socialist*, no. 43, vol. 11, 1986, pp. 38–40.

26 D. Webster, *Looka Yonder! The Imaginary America of Populist Culture*, Routledge, London, 1988, p. 179.

27 Hebdige, 1982, op. cit., p. 216.

28 Bigsby, op. cit., p. 27.

29 Webster, 1988, op. cit., p. 210.

30 I. Ang, *Watching Dallas: Soap Opera and the Melodramatic Imagination*, Methuen, London, 1985, p. 18.

31 J. Tomlinson, *Cultural Imperialism*, London, Pinter Publishers, 1991.

32 A. Klein, 'Baseball in the Dominican Republic', *Sociology of Sport Journal*, no. 6, vol. 2, 1989, pp. 95–112; A. Klein, *Sugarball: the American Game, the Dominican Dream*, New Haven, Yale University Press, 1991.

33 J. McKay and T. Miller, op. cit., 1991.

34 This debate began towards the end of the 1940s when a group of Latin American economists working for the United Nations Economic Commission for Latin America (ECLA) criticised the way in which the Western world has tended to explain the developmental gap between the rich and poor countries.

35 For a general review of this area see the following writers: M. Blomstrom and B. Hettne, *Development Theory in Transition*, London, Zed Books, 1984, B. Hettne, *Development Theory and the Three Worlds*, London, Longman, 1990; J. Larrain, *Theories of Development*, Cambridge, Polity Press, 1989; and L. Sklair, *Sociology of the Global System*, London, Harvester Press, 1991.

36 R. Prebisch, *The Economic Development of Latin America and its Principle Problems*, New York, United Nations, 1950, p. 64.

37 ibid., 1950.

38 Sunkel and Paz, 'Big Business and Dependencia', *Foreign Affairs*, no. 34, 1972, pp. 20–42.

39 O. Sunkel, 'National Development Policy and External Dependency in Latin America', *Journal of Development Studies*, no. 1, vol. 1, 1969, pp. 16–34.

40 ibid., 1969.

41 F. Cardoso, 'Dependency and Underdevelopment in Latin America', *New Left Review*, no. 74, July, 1972, pp. 10–18.

42 Cardoso and Faletto, *Dependencia y Desarollo en America Latina*, Mexico, Siglo, 1969, p. xxi.

43 F. Cardoso, op. cit., 1972.

44 See for example Raul Marini, *Dialectica de la Dependencia*, Era Mexico, 1973.

45 See discussion in M. Blomstrom and B. Hettne, op. cit., 1984, p. 66.

46 F. Cardoso, op. cit., 1972.

47 ibid., 1972.

48 ibid., 1972.
49 Dos Santos, 'The Structure of Dependency', *American Economic Review*, no. 60, vol. 21, 1970.
50 ibid., 1970.
51 ibid., 1970.
52 G. Frank, *Capitalism and Underdevelopment in Latin America*, New York, Monthly Review Press, 1967.
53 I. Wallerstein, *The Modern World System*, New York, Academic Press, 1974.
54 G. Frank, *Critique and Anti-critique: Essays on Dependency and Reformism*, London, Macmillan, 1984, pp. 245–8.
55 I. Wallerstein, 'World Systems Analysis', *Cencrastus*, Summer, no. 26, 1984, p. 15.
56 ibid., 1984.
57 R. Gruneau, 'Modernisation or Hegemony: Two Views on Sport and Social Development' in J. Harvey and H. Cantelon, (eds), *Not Just a Game: Essays in Canadian Sport Sociology*, Ottawa, University of Ottawa Press, 1988, pp. 9–32.
58 W. Baker, *Sports in the Western World*, Totowa, NJ: Rowman and Little-field, 1982; R. Clignet and M. Stark, 'Modernisation and the game of soccer in Cameroun', *International Review of Sport Sociology*, no. 9, 1974, pp. 81-98; M. Krotee, 'The rise and demise of sport: a reflection of Uruguayan society', *Annals of the American Academy of Political and Social Science*, no. 445, 1979, pp. 141–54; R. Mandell, *Sport: A Cultural History*, New York, Columbia University Press, 1984; E. Wagner, (ed.), *Sport in Asia and Africa: A Comparative Handbook*, Westport, Greenwood Press, 1989; E. Wagner, 'Sport in Africa and Asia: Americanisation or mundialisation?', *Sociology of Sport Journal*, no. 7, 1990, pp. 399–402.
59 E. Wagner, op. cit., 1990, p. 399.
60 ibid., 1990, p. 400.
61 ibid., 1990, p. 402.
62 See W. Baker and J. A. Mangan, (eds), *Sport in Africa: Essays in Social History*, New York, Africana, 1987; J. A. Mangan, *The Games Ethic and Imperialism*, London, Viking Press, 1986; R. Cashman, *Patrons, Players and the Crowd: The Phenomenon of Indian Cricket*, Bombay, Orient Longman, 1980; H. Eichberg, 'Olympic sport: neocolonism and alternatives', *International Review for the Sociology of Sport*, no. 19, 1984, pp. 97–105; J. Arbena, 'The Diffusion of Modern European Sport in Latin America: a case study of Cultural Imperialism?', paper presented at the annual meeting of the Southern Historical Association, Lexington, Kentucky, November 1989.
63 Eichberg, op. cit., p. 97.
64 ibid., p. 102.
65 J. L. Arbena, *Sport and Society in Latin America: Diffusion, Dependency and the Rise of Mass Culture*, Westport, Greenwood Press, 1988; B. Stoddard, 'Cricket and Colonialism in the English-Speaking Caribbean to 1914: Towards a Cultural Analysis' in J. A. Mangan, (ed.), *Pleasure, Profit and Proselytism. British Culture and Sport at Home*

and Abroad 1700–1914, London, Frank Cass, 1988, pp. 231–57; B. Stoddart, 'Sport in the social construct of the lesser developed world: a commentary', *Sociology of Sport Journal*, no. 6, 1989, pp. 125–35; A. Klein, op. cit., 1989.

66 G. Jarvie, *Highland Games: The Making of a Myth*, Edinburgh, Edinburgh University Press, 1991.

67 ibid., pp. 104–5.

68 B. Kidd, 'Sport, Dependency and the Canadian State', in M. Hart, and S. Birrell, *Sport in the Sociocultural Process*, Brown, Iowa, 1981, pp. 707–21. See also debate in the *Sociology of Sport Journal* between J. Maguire, op. cit, 1990; B. Kidd, 'How do we find our own voices in the "New World Order?" A Commentary on Americanisation', *Sociology of Sport Journal*, no. 8, pp. 178–84; A. Klein, 'Sport and Culture as contested terrain: Americanisation in the Caribbean', *Sociology of Sport Journal*, no. 8, 1991, pp. 79–85 and A. Guttmann, 'Sports diffusion: a response to Maguire and the Americanisation commentaries', *Sociology of Sport Journal*, no. 8, vol. 2, 1991, pp. 185–90.

69 B. Kidd, op. cit., 1981, p. 713.

70 ibid., p. 714.

71 A. Klein, op. cit., 1991

72 ibid., p. 3.

73 See the collection of papers in J. Bale and J. Maguire, (eds), *The Global Sports Arena: Athletic Talent Migration in an Interdependent World*, London, Frank Cass, 1994.

74 J. Tomlinson, op. cit., 1991. In contrast, see the debate contained in R. Rollin, (ed.), *The Americanisation of the Global Village*, Bowling Green, OH, Bowling Green University Press.

75 Featherstone, op. cit., 1991, Robertson, op. cit., 1992 and Tomlinson, op. cit., 1991.

76 Featherstone, op. cit., 1991, Robertson, op. cit., 1992.

77 Appadurai, op. cit., p. 308.

78 If the analysis moves towards a concern with what Sklair describes as transnational practices, then the observer is better placed to note that there is something more at work than solely flows between nation-states. It may well be that transnational practices, which take a variety of cultural forms, gain a degree of relative autonomy on a global level. See L. Sklair, op. cit., 1991.

79 A. Giddens, op. cit., 1991. His analysis clearly has implications for the tradition we examined in Chapter 9.

80 See Robertson, op. cit., 1992, Chapter 9, for a discussion of these issues and of Giddens' work on globalisation more generally.

81 Giddens, op. cit., 1990, pp. 175–7.

82 ibid., p. 64. See also D. Harvey, *The Condition of Postmodernity*, Oxford, Blackwell, 1989. See, in particular, in part three his general analysis of time and space and also his discussion of these elements in what he terms 'postmodern cinema'.

83 ibid., 1989, p. 79.

84 A. Giddens, *Modernity and Self-identity*, Cambridge, Polity Press, 1991, p. 21.

85 Giddens, op. cit., 1990, p. 175.
86 See Robertson, op. cit., 1992, chapter nine.
87 ibid., p. 135.
88 ibid., p. 133.
89 ibid., p. 130.
90 ibid., p. 51.
91 ibid., pp. 57–60.
92 ibid., p. 59.
93 ibid., p. 130.
94 The question of identity is explored in the following readings: E. Gellner, *Nations and Nationalism*, Oxford, Blackwell, 1983; S. Hall, 'The question of cultural identity', in S. Hall, D. Held and T. McGrew, (eds), *Modernity and its Futures*, Cambridge, Polity Press, 1992, pp. 274–316; E. Hobsbawn, 'Mass-producing traditions: Europe, 1870–1914', in E. Hobsbawn and R. Ranger, (eds), *The Invention of Tradition*, Cambridge, Cambridge University Press, 1983, pp. 263–307; A. K. King, (ed.), *Culture, Globalisation and the World-system: Contemporary Conditions for the Representation of Identity*, London, Macmillan, 1991; A. Mazrui, *A World Federation of Cultures: An African Perspective*, New York, The Free Press, 1976; B. Schwarz, 'England in Europe: reflections on national identity and cultural theory', *Cultural Studies*, 1992, pp. 198–206.
95 The question of globalisation, sport and identity has been recently examined by J. Maguire, 'Globalisation, Sport and National Identities: the Empires Strike Back?' *Leisure and Society*, (vol. 16, no. 2, 1993, pp. 293–322) and G. Jarvie, 1993, 'Sport, nationalism and cultural identity', in L. Allison, (ed.), *The Changing Politics of Sport*, Manchester, Manchester University Press, pp. 58–83. For further discussion see also K. S. Inglis, 'Imperial cricket: Test matches between Australia and England 1877–1900' in R. Cashman and M. Mckernan, (eds), *Sport in History*, St Lucia, University of Queensland Press, 1979, pp. 148–79; C. L. R. James, *Beyond a Boundary*, London, Stanley Paul, 1963; P. James, 'The ideology of winning: cultural politics and the America's cup', in G. Lawrence and D. Rowe, (eds), *Power Play: the Commercialisation of Australian Sport*, Sydney, Hale and Iremonger, 1986, pp. 136–50 and S. Reynolds, 'The influence of sport upon national character', in *Australian Society for Sports History Bulletin*, no. 16, April, 1992, pp. 1–16.
96 R. Robertson, 'After nostalgia? Wilful nostalgia and the phase of globalisation', in B. S. Turner, (ed.), *Theories of Modernity and Post-modernity*, London, Sage, 1990, pp. 45–61.
97 M. Featherstone, 'Local and global cultures', *Vrijetijd en Samenleving*, nos. 3/4, 1991, pp. 43–58.
98 Featherstone, op. cit., 1991, p. 122.
99 ibid., p. 127.
100 G. Mclennan, *Marxism, Pluralism and Beyond*, Cambridge, Polity Press, 1989.
101 P. Bourdieu, *In Other Words: Essays Towards a Reflexive Sociology*, Cambridge, Polity Press, 1989, p. 35.

Index